BETWEEN TWO WORLDS

Between Two Worlds

The Canadian Immigration Experience

Edited by

Milly Charon

Quadrant Editions 1983

Published by Quadrant Editions, R.R. 1, Dunvegan, Ontario, K0C 1J0. Quadrant Editions are distributed in Canada by Volume Incorporated, 3636 boul. St. Laurent, Montreal, Quebec, and in the United States by Flat Iron Distribution, Dover Book Distribution Centre, 51 Washington Street, Dover, New Hampshire, 03820, U.S.A.

Published with the kind assistance of the Ontario Arts Council and the Canada Council.

The editor and the publisher would also like to express their gratitude to the Secretary of State, Department of Multiculturalism for a grant without which the publication of this work would not have been possible.

Typeset in Paladium by Resistance Typographers, Edmonton, Alberta. Printed and bound in Canada by Hignell, Winnipeg, Manitoba.

CANADIAN CATALOGUING IN PUBLICATION DATA
Main entry under title:
Between two worlds

ISBN 0-86495-030-6 (bound). — ISBN 0-86495-024-1 (pbk.)

1. Canada — Emigration and immigration — Biography. 2. Canada — Emigration and immigration — History. I. Charon, Milly.
FC104.B48 1983 971.06'092'2 C83-091461-7
F1035.A1B48 1983

DEDICATION

This book is dedicated to:

the millions of immigrants who worked
so hard and endured so much to become
a part of the Canadian mosaic;

my parents whose pain and suffering
taught me the meaning of patience
and compassion;

the special friends who believed in me
when I doubted myself;

and above all, Gary Geddes, whose
encouragement and advice helped make a
twenty-year-old dream come true.

STORY CONTENTS

INTRODUCTION

In the last ten to twelve years, there has been a significant increase in "Ethnic Studies" research in both Canada and the United States. It may be that the more the mass media reduce our world to a village overcoming the boundaries of space and time, the more we attempt to define our role and status in this "global village". The need to belong is compelling and in response to this need many of us are bringing to light how and why we belong.

Other factors, too, have contributed to this phenomenon. As first, second or third-generation descendants of immigrants, we find ourselves in an entirely different context from the one which faced our forebears. We can communicate in the language of the country; we enjoy social and financial security; we have leisure time. Those who preceded us often could speak neither English nor French; they moved from one job to another and learned from experience that this hospitable land was not without its exploiters; they sought steady employment and worked unceasingly and tirelessly to assure that their children, and their children's children would fare well in this land. Hence, it is in recognition of their effort and in order to distinguish clearly their contributions to Canadian society that ethnic studies enjoy this new interest.

There is, finally, the factor of the place of these immigrant communities in Canadian history. Canada is perceived as a country composed of three distinct entities—the native peoples, the descendants of the French and English colonists commonly referred to as Canada's "two founding peoples" and, finally, the ethnic communities. Although the role of the native peoples and especially of the French and English constitutencies has received extensive attention in the writing of Canadian history, the same does not apply for the ethnic communities. Specific events, rather, stand out in the historical treatment; for example, the Irish immigration following the great potato famine in the mid-nineteenth century, the importation of Chinese laborers in building the national railroad and the great immigration waves that followed, especially after World War II. No doubt people of ethnic origin contributed significantly to the historical development of their country throughout these years. For the most part, however, their role has been forced to the background because of the English/French tension. Paradoxically, this same phenomenon has enabled ethnic communities in Canada to retain their community and culture from generation to generation. Indeed, for most ethnic communities in Canada, language and culture of origin live; the identity is genuine rather than folkloric.

Within this context, Milly Charon's work is an important contribution. It is more than a testimonial to different people of various ethnic origins. It is a living reminder of the forces, determination and courage which motivated people to come to a strange land, to face new languages and cultures, in order to better their lives and the lives of those who would follow. Each story strikes home to us; each contains characteristics common to the Canadian ethnic experience. Indeed, Charon's relentless pursuit to put this work together and her steady perseverance are a worthy reflection of the values our immigrant parents and grandparents displayed before us. And as they succeeded, so has she. There is, moreover, an element in these recollections which one cannot ignore. Nationalism is not one of Canada's stronger points. We hear it so often that we have become accustomed to it—to the point of being proud that we are not strong nationalists. As we read these recollections and see and hear how much Canada means to the immigrant, we appreciate more what this country has provided for us and what it offers us in the future. The least we can do for our ancestors is to contribute, to forge and to shape this country so that it will continue to reflect those values and opportunities which attracted them to this land.

Dr. Don J. Taddeo
Dean of Arts and Science
Concordia University
Montreal, Quebec

PREFACE

This book and others I am planning have been rattling around in my brain since my late teens. Years had to elapse before I could get the first phase under way. I returned to school, deliberately choosing courses designed to improve my writing and editing skills.

My early years were spent in the Montreal immigrant ghetto in the mid-thirties and forties. My parents had come to Canada with stars in their eyes and dreams of improved economic conditions and a better future. They sought a haven free from war, hunger and disease. Instead they became trapped by their illusions when reality proved too hard to face and they ended up bitter, angry and alienated.

My father had been an officer in the Czechoslovakian army, and he met and married my mother in Canada. Both had left Europe during the 1928 wave of postwar emigration, fleeing like so many thousands of others from inflation, depression and Communism sweeping over one war-battered country after another.

Four years later, Papa developed skin cancer from a bad sunburn and spent years in hospitals hoping for a cure. Very little was known about the disease in those days. With no money coming in, Mama had to go to work in the usual places open to immigrants who didn't speak the language—the sweatshops on St. Lawrence Boulevard—where she toiled over a sewing machine for a mere pittance. As babies, my sister and I were placed in the care of others while Mama tried to keep food on the table and a roof over our heads.

When no doctor could help him, Papa tried to take his own life. In silent sympathy, his friends collected money to send him back to Europe where research into skin ailments had reached a high degree of success.

It was 1936.

From a clinic in London, he went to another in Belgium, then to a hospital in Austria. He was in Vienna when Germany annexed the country in an almost overnight takeover. He left for Germany and spent more than six months there under the care of a German skin specialist who cured him. The scars never disappeared, but they were no match for the ones he carried on his soul.

Wandering from one country to another, from clinics to hospitals, my father became engulfed by the mass mania of German nationalistic aspirations. All around him the madness was escalating, and he was trapped in fear right in the heart of the whirlwind.

As soon as his treatments were finished, he left for Czechoslovakia to warn his parents and family that something was about to happen.

As a former army officer, he knew the signs. He begged them to leave, to sell everything, but they believed his mind had been unhinged by his illness and ignored him.

He took the train to Hungary to visit my mother's family whom he had never met. Again he voiced his fears and urged them to leave. No one listened. He left with a growing sense of urgency and by a circuitous route managed to get back to Belgium where he had a brother and sister-in-law. They thought he was exaggerating when he warned them of what he had seen in Germany. They didn't believe him.

He sailed from Belgium just before the entire continent was plunged into World War II. My parents lost everyone. Of two large families, they were the only ones who survived because Canada had offered them a home. I grew up without aunts, uncles, cousins and grandparents.

I had no roots in the Old World. I had to grow them here.

We lived in the immigrant ghetto east of St. Lawrence Boulevard, the ghetto that was a miniature United Nations. Behind every doorway was a story. I developed my powers of observation by watching people, analyzing how they acted and interacted. I listened to their stories, honing my linguistic skills in the new tongues I had to learn, absorbing everything I could that would be useful in later years.

The differences fascinated me, but it wasn't until years later, after I had left the area, that I realized the difference between the newcomers and established Canadians.

Europeans who emigrated never quite made the adjustment to the New World. No doubt it was the same with those from other continents. It was as if they were caught between two worlds, trapped in time.

The children were the intermediaries—the ones who bridged the gap. They were pushed and pressured from all sides to make good, to be better, to do more than their Canadian counterparts.

In every family on the street where we lived, the first-born was designated from early childhood as the most responsible, unless, of course, he or she was crippled or feeble-minded. This child became the emissary, the translator, the secretary, babysitter, housekeeper, chief-cook-and-bottle-washer, and nothing short of death could change this sacred trust. This meant total responsibility—on call twenty-four hours a day—and there were no excuses or shirking of duty.

We were poor, like most immigrants in the ghetto, and we didn't have much in the way of clothes, furniture or other material things, but at least we were eating. I guess we were luckier than most. Mama was clever and she was good with her hands. She could make anything. Besides sewing all our clothes, she painted walls, put up wallpaper and even repaired worn heels on our shoes.

I think back and I realize why she never took my sister and me to places where there were beautiful and expensive things. Whenever we went to department stores, we stayed in the basement and on the first and second floors. We always skipped the third and fourth floors where all the exquisite china, crystal and furniture were displayed. She didn't want us asking for things beyond our means.

And so, because I remained in the ghetto until I was almost sixteen and didn't know that there was a division of "haves" and "have-nots", my illusions were shattered when I grew up and left our ethnic compound. Our parents had built the walls looking for a feeling of security in a strange and new land, and we had to break out to see what was on the other side.

It has been said that ignorance is bliss. Years later, after I had achieved some degree of understanding, I was inclined to agree. Mama had been right on some issues. Yet when I think back to those early years on City Hall Street, or l'Hotel de Ville, and remember my life there, I marvel at my naiveté and my ignorance. It is then I question my mother's wisdom in keeping me that way.

The ghetto was our world and was stuffed full of people from all over the globe. We were exposed to so many types we didn't always see the differences unless they stuck out like a sore thumb. One of those "sore thumbs" was the accent. All our parents had accents and anyone who didn't became special in our eyes. Lack of an accent classified you as a step above the immigrant. You were more important, more educated, smarter. I know some of the children, once they started school, were ashamed and embarrassed by their parents' heavy, ethnic accents.

Faced with the reality of the outside, we rapidly shed our illusions. We learned to question the Gospel according to family rules and mores; we quickly discovered a new vocabulary that included such colourful words as Hunky, Wop, Kike, Kraut, Bohunk, Chink and Nip. Though we were born here, with roots deep in Canadian soil, part of our minds and souls still carried the indelible stamp of the old country. In a way we were split personalities, bearing the mark of two worlds.

Our parents never made the transition, their thick accents and Old-World customs clinging to them like burrs. Their displacement was physical; ours was psychological. And so, we longed to produce children who would be 100-per-cent Canadians with neither accents nor hangups. It was as if, secretly, we were ashamed.

Often, however, we wear our duality as a badge of honour. We are proud of our origins, proud of what our parents accomplished and proud of the land that gave us a chance.

But every year more immigrants come to this country and every year the same pattern is repeated, no matter what the country of origin. Why do two generations have to elapse before the transition is complete? Perhaps understanding and sharing will help to break the cycle, to make the displacement easier, the adjustment quicker and less painful.

This, then, is the rationale for *Between Two Worlds*. I have collected articles, essays, short stories, interviews and personal testimonials in celebration of our diversity. Each piece is a unique thread in the national fabric. While the finished product may appear to have three sleeves, a back-to-front collar and an uneven hem, I am hoping the sincerity and genuineness of the copy will add quality to my efforts. Haute couture it is not, but many of us are content with the ready-to-wear garment.

Those who could write submitted manuscripts for editing. Those who had no writing skills were interviewed. There were many who could barely speak English or French. Some stories evoked so much emotion—memories were so painful—that the subjects broke down and cried. I must confess I cried with them, but it established an even stronger rapport between us. We understood one another, and there was empathy despite the language barrier.

If this book arouses some emotion in the reader, if it gives some understanding of the immigrant's plight, if it helps to dissipate the blind, unreasoning prejudice some people have for displaced persons, then I will have succeeded beyond my wildest expectations.

This book might not have been finished, if not for those special friends who believed in me. And so, my deepest affection and thanks go to Linda MacDonald, proofreader, adviser and confidante; Enn Raudsepp who freely gave suggestions, advice and encouragement; Andy Melamed whose shoulder was always available to cry on; Linda Ghan and Barbara Weiss whose support and sympathy were greatly appreciated; Barbara Lalonde, stricken with multiple sclerosis and blindness, who listened and advised and Maria Brecht, who sympathized and cared.

I would also like to extend my gratitude to resource people Ben Queenan, Harry Blank, MNA, Vancouver writer C.D. Minni and Claudine Lussier (Regional Library of Employment and Immigration).

To Alice Lévesque, who edited and typed part of the final draft, go my thanks.

My sincere thanks go to those whom I jokingly called "procurers"—Lynne Moore, Minko Sotiron, Fania Jivotovsky, Dorothy Mosel, Rachel Levy, Helen Sher, Dean Don Taddeo (Concordia University), my daughter Marla and others too numerous to list. All found immigrants and directed them to me, providing stories that appear here or, hopefully, in the sequel.

Special thanks go to the ethnic weeklies and the English dailies across Canada that printed my request for immigrant stories. They were: *Modersmaalet, De Nederlandse Courant, The Chinese Times, Vaba Estlane, Czas, the Guardian,* Charlottetown; *Evening Telegram,* St. John's; *The Chronicle-Herald,* Halifax; *The Daily Gleaner,* Fredericton; *Telegraph Journal,* Saint John; *The Vancouver Sun, The Calgary Herald, The Calgary Sun, The Edmonton Journal, The Winnipeg Free Press, The Hamilton Spectator, The Ottawa Citizen,* and the *Toronto Star*. Magazines *Heritage Alberta* and *Kaleidoscope Canada* reprinted the request in an effort to help in my search. Without the help of the media I would not have been able to meet my deadlines or accumulate such a variety of stories.

Finally my gratitude and affection go to my editor Gary Geddes for cutting, editing and clarifying the manuscript. Thanks go to Robert Allen, who helped with the editing and Andrew Wheatley, publisher of *Quadrant*.

Last but not least, a special note of thanks to Mrs. Helen Demuth, my grade-five, -six and -seven teacher who first put my feet on the path to education and achievement.

Joann Saarniit

VOYAGE TO FREEDOM

The story of Joann Saarniit, Estonian artist, was written in a series of newspaper and magazine articles between 1948 and 1980.*

Nearly 350 Europeans who had been held under immigration detention in Halifax would always remember Christmas of 1948. It was their first Christmas in Canada and it could have been their last.

Twelve days before Christmas, a little minesweeper, the *Walnut,* tied up at the French cable wharf. Nearly 350 men, women and children who had left their Russian-dominated countries poured out of this ship and presented themselves to immigration officials. They wanted to stay in Canada.

Halifax's Mayor, J.E. Ahern, heard about the group. Some were being held in the immigration detention barracks, and others at old Rockhead detention quarters. A former newspaperman, Mayor Ahern spoke to officers of the Halifax Press Club. Within a few hours, the men and women of the Press Club were planning a Christmas party for the 70 Estonian children.

At two o'clock on the afternoon before Christmas, about 30 youngsters at the barracks were waiting for Santa Claus. They were shiningly clean and dressed in spotless frocks and suits. To these youngsters, most of whom were Estonians, Christmas was as important as it was to Canadian children. Captain August Linde, skipper of the *Walnut,* was Santa Claus.

In the small auditorium in the detention barracks, Captain Linde came out on the tiny stage chortling and laughing and talked to the children in Estonian. For each child there was a toy, some fruit and candy. For these gifts each one had to recite a verse of poetry, and as a Christmas tree blinked its colourful lights, the children said the verse and accepted their parcels. Some of the mothers dabbed handkerchiefs to tear-filled eyes.

Before Santa Claus left, seven young girls sang Christmas carols in Estonian. Earlier in the afternoon a loudspeaker mounted on a police car played carols outside the building. At Rockhead detention quarters the scene was repeated. At both parties, Mayor Ahern presented the youngest boy and girl with Canadian silver dollars and

* *Halifax and Toronto*

told each he hoped the coin would be the beginning of a fortune to be earned in Canada.

Immigration officials were processing the group who had left Sweden November 15, and arrived in Halifax December 13, 1948. Shortly after, the Resources Department announced the Immigration Branch had completed the examination of the refugees who fled Sweden in the path of Soviet persecution. They would be admitted at the rate of 100 a week and would be placed by the Labour Department. The first group would be sent by train to Pickering, Ontario where employment had been arranged.

Meanwhile, one of the world's few first-hand records of the stark reality of life and death in horror-ridden Siberian prison camps—believed to be the only one in oils—rested in Halifax Rockhead immigration hospital with its owner, 39-year-old Estonian artist, Joann Saarniit, who with the other *Walnut* passengers, was awaiting official admission to his long-sought land of freedom—Canada.

For two years, Saarniit had been held in a prison camp in Russia, where he secretly made pencil sketches of atrocities committed on prisoners. After he was freed and sent back to Estonia, he translated his sketches into a series of startlingly vivid paintings. Now, at Rockhead, Saarniit displayed a number of his paintings for the first time.

Saarniit was a marked man on the books of Stalin's secret police, but his happiness in reaching Canada overcame his fears, for soon he would fulfill a promise he made to friends he had left behind in Siberia—to tell the free world with his paintings the actual story of what was going on behind the Iron Curtain.

His goal was not commercial. These paintings were not for sale. They were a record for mankind. To help Saarniit, the Halifax Branch of the Canadian Red Cross decided to sponsor one of the most dramatic events to take place in the art world of North America during that period. The 40 oil paintings Saarniit had brought from Europe were exhibited for the first time at the Lord Nelson Hotel on February 5, 1949, with admission fees going to the Red Cross. These paintings were the only existing first-hand pictorial accounts of life in a Siberian concentration camp. Combining grim realism with arresting design and powerful self-expression in every stroke of the brush, the artist's startling use of colour compelled attention.

Saarniit, who lived for almost three years under the rule of terror he so graphically depicted, wanted every Canadian to know about the evil forces at work in Soviet Russia.

* * *

*In my hometown of Tallinn, Estonia, my life had been a quest for freedom, art and colour, and it all ended abruptly one August evening in 1940 when a Communist officer came into my commercial art studio.

"Take food for five days!" he ordered. "You are being conscripted into the Red Army."

I said good-bye to my wife Lutti and my three-year-old son Matti and together with 1,200 other Estonians was herded on board a ship in the harbour. At the Russian port of Leningrad, we were shuttled into a freight train—60 men to a boxcar—with a barrel split in two for a toilet. For 11 days we traveled across the Ural Mountains to Siberia. We huddled together without food, heat or light, screaming vainly for food, only to be informed that we were being taken to a mobilization centre.

At Smolensk, each of 1,200 Estonians was finally given a salt herring and half a loaf of bread. Then we were strung out in a single line and forced to march 200 miles northward, clad only in light summer clothes and shivering all the way. If a sick prisoner slumped down on the road, the horse-mounted guards spat at him and left him to die.

Finally in the middle of the wind-swept, barren tundra, the survivors of the death march arrived at Novo-Nasselniky, a Siberian prison camp.

"This is your new home," a Red officer said jovially. He pointed to the three barracks reserved for the Red guards and to the thin tents, each of which was to house 60 prisoners. A barbed-wire fence enclosed the desolate place,and it was guarded by wolfhounds with wide snouts and big teeth.

The Red officer said, "You will build a new Estonia here."

It was like living on the edge of the world. It was so bitterly cold that even the guards refused to accompany us when we were marched out each morning to saw down our quota of trees. Five hundred of us died within six months.

At 7:00 a.m. and 6:00 p.m. we were handed two identical meals—watery potato soup, half a slice of rye bread and one square piece of what must have been horsemeat. If a prisoner didn't cut his quota of ten trees a day, he was refused even this frugal supper. If he tried to escape, he was roasted in a steel drum over flames, his corpse strung out on the barbed wire fence for months like a scarecrow as a gruesome warning. There were other methods of torture that were just as horrifying.

To avoid freezing in winter, the prisoners were allowed to dig an underground trench and cover its top with branches. About 400 men

**"Our Baltic New Canadians" Liberty, 1959 Courtesy Frank Rasky*

were huddled in this tunnel, a bonfire smoking in the centre. At night we sang Estonian ballads, recited poetry or spun out stories to help us forget our gnawing hunger. Because of hunger, you were lucky to sleep five hours. You didn't think of freedom. You thought only of food, food, food. You dreamed dazedly of all the best meals you had ever eaten—Estonian sauerkraut, cabbage rolls and our golden taffy-like pastry.

But the will to survive was so fierce that the men learned to forage like animals. They roasted acorns and made coffee of it. They nibbled the soft heart inside the trunk of fir trees. Because of the lack of salt, sugar and fresh vegetables in our diet, we all suffered from deficiencies. Once I lost my voice for two months.

"You'll be a mute dummy for life," predicted one amateur doctor. But another, an Estonian farmer, said that milk and honey were the only things that would help me regain my ability to speak.

By a miracle, a Russian peasant woman with a goat passed the camp that day. I offered her all the money I had won in card games if she would help me. She returned with goat's milk and a dab of honey, and I recovered my ability to speak within two days.

After two years of being kicked and beaten into subservience, I was asked by an officer if I would like to enlist in the Red Army as a proletariat artist. I eagerly accepted, but instead of daubing paint I was told I would be one of the 8,000 Estonians the Reds intended to thrust against the approaching Germans in the battlefields of Velikije Luki. Along with my countrymen were Red peasants who were being recruited. I was amazed at their ignorance.

Many of them had never seen a train. Hundreds of them fearfully leaped off the "monster" as it began to move and hot-footed it back to their farms. So the Red officers learned to lock the peasants into the train ahead of the others. Their life was dirt cheap. They were so poor they wore shoes made of tree branches and bark and were so starved that they once ate blades of grass.

In three months, 20,000 Estonians died. I knew we didn't have a chance if we stayed and so with 1,000 other Estonians, I deserted the Russians one night and we sneaked across the battlefield to join the advancing Germans. But they didn't trust us because we were Estonians. There was no way out, so I allowed myself to be caught by the Russians again. Now, however, the Russians didn't trust me because I was an Estonian. I was sentenced as a spy to fifteen years in Siberia. Rather than face that again and knowing full well that I could never survive, I escaped and swam a river one cold March day and was taken by the Germans once more. Now the Germans considered I was a spy as well and that I had secret information about the Russians. They quizzed me day and night, but at least they fed me—heaps of marmalade, cocoa and white bread. I tried to appear inscrutably all-knowing about military secrets.

Finally in disgust, the Germans sent me to a prisoner-of-war camp in Poland. A commander there asked me how I liked being a prisoner. I said it was marvelous. The food was superb compared to what I had had in Russia. I asked him to send me back to Estonia so I could be of help as a member of the pro-German Estonian army.

My wife, who hadn't seen me in three years, was astounded when I casually strolled into my house in Tallinn one day.

"I've been in mourning for you!" she exclaimed as she hugged me. "Your name is listed downtown as having died in Siberia. A friend signed as a witness that he saw you die."

"Some friend," I said, and went to look for myself. Sure enough, it was there. I told the German official that obviously there had been a mistake.

"I'm here, so please remove my name from your obituary column."

"But you can't be alive!" blustered the army clerk. "It reads on this list that you are dead."

The German officials were so dumb that I noticed a week later my name was still on the obituary list.

Unfortunately I had discovered my wife was living with a German. I know she thought I was dead, but if it had been anyone but a German or Russian, it might have been different. I could never forgive her. However, we stayed together only until we reached Canada because governments prefer immigrants with families.

So far as the Germans were concerned I was dead, I told my wife, and one night we escaped by fishing skiff to Finland. Although I had no visa, I bluffed my way into a job as a designer for a Helsinki film studio. Unhappily, I was collared one night at my hotel by the Finnish police.

"You don't like the Russians," the official at police headquarters told me. "You don't like the Germans. You must not like Estonia either since you escaped from there. So you must be an international spy."

After being questioned at headquarters with 100 other suspected spies, I was told to get into the black police van parked in the alleyway and to sit and wait.

My escape was simple. I just entered the back of the truck and then walked out the front. I walked away whistling.

Regrettably, the Helsinki police nabbed me later.

"This time you are arrested forever," they declared.

But I had been shrewd enough to paint some murals for the Finnish steam bath of the commander-in-chief. I told the officers to take me to their leader and sure enough, he insisted I was a patriot par excellence and that there was some mistake. I was to be released immediately.

Since the Reds were threatening to take Helsinki, my wife, my son and I crossed to Sweden in a two-masted yacht. There I worked as a dishwasher and a freelance artist until 1948 when I began to worry that the Reds might even attack Sweden.

So, along with about 306 other Estonian refugees and the rest from other countries, I decided to cross the Atlantic to Canada. We all pooled our money and with $100,000 bought an ancient English minesweeper, the *Walnut*, which had been sold as scrap to Sweden after the war.

It cost me $1,700 to cross the Atlantic in that wheezy old tub. It would have been much cheaper to book passage on the Queen Elizabeth and much safer.

The ship originally designed for fourteen men had been honeycombed, each space utilized to hold a passenger. They ranged from a nine-month-old baby to an eighty-year-old.

We felt we had to go even if Sweden was neutral because not too long before that the Swedish government had handed over 140 Estonians to the Russians, and we were afraid it might happen to us.

However, the Swedish officials insisted we have lifeboats, but we nailed them to the deck just to make it look good. Luckily we didn't have to use the useless things, and when we reached Sligo, Ireland after crossing past the north of Scotland through the North Sea, we sold the lifeboats to pay for supplies.

We dropped twelve passengers in Ireland. Some were sick and others were afraid to continue during the winter in such a small boat.

It was dangerous, and the trouble was the ship was run by a committee of civilian Estonians. The captain mistakenly headed it for South America. The green crew was seasick, the boat ran out of coal, and once even ran backwards. A storm filled it so full of water that all the passengers had to bail it out with milk cans. Since space was at a premium, my paintings were stacked on deck and I spent stormy nights miserably holding on to them to keep them from being washed overboard. During the day I wiped them down to keep them from being ruined by the salt spray.

It took the leaky ship a long time to cross and as we neared Greenland, the Canadian government sent out a plane to inform us we were heading in the wrong direction. But the pilot couldn't get a radio message through since the boat's aerial had been blown down by a storm. The pilot must have had the wits to realize this and he pointed his wings in the right direction. As we limped into Halifax, men and women crowded up on deck, cheered, wept and sang our national anthem.

And at last the rusty old "*Walnut*" steamed triumphantly into the arms of Canada and into history.

Ottawa, February 14th, 1949

Dear Mr. Saarniit:

I have just received from Mr. Christie the beautiful album compiled by you and your fellow passengers on the *S.S. WALNUT* and wish to express my very great pleasure in this artistic record of your journey to Canada. I feel that not only I but the Director of Immigration and other officers of the Department who were concerned with your landing in this country share in your gift.

We in the Department extend to all of you our good wishes for your future in this Canada of ours and now to be yours, and hope that this will prove to be the promised land at the end of your exodus.

Yours sincerely,

H. L. KEENLEYSIDE,
Deputy Minister

January 18th, 1963

Mr. John Saarniit,
567 Roehampton Avenue,
Toronto 12, Ontario.

Dear Mr. Saarniit:

Re: Your painting entitled:
"Sudbury Mines"

On behalf of the Province of Ontario, I write to you to thank you for your courtesy and generosity in making available one of your own works which will grace the premises of Ontario House in London, England, as part of a display by Canadian artists. We are very proud of your contribution, and as soon as the renovations on Ontario House are complete, we shall ship your painting along with some others of which you are aware, to England.

I am writing to the Agent General to advise him that your painting and a number of others are now ready to travel to England and it may be that a public exhibition will be possible, sponsored by Mr. Weston in London prior to the paintings being incorporated into Ontario House.

In the meantime, may I again thank you for your painting and for the time and care which went into it. It will be treasured by our people. These paintings will be a major contribution in our efforts to create an awareness in other jurisdictions in the world that Canada is a nation of the highest quality and her people are creative and industrious.

With kindest regards,

Yours very truly,

Robert W. Macaulay

I went to Toronto with a group of Estonians once I was processed and for three years worked as a $40-a-week floor cleaner at a Toronto Hospital. Then I was a window display artist for the T. Eaton Company. Finally I found a position as a commercial designer with the Wolfe Brothers Advertising Industrial Agency. I stayed there for 26 years and in my free time kept painting in my studio at home. Over the years I had many exhibitions and my paintings were exhibited in many parts of the world. They are represented in the permanent collections of many prestigious galleries, including The Smithsonian Institute in Washington; Canada House in London, England; The Chicago Tribune; the S.J. Zacks collection and many others.

In 1969 when I was in New York, I met and later married an Estonian who was working as a dressmaker. She also wrote poetry. Today we live in a house on Roehampton Avenue and I am still at work in my basement studio. I have continued painting, trying every possible technique, and have exhibited in various group exhibitions organized by the Estonian and Canadian communities. I also had a number of one-man shows and won awards and prizes. My son and daughter are award-winning artists as well. I am a member of the Ontario Institute of Painters and The Society of Co-operative Artists.

My horror paintings of the Siberian prison camps are hanging in my basement gallery, and I use them as reminders to warn the world about Communism. The paintings have been exhibited at anti-Communist exhibitions and in Geneva, as well as many times here in Canada. Canadians take the Communist threat too lightly. They don't realize the danger. We have spies in Canada, but nobody is alarmed about it. Young people don't see any danger in Communism. They don't understand. How can they? They haven't suffered at Communist hands.

As a contrast to the prison-camp paintings, I have also put on canvas my impressions of Canadian landscape. When I compare Estonia and Canada in terms of colour, Estonia is gray, brown and ochre. Canada is blue, orange and scarlet. All the colours here are brighter and more beautiful—just as the country itself is brighter and more beautiful to all freedom-seeking refugees.

Today there are close to 10,000 Estonians established in Toronto and the area. None of those who arrived on the *S.S. Walnut* returned to Sweden. The Estonians prospered in Canada and made a significant contribution to the culture and economy of their adopted country.

And what became of the *Walnut*? When the owners tried to sell her, it appeared her papers were not in order. Originally the ship, which had been built in 1939, had been a trawler on the Dogger Banks. It had been taken over during the war for minesweeping and escort duties before being sold to Sweden. The ship had sailed from Sweden under a Honduras flag, but was not registered, and her papers were unofficial. A buyer could not be found, and eventually she sank to a watery grave in Halifax.

The *S.S. Walnut* had served the British well as a minesweeper in 1942, but she had not been built to cross oceans. Her greatest challenge came when she carried 347 refugees to new lives in Canada.

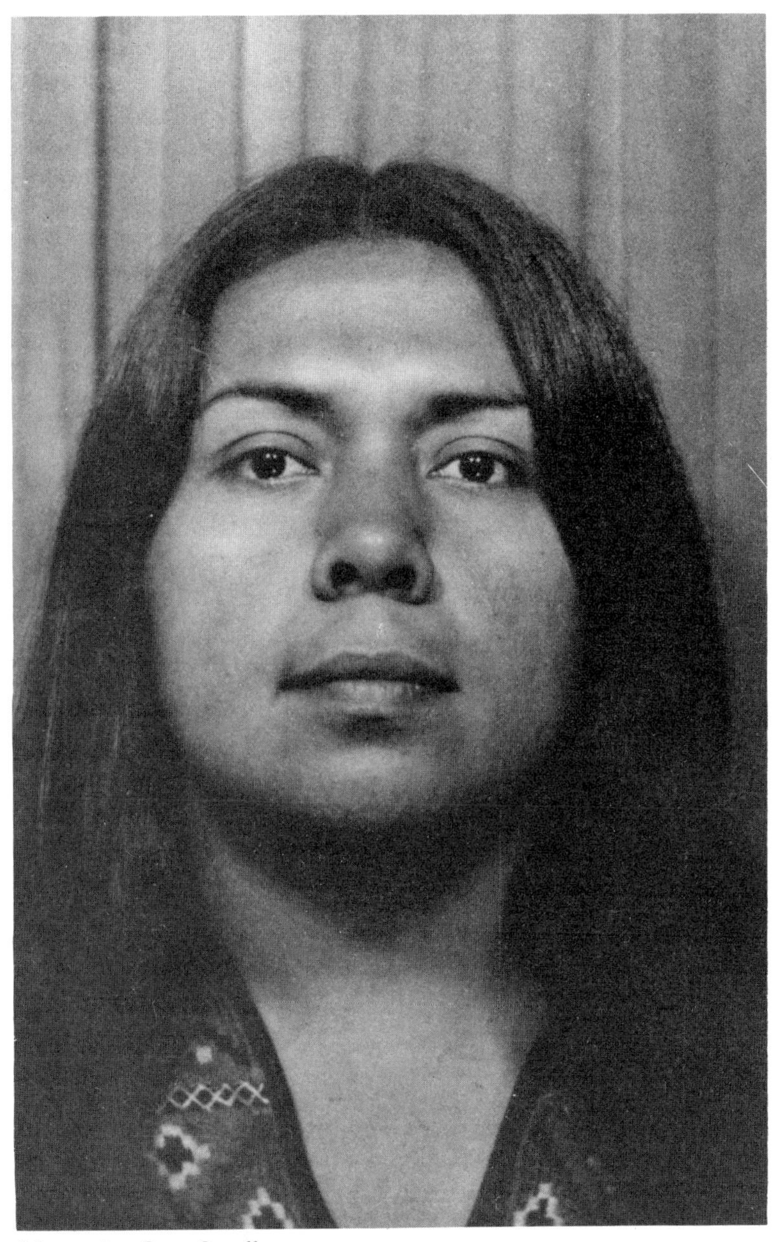

Margarita Cruz Sandborn

EXILE OR DEATH:
THE PRICE OF SOCIAL CONSCIENCE

From an interview with Margarita Cruz Shandborn

It was July, 1976, and Montreal was playing host to hundreds of thousands of visitors from all over the world. The Olympics were in full swing, and the city was caught in the competitive madness that turns a host metropolis into a frenzy of activity.

Shortly after 11:00 p.m., a plane arrived at Dorval Airport from Atlanta, Georgia, U.S.A. No one looked at the tiny, dark-haired girl with the large, black eyes, now blurred by lack of sleep. In their depths lurked a spark of fear only a trained observer would have noticed. She kept glancing about her as if searchng for someone.

She knew only a few words of English and no French. The immigration official found someone to question her in Spanish, her native tongue. Her name was Margarita Cruz, she said, and she came from San Salvador, Capital of El Salvador. She produced her university papers and a student card together with a visitor's visa. Taking all this into account, the officer allowed her two weeks in Canada.

What he didn't know was that she was fleeing certain imprisonment or death. Her crime? Possession of a social conscience — caring about the poor in her poverty-stricken land ruled by a dictator and administered by military police.

Six years later, her lashes blinked away the tears gathering in the corners of her eyes as she tried to explain the reasons for running away.

"It was with much sorrow I left my family, but I couldn't stay in the country. It was too dangerous for them and me. My parents thought it wise for me to leave until things had quietened down, but I felt like a traitor leaving at this time. I love my country and I was always against people who deserted their native land, taking the easy way out, and here I was doing it."

She felt she should have dropped out of sight in the interior of Salvador and fought from hiding for reforms. She was torn emotionally because her family wanted her to leave as quickly as possible. Many Salvadorians had already fled to the United States because of its proximity. Margarita came to Canada because she had a cousin here, who had left a few years before because he was being harassed. A technician at the National University, he lost his job when the soldiers closed it for a year in 1972.

Margarita, 28, is the oldest of three children. Her mother, a brother of twenty and a sister of nineteen have since left El Salvador, following Margarita northward. Her father remained behind. It was his concern and compassion for the poor that indelibly marked Margarita from the time she was five years old.

"Originally my parents had been country people and then became merchants in a small market in the capitol. From the time I was a child, my father educated me in the realities of life around us. He showed me what misery and injustice meant and the different sets of laws for the rich and the poor. This helped me develop a social conscience."

She felt her family had more privileges than the majority of the population because they were able to attend school. She, herself, was in university. Enrolled as a psychology major, she had two and a half years of higher education when she had to leave.

"When you think that sixty per cent of Salvadorians can't read or write, you can see how lucky I was. I didn't leave because I disliked studying; on the contrary I loved it, but I felt that there were people dying of hunger and it was more important for me to get involved with that. I had to do something for my people."

Most North Americans are unaware of the situation in El Salvador. In the mid-1800s the commercial lands used by the peasants to grow food for their own consumption had been expropriated by government decree and consolidated into large farms to grow coffee. "Fourteen Families", the core of the emerging oligarchy, controlled the export crops, particularly the coffee.

The 1930s were a period of intense worker and peasant marches and protests against this control. Minimum wage and relief centres were demanded for the unemployed. The oligarchy responded by giving a mandate to the military to rule El Salvador, and the Communist Party issued a call for uprisings protesting the refusal of the government to recognize their candidates who had won in municipal and legislative elections. The leaders were arrested a few days before the march, and 4,000 peasants and workers, who were unaware of the loss of their leaders, converged on the capital. They were massacred by the military and paramilitary and within a few weeks, the soldiers killed over 30,000 people and hanged the leaders in the town square. Four per cent of the population was butchered, the Communist Party was liquidated, the Workers' Federation destroyed, and the Indian population forced to abandon their native dress, language and customs.

From that period on, El Salvador saw the emergence of one reform party after another, many vying for control while the military repressed any attempt to reform the economy, education, improve the lot of the peasants and workers and bring democracy to the tiny country. All attempts at democratic elections were met with repressive force. Fraud and manipulation of elections in 1970 and 1972 by the military proved that meaningful reforms were impossible. Revolutionary committees attempted to bring about change, but to no avail.

Margaria Cruz's concern escalated in her teens. She made friends with many of the poor people, visiting them and trying to find some solution to their appalling living conditions. Again and again, she asked herself why families of four, five and six lived in one-room shacks with a dirt floor, without water, toilets, privacy or food. It was pitiful, and she felt powerless to change it.

"It was one thing to give them friendship, but that wasn't enough. What they needed was food."

Her outlook changed even more when she looked at religion in a different way. She began to question her Catholic upbringing in order to reorient herself to the new theories and the theology of liberation—that religion should not teach people to be content with poverty and injustice.

"I thought it was wrong and could not understand a religion that kept people ignorant, poor and subservient."

There was a new group of young priests who were actively preaching this new theory of activism, and she became involved. Using simple terms, she began to teach young children what was happening in their society. The way things were, there wasn't much hope for their future, she said sadly.

"I suppose I had been looking for something as well, but I kept studying while I worked with the Christian Workers' groups. All this created emotional problems for me because my parents, like all poor families, hoped that their children would become professionals in order to improve their economic condition. My parents wanted me to become a doctor, and when I was so occupied with these poor people, I realized I would have to overlook their suffering while I was working on *my* future and improving *my* lot."

In her early years at the university, Margarita could see the problems the students faced. The quality of education was poor, and the students began organizing to improve it. The struggle began when the government tried to stop the marches, and Margarita's first encounter with military force came when an enraged soldier hit her with the bayonet of his rifle, drawing blood. Rather than dissuade her, the attack made her angrier and more determined to continue. At the same time, the teachers went on strike, and in the clash of demands and ideals, the government closed the university for a year.

"If I hadn't lost that year, perhaps I might not have dropped out, but rather than waste time, I devoted every minute to working with the peasants, helping them, exhorting them to organize for better working conditions. You could say I became irrevocably dedicated to the cause, and so when the university opened a year later and I went back, I began to ask myself what I was doing there. I was still working with the peasants on weekends and I tried to explain my predicament to my parents. They didn't understand what I was doing and why, but they respected my decision. And so, I dropped out of school and began to work full time in what was a popular revolutionary organization in El Salvador."

By 1976, the government began even harsher repressive measures against those involved in this program for social change. Thousands of people from the worker, peasant, teacher, student and church sectors combined in the popular organizations, using mass protests and civil disobedience. Under General Romero, selected by the Party of National Conciliation (PCN), there was a major escalation of government terror.

"We were continually harrassed, picked up and imprisoned. Many just disappeared and we were certain they had been murdered. In spite of this, I could not stop what I was doing. At the same time, other splinter groups began revolutionary movements in the country. They were weak, but with time they could have become stronger. However, they were riddled with internal problems and were powerless to effect any kind of improvement in the country. When our efforts bogged down, I became depressed, disillusioned and lost hope. At the same time, I was becoming a danger to the government, so I had no choice but to leave."

It was the first time Margarita had traveled so far. She had been in neighbouring Central American countries, but only by bus. It was her first flight, and she was nervous. She was also terrified the military police would arrest her at the airport, but luckily she was not stopped.

"I wasn't conscious of what I was doing. I was totally numb, and the problems I had with the trip made it worse. The reservations somehow got mixed up, and I had to spend three days in Mexico. It cost me more to get up here. I didn't want to go through the United States because I was afraid I would have trouble with the immigration people, but I had no choice. Even at the Atlanta airport, I could feel the discrimination. If you weren't an American and were in transit, you were treated like a criminal.

"The official stationed someone at the door of the room where I was detained and questioned so I wouldn't escape. I didn't even want to stay there; I was on my way to Canada. They looked at my passport. Clearly marked in it was my destination—Canada. But they said the photo didn't look like me and they inferred that perhaps it wasn't in order—little things like that which made me feel even more like an alien. I was really upset, and when I finally got on the plane I was so happy."

She admits her worst problem on arriving at Dorval was the language. All she spoke was Spanish and a few words of English. Her cousin was supposed to pick her up, and because her flight was delayed, he assumed she was not coming and returned home.

"Here I was, stranded in a strange country, not knowing the language and no one to help me. It was after midnight, and I went out all alone to hunt for a taxi. I had the address written down and showed it to the cabdriver who took me to my cousin.

"My cousin helped a great deal those first weeks in orienting me. For me, the city was another world, very different from what I had been used to in San Salvador. I didn't know what I was going to do here."

He took her to an immigrant aid society on De Maisonneuve Boulevard, run by nuns, who gave Margarita advice and obtained a temporary work permit for her that could be renewed after a period of time. Although she considered herself a political refugee, she was afraid to ask for asylum because she didn't trust it. She was frightened she would be subjected to all kinds of questions—interrogations that would be dangerous for all those people, many of them friends — involved in organizations in her homeland.

"I didn't know what kind of diplomatic relations Canada had with El Salvador and I didn't want to be the one to pass on information that would place others in jeopardy. That was why I couldn't ask for political asylum. Perhaps it would have been easier for me if I had. I don't know. Maybe I was too suspicious, but you must understand I was so used to a country of repression that I was naturally afraid."

The nuns found her a job, but there was no other choice than that of a domestic in a private home with a family who had a five-year-old child. The job paid $70 a week, room and board. According to the immigration department this was the only type of work she was permitted to do. She was told to look after the house, the child, she had weekends off, and her work permit was good for six months.

She found it a difficult and restrictive experience. Before, she had been used to an independent, active life, going where and when she pleased, and suddenly she was locked up in a house all week, doing housework. It was a hard adjustment.

The language was another problem. Her employers were French Canadian and she couldn't make herself understood. She was forced to resort to a dictionary to communicate with the family. It was a frustrating position to be in for the family did not have much patience.

"They must have thought I wasn't too intelligent because I could not understand them. I took night courses twice a week in French and picked up the basics in the language. Slowly I began to learn, but I had a feeling of inferiority. There was some prejudice because they treated me as if I came from an uncivilized country. They made me feel stupid when they showed me how to use the electrical appliances, even the radio. We had a radio back home. I guess they had an image of my coming from a really backward country and it bothered me."

Margarita discovered that not only was the food different from her country's cuisine, but she didn't eat the same meals as her employers. She had hamburger and vegetables, and they ate more costly foods such as salmon and steak.

She had to get up at six o'clock in the morning to walk the dog, even in the winter.

"I thought that in this country, dogs were more important than people. From what I saw they were treated better than people. The family was so careful with the dog, and I was given all kinds of instructions how to handle it and what not to do with it.

"There were so many details I had to pay attention to. The man of the house was very nervous, and he would yell and scream for all kinds of things and every little thing was a catastrophe. That bothered me, too."

Her room, which was very small, was just off the kitchen and had probably been a pantry at one time, she says. It was no bigger than a large cupboard.

"It gave me claustrophobia and also, there was no privacy. I was on call all the time. There were times when I was sleeping and they would wake me up to do something. It was very disturbing. I did everything there, and I worked more than eight hours a day."

A year passed in this way, and her permit was renewed after six months. Because of a new law making it mandatory for new immigrants to apply from outside the country, she was forced to leave Canada in order to become a landed immigrant. What bothered her more than this interruption was the kind of working conditions she had that made her feel like a slave. She wanted to be able to change employers when she felt she was being exploited.

"I didn't want to be forced to work this way by Canadian Immigration. I was also at the mercy of the employer. He could complain to

Immigration Canada that he wasn't satisfied with my work, and I could be deported. I always felt uneasy, afraid that this could happen to me and where could I go? Certainly, not home.

When I left, I chose to go to Boston. My employer offered me a work contract so that I would have employment when I re-entered the country. It made things easier having a job waiting.

She was told by Immigration Canada that the process would take two months. But the time dragged on and on, and her papers did not come. Her money was running out, and she was living like a miser, unable to work. She had a tiny, sparsely furnished room and one suitcase with her personal belongings. The two months stretched to eight and she still hadn't received her papers. Every week she went to the Canadian consulate to ask what was happening and why it was taking so long.

"They told me they were checking my dossier in Salvador. I couldn't understand why it was being held up. There was a girl I knew who was going through the same thing as I, and she had her papers much faster. When I complained, I was told it was because I came from a small country like Salvador and it was harder to get information. But this girl came from the same place I did, and she didn't have any trouble. I was beginning to suspect that the delay was deliberate."

She was in a state of anxiety, fear and anger during the nine months in Boston. She felt stranded. She didn't speak any English; her visa permitting her to stay in the U.S.A. was expiring; her money was almost exhausted, and she couldn't work without a permit. Luckily a friend allowed her to launder napkins, tablecloths and clothes in return for food, and she struggled on. To break the monotony of that bleak period, several times she visited friends from home who were living in New York City and Washington.

Finally after nine months, the papers arrived and she was allowed to re-enter Canada. Her former employer was taking his family to Europe on holiday and needed someone to look after the house while they were gone. He had obtained a temporary work permit for her, but somehow she found the relationship with the family even more difficult now. Because they felt they had done her a service, they expected more of her. As a result she was working even harder at the same salary. In addition, when they left for Europe, they refused to pay her the $70 a week she had been earning. They cut it in half because they were not there and she wouldn't be doing as much work. They insisted she stay in the house the entire time.

It was 1978 and before leaving for Boston, Margarita had met a young man who later was to become her husband. A relationship had been established, but Margarita was afraid to think of something more stable, more permanent. He had proposed marriage before she left and she had been afraid to accept.

"I thought of it as an urgency created by my immigration problems that I would be forced to accept because I had no other choice. I was also afraid of another culture, another way of thinking. Everything was so different here."

But when she returned to Canada, they met again, and he spoke of marriage once more. However, because her position at work was so tense and difficult, she wanted to wait until her contract was up.

"I know now that he did this to help and not to take advantage of me. I believe he loved me. He was correct in every way, but I felt it wasn't a free choice; immigration had precipitated the situation. I wanted to continue working after I got married to earn some extra money, but my boss wanted me to live in the house even after I got married. I insisted on working days and going home to my husband at night. My employer said no, that if I was to sleep out, it would be only after they didn't need my services in the evening. That meant I couldn't finish until 9:00 p.m. They wanted to go out and they needed a babysitter. I wanted a private life of my own, and they wouldn't let me have it. It was unreasonable."

Finally she refused to take any more of their demands. With a new husband and a new family obligation, she had no choice but to give notice.

"This whole domestic experience hurt me. But I knew of other girls working as domestics who had it worse than I. They were only being paid $25 a week and weren't allowed to go out at all. One girl I knew came from the Dominican Republic. Like me, she was placed with a family, and when her employer didn't want her any more, he passed her on to a friend without making any papers or anything, as if she was a piece of property he was lending."

There were many cases like this, she said, and because she was concerned, she became involved in establishing an association for immigrant female domestics. She did this while she was still employed and after she stopped working, continued helping others.

"It was very difficult to do this sort of thing with isolated girls located in houses scattered all over the city. Believe me, there were many in this position. They were afraid to do or say anything because they thought they would be deported. They didn't know the language, didn't know anyone here and they lived in fear. What we did was meet and give each other encouragement and support. We began checking into our rights, what to do, how to act, and we formed an association to protect domestics from mistreatment and exploitation. In addition, we wanted to set up a system where domestics could come under the minimum wage law."

This was difficult to accomplish because many of the women were afraid to organize, especially the immigrants. It was almost impossible to make employers and the public understand that domestic work is labour like any other profession. They thought of housework as normal and as natural for women as breathing, and not worthy of recognition in the work force.

"When we demanded the minimum wage, employers considered our demands as unimportant and secondary. Even the government refused to regard domestics as workers.

"Eventually, after many meetings and discussions, we advanced a very short distance. We were included in the minimum wage, but domestics who lived outside were excluded. There were so many things that needed changing, and they still do today."

About this time, the situation in El Salvador worsened, and the war escalated. Margarita wanted to do something for the Solidarity Movement and therefore had to make a choice. She could continue her struggle for the immigrant workers here, or work for the good of her country. She chose her country, yet felt she was torn into two parts.

"You see, as immigrants we are far from our countries of origin and we can't go back, but we don't feel as if we belong here, not yet. We are caught in the middle. Where are we? I had to make a decision because in my heart I was still thinking of going home one day. That was always my hope, my dream, to go back and continue my work for the welfare of my people. Because it wasn't safe, I had to stay here and keep thinking . . . maybe next year or the year after I will be able to return."

All she could do was try and find some support in Canada for her countrymen. She began forming small groups with other Salvadorians to try and sensitize people to their plight. It was almost impossible to get a response from Salvadorians who had left ten years before for economic reasons. They had never been involved in the struggle for reform in their homeland. They were not conscious of the situation, and many reacted adversely.

"Some of these people called us Communists and asked us what we thought we were doing? We weren't Communists, and we continued to form our first committee of Solidarity, to write manifestos, news bulletins and releases on what was happening down there. We arranged group gatherings to disseminate the information. It was already 1979, and very little had been done to change conditions in El Salvador."

Just about this time, she felt an urgent need to return home, not only to see her family and friends, but to determine exactly what was happening there. She had to know. There must have been many changes since she left the country, she thought. She and her husband decided to visit Central America at the same time. It was December, and even if it was dangerous, Margarita had to make contact with her origins, her home, her roots. Without this she felt she would be living in despair and frustration for the rest of her life.

Her husband did a great deal for her, she says. He had been helping her all along with the immigrant problems. He bolstered her, encouraged her and also worked on the Solidarity Committee. He began to learn Spanish to make communication easier.

They visited Costa Rica, Nicaragua and then entered El Salvador, still uncertain they would be permitted into the country. She had not told her family they were coming. It was Christmas and her arrival was to be a holiday surprise.

The threat of imminent arrest hung over them, but Margarita was helped by a state of confusion within the government. International pressure on the military regime was forcing some movement toward democracy. In addition, Margarita gained some anonymity through use of her married name and as a result she was not on the "stop and detain" lists. Because it was Christmas Day and she was arriving at a border crossing and not an airport, the guards were more relaxed and friendly. She was not arrested.

"I only stayed a week. I couldn't stay any longer. I contacted people who were still working for the cause, but I couldn't see all my old friends because many of them were working clandestinely and remained in hiding. With the activities of the military police so much in evidence, they were afraid to come and see me.

"I was terrified I might not be so lucky leaving the country as I had been entering it. There was a law that stated all Salvadorians leaving the country must register and get government permission. While you waited, the government researched your background to see if you were dangerous or had been involved in the reform causes. I would never have made it out.

"Luckily I was with a Canadian, and because there is so much corruption in the government, we offered someone money to forego the usual check of my past activities. That was the only way I succeeded in leaving the country without being arrested."

Safely back in Canada, the Sandborns saw a TV documentary about Salvador a few weeks later. Filmed by the existing military government, it described the rebel causes and the militants involved in the struggle. To Margarita's dismay and surprise, she was in the film and was portrayed as one of the militant enemies of her country.

The man who produced the documentary was Roberto D'Aubuisson who is now President of the Constituent Assembly.

"He is said to be a fascist and the one who planned the assassination of Bishop Romero. This man is regarded as a terrorist by those who are fighting for reform in the country," explained Margarita.

Her classification in the film convinced Magarita that she could not return to her homeland and in December 1981, she applied for Canadian citizenship. She never received an answer. She inquired in February to see what was holding up the procedure. In June she received a visit from the RCMP. She knew why they were coming to see her.

"They were checking on me and watching me, although I had not done one thing that was dangerous or a threat to Canada. All I had tried to do was help my people by going on speaking tours to make Canadians aware of the situation in El Salvador. I tried to get some suppport for the poor and underprivileged in my country."

However, Margarita was quick to point out that there is a law that states an immigrant seeking citizenship must refrain from involvement in any political cause outside the country or face deportation. Margarita sees what she is doing as a social cause and not a political one.

"All I do is talk, nothing more. I don't agitate for anything subversive. As the representative of one of the Democratic Revolutionary Committees, I made public speeches and had announcements placed in newspapers to disseminate information on events in El Salvador."

She was upset by the way her citizenship application had been handled and the harassment she felt was directed at her because of activities involving her homeland.

"When the RCMP appeared at my door," she said, "I knew they had been looking for me at the different offices I worked out of. Someone forwarded the message they wished to speak to me, but I was in Vancouver at the time on a cross-country speaking tour. The economic summit was in progress in Ottawa, and President Reagan was in from the United States. I wondered if the Canadian government thought my work was a danger to national security because of the summit. What else could I think? Why were they looking for me? What crime had I committed?" she asked.

Obviously the government was informed on events because members of parliament, NDP leader Ed Broadbent and Conservative Flora MacDonald, had both taken a fact-finding trip to Salvador. It made Margarita wonder why *they* were concerned, and she had to refrain from informing the Canadian public.

"There were times I felt I was banging my head against the wall with this ridiculous law that wedges immigrants into a corner. That's just one complaint, but another and even more serious one is that my mail was being opened, always, even now. My letters arrived unsealed. I know they were being opened and read. I wanted to know why. I thought Canada was supposed to be a democratic country. I know Canada is not like Salvador because if I were in my homeland now, I would be dead for speaking out and doing what I am involved in here — trying to make Canadians aware of our struggle for democracy."

The two RCMP officers had asked to see her papers and passport. She asked why. They answered it was a routine interview because she had applied for citizenship. She thought it was strange she had been chosen, because she knew of Salvadorians who in the last few years were being treated as Communists or terrorists, only because they came from a country that was in a state of war.

"I told them I would answer any question that was pertinent, but none that I felt were unreasonable. I showed them all my papers and answered questions about when I had arrived, where I had worked, things of that nature. But they also wanted to know if I was still married, what did I think of the elections in El Salvador which had taken place in March when D'Aubuisson was elected. I realized this was not a routine question and said so."

"No, no," said one of the agents. "Our government realizes what is happening in certain countries and needs to have eyewitness accounts from immigrants from these lands. We are doing the same with the Chilean immigrants."

"I answered that it seemed a funny way for a government to inform itself about the conditions of other countries when there was a Canadian embassy or consulate in Salvador and it would have been more logical to get information from their staff who were on the spot, rather than from a Salvadorian thousands of miles away. I suggested that if they really wanted more information, they could do an official parliamentary inquiry and send a committee down there to see for itself.

"Rather than questioning immigrants this way and making them feel they have done something criminal, perhaps it would be advisable for a group to go to Ottawa in a semi-official way so no one feels intimidated and frightened. I think there are other and better methods of procedure. We may be immigrants but we are people, too, like Canadian citizens, and we have the right to be respected. We should be permitted to receive letters and phone calls without having our mail opened or phone tapped. I am not afraid, but there are many immigrants who are terrified by all this," she said.

Margarita refused to answer any of the politically oriented questions, and said she would ask her lawyer if this was normal procedure for citizenship application. The officer insisted she answer, and she countered with: "Does my answering or not answering the question have any effect on my receiving the citizenship papers?"

The officer left his card and said she should call him back if she decided to talk about it. Margarita consulted her lawyer who told her the procedure was abnormal. Only a citizenship court judge should have asked these questions. He agreed it was a form of harassment.

Another thing Margarita said she had seen were cases of discrimination by the public as far as colour was concerned. Traveling across the country, she realized it was worse in Ontario and escalated the farther west she went.

"I have seen it in the immigration offices as well," she says. "The staff isn't too courteous. They treat people as if they were doing them a big favour. I know there is a program in effect for helping immigrants in their settlement here, but very often there is a long process of appointments and interviews, and some interviewers are pejorative and almost insulting. Very often, immigrants are made to feel like thieves. Perhaps it is the way we dress and we may look suspicious because we aren't fashionable, but most of us don't have much money for clothes. But then again, maybe I am less trusting and suspicious of others because of all the things I have gone through."

Despite the negative things, Margarita has found much that is positive in Canada. There is more democracy here than back home, she says, and she finds the size of the country with its sparse population fascinating. Her homeland has almost five million people packed into twenty square miles.

Margarita is struck by the abundance of opportunities in Canada and the ambition people have to get ahead. She finds it unusual that information is so freely given here and you can know more about the country and government than in Salvador. Another positive thing is that women's rights are more highly developed than in Latin America, where women are considered to be very low on the human scale.

"It made me feel good when I came here to see the struggle for women's rights and the progress being made in the search for equality. The way women are treated in Salvador bothered me very deeply. They have no rights."

In the last three years, in her travels across the country working for Solidarity, Margarita has discovered that many Canadians are sympathetic and care about the struggle for reform in her country. She believes that people everywhere should know about the problems of Third World Countries less developed politically, socially or economically.

In terms of change, she finds Canadians generally are apathetic, perhaps because there is less need for active reform here than in El Salvador. People are much better off here, and the standard of living is much higher. There is less to change.

As an immigrant, she has found many things difficult to understand — things like the culture, the manner of living, and the way of thinking.

"There are so many differences, and it isn't easy adjusting to them, especially the mixture of different cultures and ethnic groups. Everything and everyone is accepted here, and people keep their backgrounds, not like in the States. I am just beginning to understand things better, but I don't know if I will ever be able to become a part of it."

If she had a choice, she says, she would have preferred to remain at home. But since she couldn't she probably would have been happier in another Latin American country, but only because she would have been near her own land. Canada is so far away, she explains sadly.

"I think my problem is that I haven't made the adjustment to the way of life in Canada. I am stuck in the middle, but more of me is in El Salvador than here. I still have much hope that one day I will be able to return and things will have improved in my land. I know it will take much time, but in the meantime, I feel I should be realistic and learn all the positive things about this country. I know I can do more for my poor people up here in Canada than sitting in prison down there, or dead, because of my social conscience."

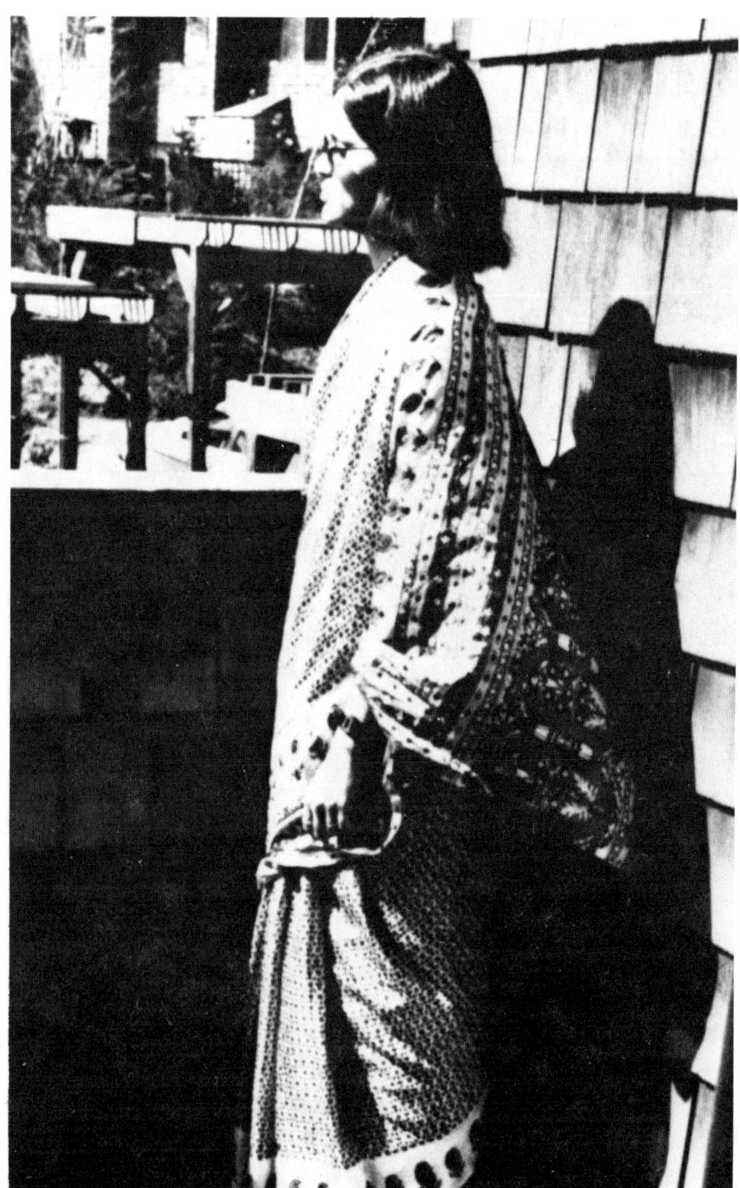

Meera Shastri

CANADIAN EXPERIENCE
by Meera Shastri

People constantly ask me why I came to Canada. I wish I could reply that it was a desire to be a part of this great country, but that was not the reason.

I grew up in an upper middle-class (East) Indian home and was fiercely patriotic. My goal was to become a teacher and educate the illiterate masses of India. To prepare myself for this profession, I went to university. How can I explain to my Canadian friends that the institution of arranged marriages, unheard of in Canada, was responsible for my emigration to Canada? Yes, I had decided that my parents would choose a life partner for me. I know that most Canadians will be shocked at that statement, but I have seen how dearly my parents love one another and how successful their arranged marriage has been.

My parents corresponded with many people and eventually heard of Ray. Our horoscopes, which had been prepared and based on planetary positions at the precise moment of birth, were duly compared by an astrologer who declared us to be highly compatible. Ray and I were brought together, and my first reaction was: "Oh, God! I hope my parents approve of him!" Perhaps it was what is called "love at first sight", but I will not give my intuitive reactions such a glorified expression.

I had been under the impression that Ray was studying and training in the United States and Canada and would be coming back to India. It came as a shock, therefore, when he mentioned he had just emigrated to Canada and would be returning to look for his first job. My heart sank. Immigration seemed so final and involved giving up so much. I nearly backed out of the marriage, but my parents pointed out that they had migrated from Southern India to Northern and that had been a major step. Northern and Southern India are poles apart linguistically and culturally—dress and food are totally diferent as well.

Although our parents were from the south, both Ray and I had been raised in the north, and we spoke three different languages—not dialects—fluently. Because we had traveled back and forth visiting grandparents each year, we were equally at home in both parts of the country and thus, had retained our southern heritage. Taking all this into consideration, I finally allowed my initial hesitation to vanish and decided to marry Ray and emigrate to Canada.

My parents had traveled extensively in Europe, and their stories of the friendliness of people, many of whom had asked to photograph my mother in her beautiful saris, gave me the idea that I would be like an ambassador of goodwill to Canada. Idealistically, I thought I would be building a bridge of understanding between two cultures. The literature distributed by Canada Manpower in India strengthened this view even more. I was eagerly looking forward to becoming a part of Canada's ethnic mosaic.

Little did I reaize that I would be coming to a country where people would refer to me as an East Indian; a large percentage of the population would have the preconceived notion that I stank; that I couldn't speak English; that my house would reek of curry and that I should consider myself lucky to find a job as a berry picker or at most, a nurse's aide. I must admit it took a while for my bubble to burst and for me to realize what most Canadians thought of the East Indian immigrant.

My first impression of Toronto was great. Immigration staff at the airport seemed brusque at first, but became very friendly when they found I could speak English. I was very impressed by the way they handled everything with a minimum of red tape—a contrast to India.

Ray expected me to be gasping in wonder at everything I saw in the city, but when you have read about life in the western world and have been exposed to it through the media, the reality does not surprise or delight you in the same way. What impressed me the most was the cleanliness which was a stark contrast to Bombay or Calcutta where I grew up.

The first adjustment I had to make was to the weather. I had left the tropics and walked into a blizzard! I stood outside in the snow, savouring the delights of my first snowflakes. Within a week of my arrival in Toronto, I realized that the sari was not a practical outfit for the Canadian winter and took to wearing pants. It was just a short while before I began to feel self-conscious about wearing saris even when the weather was good. Now I wear pants most of the time, but to this day I have not been able to wear a skirt. The sari was designed to conceal rather than reveal, and I am inhibited about showing my legs.

My first lessons in humility began when I looked for a job. The University of Toronto graciously evaluated my Master's degree and gave it the equivalent of a Bachelor's at their university. Without a teaching certificate, however, I could not teach in this country so I decided to enter the clerical force. Unfortunately all new immigrants must have faced the Catch-22 situation of requiring "Canadian experience" for a job and needing a job to get that experience. I suppose I was luckier than most new immigrants because I could speak English fluently with little trace of accent. In fact, several people pointed this out to me and with delight, I mentioned it to my husband. He retorted: "The next time someone says you speak good English, you should say, 'so do you'." I was shocked at his cynicism, but I understand it now because I have heard people say it patronizingly. There is no rule that says an immigrant should speak "pidgin" English! I can imagine what my son's reaction would be twenty years hence if someone said to him: "You speak good English!"

At a personnel agency I was given a test, and the counsellor who interviewed me raved about my sari and said I wouldn't have any trouble getting a job with my intelligence. But, she said, most jobs required typing. I was quite flattered by her praise and too naive to realize that it was my first "Don't call us, we'll call you". However, she did give me a friendly tip for which I shall be eternally grateful.

She had asked the significance of the red dot that I had painted at the centre of my forehead. Very diplomatically she suggested that I would improve my chances of finding employment if I relinquished the dot. I had not even been aware of this. In India the red dot is important for it denotes a woman is married. No dot is a sign of widowhood. I did a lot of soul searching and from making it less prominent at first, I finally dropped it altogether. Later I was told that Canadians find the dot offensive. In fact, a five-year-old boy once told me it looked stupid.

However, I recounted this experience to my immigrant and non-immigrant friends, and they all said that the lady counsellor had no right to advise me to remove it and that I should have complained to the Human Rights Commission. But I felt she was not discriminating; she was warning me of the possibility that others might discriminate, and for this I was grateful.

My first proper job interview was for a junior clerical position in a Downsview factory, in a Toronto suburb. I learned my interviewer was a Mr. Mishra which indicated he was of East Indian origin. His first statement after he introduced himself was that he did not come from India and had never been there. He was an Australian immigrant. He seemed to feel I would take advantage of the fact that we had common ancestors and he took great pains to convince me that we had nothing in common. Because I was there on the basis of my qualifications and not my race, his attitude irritated me. He barely touched on my ability and suitability, and in the half hour I was there, related his own views on immigration and expounded in great detail the shortcoming of immigrants from India.

Needless to say, I was not hired. Although I was not disappointed at not getting the job, this incident sowed the seeds of doubt in my mind. Would my children and grandchildren someday be subjected to this, and would they feel ashamed of their Indian ancestry the way Mr. Mishra obviously did? Because I was an optimist, I pushed away such thoughts then, but today I am convinced that most second- and third-generation immigrants react this way, and my child is not going to be an exception.

My job search was hardly a month old when Ray began discouraging me.

"It's no use, Meera. It's quite impossible for a new immigrant to get a clerical job without Canadian experience. One of my friends said he could get you a job at the airport. Do you want to try it?"

At first I was excited and then discovered that it meant standing in an assembly line filling trays with pre-packaged food. I was determined not to become a mindless robot without exploring all the avenues open to me. Of course, the salary for this job was disgustingly low, and practically all the employees were immigrant women, most of whom couldn't speak English.

After a week of filling out forms and making phone calls, I finally found something. An insurance company where I had applied in answer to an ad, called me for an interview which lasted three hours and included tests. I sailed through everything without trouble and got the job. It was just a junior clerical position, but I was delighted for I had proved to Ray that a new immigrant without experience could get office employment.

At last I was exposed to the Canadian business world and loved every minute of it. My work proved far more exciting than I had expected. For the first time in my life, I was involved with the vagaries of a computer and found it fascinating. Within a month I was teaching the girl who had trained me better ways of doing the job. Luckily she didn't resent it.

I mentioned to Ray that about fifty per cent of my co-workers were immigrants and remarked how fair my employers were. In his usual cynical way he retorted that their salary level would never attract Canadians.

Six months later I was offered a ten per cent raise. I wasn't happy about it because I felt I had proved myself and deserved more.

"You claim you are doing a great job and that you are almost indispensible. Why don't you go and ask for a better salary?" Ray goaded.

Although I had been prepared to work for less, Ray egged me on to see the manager and state my case. He was very sympathetic and even though it involved certain technicalities, he went to the "top brass". Two months later I was given a fifty-four per cent retroactive raise and told my position had been up-graded two levels. It was a great victory, and I felt quite smug. Ray was suitably impressed.

While my work experience was improving, our social life, however, was practically non-existent. Neither one of us had any family in the city. In addition, Ray had spent four years in the United States as a student and a worker and had felt he had been accepted there as a professional. Yet here in Canada he was an immigrant first, and his professional status was resented by some of his colleagues who saw immigrants in menial roles. I tried to assure him it was his imagination, but I don't think my words had any effect. Already the seeds of discontent had been sown in his mind, nurtured by stories of rampant racism in the press and in our circle of friends. Soon Ray began talking of returning to India. I was shocked by his defeatist attitude and tried my best to dissuade him. However, the idea was still in his mind.

One evening when I arrived home from work, I saw a message scrawled in bold letters at the entrance to our apartment building. "PAKI GO HOME!" It was the first time we had seen it so close to home, and it really disturbed and hurt us. We were living in a posh residential neighbourhood and the thought that we had neighbours in the area harbouring such feelings was too much to stomach. Thus I fell in eagerly with Ray's plans to return to India, and within three months we had wound everything up and were saying good-bye to Canada.

Miraculously, Ray got a fairly decent job within a few weeks of our arrival, and we were all set to start a new life. Within a few days, however, we discovered that our lifestyle would be drastically altered by another factor—I was pregnant. In addition, our stay in Canada had made us misfits for the Indian way of life. Although we had been prepared for this, we still had to make a lot of sacrifices.

Toward the end of my pregnancy, I moved in with my parents in another city while Ray continued at his job. He found it more and more frustrating for his colleagues were continually sneering at him for his Canadian ideas. Just a month before Sameer (Sam) was born, Ray came to see me and broached the subject of returning to Canada. He was quite convinced this was the best course for both of us and our unborn child. I was shocked and so were our families. All our efforts to persuade him to stay met with failure. It wasn't a case of the "grass being greener somewhere else". Ray had thought it out carefully and had come to a decision. I had to support him and give in.

I will never know what caused it, but after Sam was born, I changed and about three months later had a complete nervous breakdown. With the help of electric shock treatment and drugs, I was restored to some semblance of normalcy after five months of therapy. During one of these sessions, I blurted out that I did not want to leave my family again. Perhaps this affected my feelings, for this time I did not look forward to living in Canada with the eager enthusiasm of the first time. Even though I was more worldly wise and less naive than before, I was apprehensive.

Ray left for Vancouver after I had been pronounced fit, and it was a good six months before he was able to find a job and our son and I could join him. For the first few months Ray's salary was barely enough to cover our basic needs, but we were optimistic that things would improve. This time I did not look for work because I preferred to look after my son until he was at least two years old.

One day as I was walking down the street with Sam in his stroller, a man stuck his head out of a passing car and yelled, "I hate f---ing Pakis; they stink! Why don't you go home?"

It is difficult to express how one feels at a moment like this so I will not even attempt to do so. With time, however, one learns to develop a thicker skin, but the hurt never goes. And yet I have to say that there had been times when I was out with Sam and people had stopped to say: "Oh, what a cute child!" or "What gorgeous eyes!" These remarks went a long way in assuaging my fears and helped to ease the pain of the other stupid insults.

My family doctor advised me to consult a Vancouver psychiatrist about the medication I was taking. She took one look at my report and said: "Bullshit! There's nothing wrong with you. All you need is to get back to work. You can stop all those drugs."

I was really excited by this vote of confidence and began looking for a babysitter and employment. It wasn't long before I landed both, but within three months I quit the job because of a personality clash with my boss who was himself a European immigrant. I noticed that all my colleagues were immigrants, and most were handicapped by their inability to speak English too well. As a result they were constantly being exploited by my boss. As his tyranny increased, I realized that I had been hired not because I was the most qualified to do the job, but because I was an immigrant and therefore would be more submissive. This knowledge hurt so much that I quit at once. If it is bad *not* being hired because you are an immigrant, it is worse to be hired because you are one. It is as if you are hired not on the basis of your merits, but because of your weakness.

This experience proved so shocking that I almost had another nervous breakdown which served to highlight the fact that my psychiatrist had erred in her diagnosis. I was still emotionally unstable and incapable of managing without drugs.

Instead I fled back to India on a holiday with Sam and into the care of my former psychiatrist who prescribed medication that brought me back to my senses. When I returned to Canada four months later and contacted my Canadian psychiatrist, she was sensible enough to say that she didn't think she was qualified to treat me because my problem seemed to have a cultural basis of which she was totally unaware. I was transferred to an Asian psychiatrist who diagnosed my problem, and we have managed to keep it under control since then.

Meanwhile Sam was growing up a beautiful and intelligent child. What filled our hearts with delight was purchasing a house for him to grow up in. Despite being so far from our families, everything seemed worthwhile here in Canada because we felt certain that Sam would have a better life in this great country. It was in our first home that an event occurred I shall never forget.

It was our first Christmas, but because we are Hindus, this holiday had no religious significance for us then. Today we do have a little tree with gifts for Sammy, but then he had been too small, and all we did was send cards to our friends. We had also sent a card to our neighbours, Fred and Alison. Imagine our surprise to find a gift for Sammy on our doorstep when we awoke on Christmas morning.

At about 4:00 p.m. that afternoon, Fred walked into our house and found us watching TV.

"TV on Christmas day!" he boomed. "I can't have that. Get ready and come over to our place. Alison is cooking a great dinner, and you must join us."

And just like that we were part of an intimate family Christmas dinner! We were deeply touched and from that day on felt an integral part of Canada.

It was only after I was working again and Sammy was at a daycare centre that I realized he was going to have problems, too. I had always thought that because he was growing up in Canada, he would be spared much of the agony of wondering if he would be accepted in Canadian society. Suddenly one night last year he asked me, "Mom, how come I'm white at home and become brown when I go to daycare?"

This incident drove home rather forcefully the point that he and maybe his children and grandchildren would be different as well. I dismissed the question as natural childish curiosity and didn't think he was being sensitive. However, I was wrong because one day he asked, "Mom, if you and Dad had lived in Canada when I was born, would I look like a Canadian?"

I tried to tell him he *was* a Canadian and that he *did* look like me, but he was not convinced. "Oh, come on, don't kid me. I don't look white," he said.

I felt like a real hypocrite then. Yes, he would have to sort out a lot of problems in his little mind in the years to come, and all I could do was hope that he would develop a sense of belonging.

He's just a child, but he is incredibly patriotic. He takes great pleasure in singing "O, Canada" at every opportunity. He is annoyed that all his favourite TV shows are made in United States and not Canada. His face lights up when he sees a maple leaf. I have every reason to believe that in him Canada has a citizen to be proud of, but...I have been doing much soul-searching and I find that his upbringing is definitely not Canadian. We have tried our best to assimilate into the outside world, but at home we are still very much Indian. Our food, our music, our religion, everything is different. How can we expect our child not to be confused?

Then there is the issue of stereotyping. Ray goes to a very good barber near our home who is a jovial type. But whenever he sees Ray, he asks: "So what sawmill do you work in?" Ray has told him repeatedly that he works as a management consultant, but the man just can't seem to accept this. I have also been asked several times if I work as a nurse's aide. Now there is nothing demeaning in these professions, but I find it a little irksome that people should jump to the conclusion that I am capable of doing only certain kinds of jobs.

I have talked to several Canadian "WASPS", who are close friends, about these issues, and their reaction has almost always been: "I'm not a typical Canadian because I'm not a racist at all, but . . . ." My conclusions based on several such discussions are that the average Canadian's attitude toward the immigrant is—"They can't help the way they look, so we'll accept that, but that's as far as we'll go. They will have to accept our ways and mannerisms in everything else. If not, they can do what they like in the privacy of their home, but outside they should conform."

Therefore, this is the approach I have chosen for myself. At home I am almost entirely Indian, but outside I ape every Canadian mannerism possible. I must confess that since there is no definite Canadian identity, this is quite difficult. Of one thing I am convinced and that is the "ethnic mosaic" is a myth.

Our lives now are typical immigrant success stories. Ray and I both have jobs where we are respected, and we live in our own home in a very respectable neighbourhood. We have an adorable child, but are we really happy? Will we ever regret our decision to make Canada our home?

Sammy's future is what will decide that. The decision to come here was ours, but the consequences are something he will have to face. We don't want him subjected to emotional hurt he wasn't responsible for, but will we be able to prevent it? Only time will tell.

Kerop Bedoukian

MIKE'S FAMILY
by Kerop Bedoukian

This is not my story. I was born in Sivas, Anatolia, Turkey in 1907 and survived the Turkish massacres. I wrote a book, *The Urchin* in which I recounted the true and chilling story of the long death march — how I, my family and thousands of others were driven by the Turks from our Sivas home in 1915, through the mountains, over the Euphrates River and across the deserts of the Ottoman Empire. With the remnants of my family, I escaped to Bulgaria and in 1926 emigrated to Canada, becoming a naturalized Canadian in 1931.

No, this is about three brothers who came to Canada from Egypt at two-year intervals.

They had left behind their father, mother and a younger brother, 16-year-old Steve. The time now arrived to have them brought to Canada and complete the family. Mike, a Canadian citizen and businessman with a capital of eighty thousand dollars, employed twelve people and was in an excellent position to sponsor his relatives. He had no difficulty in having his application accepted.

Mike was expecting his parents to arrive within three months and made preparations accordingly. He heard from them that they had had their medical examination and were waiting to be called for their visa.

A period of waiting always seems like an eternity for an anxious person. In the case of Mike, his patience was exhausted after four months, and so he decided to inquire in Montreal what was holding up his parents' visas. He was told that his younger brother, Steve, was "inadmissible" because he fell into one of the most serious "prohibited" classes in the Immigration Regulations — mental retardation.

Armed with his bank book, Mike presented himself to the Immigration Appeal Board. He explained that although his brother might not be the brightest child, he certainly was no moron and proved it with statements from half a dozen doctors who had examined him in Egypt. He proved his financial ability and would sign any document to guarantee that this brother would never become a public charge.

The Board ordered a re-examination of the young boy. Again, in Egypt, the child was examined by a Canadian doctor and again he was classified as mentally retarded and inadmissible.

Mike's lawyer, his influential friends, even his Member of Parliament tried to intervene. In each case, the strictness of the law prevailed.

* * *

It was at this time that Mike came to me for help . . . not because he knew me, but because he knew of an Armenian family from Egypt who, under the same circumstances, had succeeded in bringing to Canada a 14-year-old girl. This girl was not only of very low intelligence, but also was mongoloid in appearance. How was she permitted to come? That's what Mike wanted to know.

At the time when this girl's family were struggling with the problem, they had involved me. I was able to help because I knew a cabinet minister personally who consented to intervene with the Minister of Immigration. The Minister of Immigration can, if he wishes, overrule any regulation by a "Special Ministerial Order". Although this privilege is rarely used, in this case, he could hardly refuse a colleague. Evidently Mike had extracted this story out of the girl's parents, in spite of their promise to me not to reveal the source of their achievement.

I told Mike truthfully that since then, not only had my friend lost the election and was out of politics, but his party had also fallen out of power. Really, there was nothing I could do. He neither liked nor believed what I said.

Mike did not give up his search for a solution. As an elder son, not only did he feel responsible for the unification of his family, but also the desperate letters from his parents were keeping him under pressure. His continuing inquiries among the Armenians who, in one way or another, had had difficulties in their immigration procedure, had led inevitably to me, and I had already rejected him.

Six months went by. One day Mike phoned me and said that the President of the Central Committee of Egypt (Parekordsagan) was in Montreal and would like to see me. Could he and his mother, who had come for a visit, accompany him?

Yes, of course they could.

The appointment was made after hours in order to talk without interruption. They arrived punctually and after the introduction, I braced myself for the confrontation. I was hoping I would be able to make them understand that my position was not one of stubbornness but a genuine inability to act on their behalf.

The president recounted how often he had heard of me. He praised me for helping all those who wished to immigrate to Canada and followed with the wish that I would continue doing so. At first I felt flattered, then embarrassed and finally resentful of his exaggerated praise. In conjunction with the president, the mother made her plea. She said, "I have come all the way from Egypt especially to see you.

We have tried everything without success; you are our only hope." She told me about her despair as a mother; the thought of being permanently separated from her sons; and the intolerable life in Egypt.

Now came the "heavy artillery" of the president. He told me he had assured this family that I would not refuse him, that he had taken a side trip from his U.S. tour especially to see me and say how deserving this family was. After further elaborating on the importance of this case, he ended by saying that he would consider this a personal favour.

My answer still should have been no. I should not have raised their hopes. I, myself, had no hope. The problem was they still thought I could do it. Under the circumstances, if I refused them outright, this would be interpreted as unwillingness and would embarrass the president. The only solution I could think of was to try and fail and in so doing, prove to them that it was not because of lack of concern, but because it could not be done.

So, I said, "Look! Just because I did it once, does not mean that I can do it again. I have no way of reaching the minister. All I can promise is that I will try."

The president was delighted. He said: "That's all we want," and turned to the mother and said "Yeghav, yeghav (it got done)." He again expressed his confidence in me and showered me with praise which almost made me feel sorry for committing myself.

Have you ever hated yourself? Well, that's the way I felt. I felt cornered. I did not even know where to start. Reaching the minister, impossible as it was, would not accomplish anything. He would certainly say no. Why should he act against his own law? He hadn't even heard of me.

The request had to be made by a person whom the minister would find it difficult to refuse. A relative? Hardly; no relative would fight for me hard enough to get the minister's consent. A politician? Perhaps; but the only politicians I knew were members of parliament; they would get a lecture on upholding the law instead of asking for it to be broken. Nothing less than the Prime Minister would do and I considered this thought to be the most ridiculous.

I could not get the problem out of my mind. I thought about it during the day and dreamt about it at night. It was during the night two weeks later than an idea occurred to me. About a year before, one of my customers had mentioned that her mother was the President of the Women's Federal Liberal Party. I had filed this information in the back of my mind for a probable use in the future, but I could not recall the name of the customer. I went through my files and within an hour I came across the name and recognized it.

I called upon my customer and explained my dilemma. I wanted to know if her mother would be willing to help me.

"I don't know," she said, "would you like to ask her yourself?"

Yes,I would.

She called her mother on the telephone and after talking about each of the grandchildren, introduced me and passed the telephone to me.

I avoided telling her the nature of my problem. I expressed my wish of telling it to her personally. She said that she was leaving the next day for a lecture tour across Canada, but was able to give me an appointment two weeks hence.

When the date of the appointment arrived, I dared not telephone her. I was afraid she would make an excuse and postpone it, which might call off the whole thing. I rang the doorbell at 6:30 p.m. sharp. A charming lady of about 65 years ushered me in. She was a picture of French aristocracy, and her apartment reflected her personality—graceful, tasteful and luxurious.

After some small talk, she offered me a drink, adding it would relax me. (Had she noticed my confusion?) In no time at all she put me at ease. She told me all about her trip, her public talks, the philosophy of the Liberal party and the women's role in the Liberal party. We spent two and a half hours talking, and I enjoyed every minute of it.

Then she asked me what she could do for me. First I talked about my own background; my work with the immigrants; problems of resettlement; the heartaches of divided families and the plea of a mother to join her sons. She was polite enough to hear me out, so I went into further details of Mike's success in Canada and his sadness because he could not help his youngest brother.

When she felt I had finished my story, she said, "That shouldn't be hard. I shall be in Ottawa next week and I'll speak to Claude," calling the Minister of Immigration by his first name. I warned her that this was not a normal request. The minister would quite likely be reluctant to override the law. She pooh-poohed me, but then she had a second thought and asked me to present my request to her in writing.

At the time of my parting, she asked me to let her know if I did not hear from the Immigration Department within two weeks. I departed in a mood of exhilaration and had one of the most comfortable sleeps I had enjoyed for weeks.

Twenty-four days after I had mailed my letter of request, I heard from the Deputy Minister. I was told that the Minister of Immigration had given his consent for the move to Canada of Steve and his parents. I passed this information on to Mike and my benefactress.

In Egypt, the visa officer, before giving them their visas, requested a confirmation of the Ministerial Order from Ottawa. Again, upon arrival of the immigrants two months later, they were detained at the Montreal Airport for five hours until the admitting officer checked with Ottawa and was satisfied that such an order had been issued.

Months later, upon the continuous insistence of the mother, my wife and I accepted an invitation to dinner. Their expression of gratitude was overwhelming. Because I knew that such a heavy weight of gratitude usually turns to resentment, I minimized my role in the matter and told them that all I had done was make two phone calls and write one letter.

I cannot help thinking that it was their faith which performed the miracle because without it, I would not even have tried.

Editor's note: Because Kerop Bedoukian never forgot his heritage and his childhood experiences, he became involved in helping more than 2,500 Armenians from Turkey, Greece and Egypt to emigrate and settle in Canada. For 20 years he served as President of the Montreal Chapter of the Armenian General Benevolent Union and for 15 years was a member of the Central Committee of America for the same organization. In 1967 the Canadian government honoured his humanitarian activities by awarding him the Centennial Medal for "Services rendered to the Nation". Bedoukian died in July, 1981, following a stroke. This story, published posthumously, is from his casebook, a meticulous record of immigrant stories.

Albert O. Lee

THE PIED PIPERS OF ENGLAND

by Albert O. Lee

For he led us, he said, to a joyous land . . .
Where waters gushed and fruit trees grew,
And flowers put forth a fairer hue,
And everything was strange and new ...

Robert Browning

Early in June, 1940, Field Engineering Instructor Sergeant Albert O. Lee, 32, arrived in Ottawa from Camp Petawawa about 75 miles northwest of the city. He had a week's pass and went directly to St. George's Home for Boys and Girls on Wellington Street.

More than fifteen years had passed since he had been there, and he was amazed to find the building vacant and the doors unlocked. He walked in and saw pictures and papers scattered over the floors. Slowly he wandered through the deserted rooms, each one awakening memories etched indelibly in his mind. How strange that the nuns who had run the Home had left it in such a mess, he thought! It seemed as if they had moved out in great haste.

The Home had been an important part of Albert Lee's life. He had to know what had happened, but he wasn't sure where to go for information. Suddenly he remembered the church at the end of the block run by an order of Franciscan monks. Every morning they had come to say mass for the nuns and children in the Home.

Swinging his kitbag over his shoulder, Lee went down the block to the church. Inside he recognized a brown-robed monk and stopped him to ask: "What happened to St. George's Home and where did the nuns go?"

The monk looked at Sergeant Lee in astonishment. "I never knew," he answered.

"I don't understand you. You used to say mass every morning when I was there as a teen-ager. I remember you very well."

The monk turned and walked away without another word. Lee made a move to follow, then shook his head and left the church. For years afterwards this incident bothered him. He had been totally mystified and had the feeling that something had gone wrong. He wondered if anyone in Ottawa knew what had happened to St. George's Home. What about all the boys and girls who had lived there, waiting to be placed in homes and on farms, he thought? Who did they have to turn to now if they had a problem?

For most of the children that passed through the Home had problems. They were a small part of the many thousands of youngsters culled from the streets and back alleys, the orphanages and workhouses of England. These were children who had been orphaned at an early age, had been abandoned, neglected or had run away from abusive parents. Many had been placed in workhouses in the slums of large industrial cities. They were called "Nobody's children", "street Arabs", "Home children" or "waifs", and later were to be known as "little immigrants" — shipped to Canada as human cargo and distributed as cheap labour across the nation.

Albert O. Lee was one of these boys, but he was neither an orphan, a runaway, nor an abandoned child. Through a perverse set of circumstances, Albert O. Lee was literally kidnapped and shipped to Canada in 1920 at the age of twelve and a half.

HOME LIFE

I was born in Weymouth, England on January 27, 1908, the youngest of five children—three brothers and a sister. I am the only one left alive. When I was five years old, my father, a sergeant in the British Army, was sent to an outpost in India. My mother accompanied him, but because there were no schools in the area, she left the five of us behind. I never saw my mother again.

An older brother and my sister were placed in the care of grandparents, but two other brothers and myself were put into St. Anthony's Catholic Home for Boys in the summer of 1913. The Home was in Hatton, Middlesex, about 12 miles from London, and it worked in conjunction with a group called "The Crusade of Rescue". Their motto was "No child refused shelter."

The Sisters of Charity ran the Home. There was a Mother Superior, about twenty nuns and a priest who lived there. Other staff included a gardener and his family who had a small place on the grounds. There were at least 175 boys at St. Anthony's. The Sisters were very strict and kept us under constant supervision. They knew how to use the strap and cane very capably, believe me, for I was the recipient a good few times.

World War I broke out in 1914 and food became scarce because of the heavy loss of supply ships torpedoed in the English Channel. Often we went to bed on a supper of a single vegetable. Somehow or other we all scraped through although we were very hungry a good portion of the time.

Air raids became a way of life, and we had to blackout everything. At night we would watch our own searchlights weaving across the sky looking for enemy zeppelins. Fortunately, we were spared although we were only twelve miles from London, which suffered frequent bombing.

As if the war hadn't been bad enough, Spanish influenza hit Europe and spread like the plague westward. Millions died. I was only ten years old in 1918 when I came down with it. Of the 165 boys in the home at the time, about 80 per cent caught it, not all at the same time, of course. Miraculously we had no deaths. I heard one of the nuns say that the Home had the highest record for recovery in the country. Just south of us, there were people dying by the hundreds every day.

The flu was no respecter of age, sex or station. Some died within 24 hours; others lingered for days. When a family had a death from the flu, they placed a ribbon or piece of cloth on the front door to tell the drivers of the horse-drawn carts or wagons to pick up the dead. There were so many dying that even coal carts were pressed into service. I was told that more people died from the flu than had been killed in the war.

At the Home, all the sick boys were placed in one dormitory and the nuns watched and nursed them constantly. The first thing every morning, the nuns would walk through the school with a small hand shovel covered with live coals which they sprinkled with a type of disinfectant that created clouds of smoke and left a clean smell. Then they would feed us a dish of cooked stinging nettles for a couple of days. It tasted like spinach, and many of the boys refused to eat it. The nuns, however, forced it down them, and to this day I am convinced that this concoction had something to do with our astounding record of no fatalities.

Once this period of crisis was passed, things settled down to normal. Food was more plentiful and life was routine.

When my two older brothers turned fifteen, they were taken from the Home. One went into the British Army's Boy Service, and the other was sent to a draper's firm to learn a trade. I was left there all on my own.

One day in late September, 1920, the Sisters put on a magic lantern slide show. It was all about Canada and Australia. At the end, the nuns asked those of twelve and over, who wanted to go to Canada, to put up their hands. They took our names, and we were formed into a special group of about twenty boys and given a medical examination. No mention was made of Australia. This group was chosen for Canada.

We were told to write our parents to get permission to go. Those who had no parents were free to make their own decision. It wasn't until later that I realized this writing for permission was a ploy. I know I was in Canada long before my parents would have received my letter. Mail in those days took over two months to reach India.

When I was picked to go, I tried to get to my cubbyhole to pick up some addresses and pictures I had kept for years. On two different occasions, I was stopped by the same nun who never took her eyes off me. I had to leave everything behind, and that was when I realized that something was very wrong. It was a good thing I remembered my grandparents' address in Weymouth and managed to smuggle a letter off to them. That was how my mother discovered I was in Canada.

I also wrote a letter to the Home asking for my letters, addresses and pictures. They did answer, but told me nothing could be found. It was as if all my roots had been severed. There was nothing to tie me to my past. After I had been in Canada almost a year, a letter arrived from my mother. She was very upset and asked how and why I had gone to Canada. She had made plans for me to go to naval college as a cadet. This proved beyond a doubt that I had been packed off without permission. I kept in touch with my mother over the years. My father died in 1914 and my mother remarried in India and started another family with her new husband, who was an officer. I never met my stepfather.

Not long after our medical, we were sent to a Catholic Boys' Home in Endfield, north of London. Another group of twenty boys joined us and we were measured by tailors, who came from London, for two suits of clothing as well as other clothes and underwear. We had never been given anything like this before. In addition, two small kit bags were issued to each boy.

Two weeks later we were taken to Liverpool. At the dock a group of about thirty girls from a Catholic Girls' Home joined us. About mid-afternoon we boarded a huge ship, the *S.S. Victorian*, and six boys were packed into an eight-foot-square room with two three-tier bunks. The upper part of the walls were enclosed in wire mesh. We laughed at it even though we felt like animals in a cage. These bunks were located in the steerage area of the ship, and the stench was awful.

It was October 13, 1920, and very soon the anchor came up, and we were on our way to a new life in a new country.

THE JOURNEY

Our passage was very rough. Waves, twenty to thirty feet high, battered the old ship, and she tossed and rolled so much the second day out that all of us were seasick. We stayed that way for two days. As we approached Canada, we hit a thick fog that slowed us down to a crawl, and it wasn't until October 20 that we reached Saint John, New Brunswick. As soon as we disembarked, we were met by Sisters from St. George's Home in Ottawa. Canadian doctors gave us another quick medical, and then we were loaded on a train at the nearby station. As we passed through Quebec, children were taken off to meet farmers who had booked ahead for child workers.

That was when the tears began to fall. Long friendships were shattered. Many children broke down and sobbed. Others acted indifferent to hide their anguish. They withdrew behind a wall of silence. The train conductor must have known how hard it was for us. He made a point of helping the youngsters off the train without making them rush. He waved good-bye to all as they went off with the farmers. I am sure he had children of his own, and he felt sorry for us.

This procedure continued all the way to Ottawa. By that time, there were only two of us left, my chum, Conrad Cooper, and myself. We left the train with our kitbags and waited to be picked up. The station was crowded, and everybody stopped and stared at us as we walked to a pre-arranged spot. There we were in short pants, bare knees, Eton-type jackets and tiny caps. We must have been a sight. We, in turn, were amused at the sight of Canadian boys in long pants. Many had funny caps with ear flaps or coloured woolen toques. Later when the cold winter weather started, I was happy to have this Canadian headgear.

As long as Conrad and I were together, we were fine. Soon a fine-looking couple came along to pick up my chum. We said good-bye and both of us broke down. I watched him go off with them and I never saw or heard of him again.

I was supposed to be picked up by Mr. Clarke, Superintendant of the Ottawa Experimental Farm. The Sisters told me I had one of the best homes to go to. About an hour later, a relative of Mr. Clarke turned up at the station and told the Sisters that Mr. Clarke was in the hospital after a heart attack.

Back to the lists went the Sisters, and they came up with a Mr. O'Brien. After a few phone calls, some kind of arrangement was made, for Mr. O'Brien's sister-in-law came to the station. She took me to her apartment for four days while arrangements were made with

Mr. O'Brien. He was to meet me on Friday evening at the station, twelve miles northeast of Ottawa.

Sure enough, he was there waiting for me with his horse and buggy, and we drove about five miles to his farm where I was introduced to his wife and four-year-old daughter. I wanted to clean up a bit and was taken to my room. To my dismay, I dicovered there was no bathroom or running water. I had to be shown the outhouse and how to take water from a bucket with a ladle to fill the wash basin in my room. My days of hot water were over, and the only tub I got was a small washtub, just big enough to stand in, for use in my room. I had no other choice but to get used to it, and to the fact there was no electricity, no music and nothing of interest to read. It was total isolation.

THE FARM PERIOD

Located about eight miles north of Templeton, the farm consisted of a small two-bedroom house with an attached summer kitchen. Midway between the barn and house was an outhouse. The well was forty feet away from the house. The barn and its occupants, three horses, ten cows, some calves and chickens were to be my responsibility. There was also a pigpen outside that I had to look after. I didn't mind. I loved the animals and did a good job feeding them and keeping the stables clean.

Another job I had to do was clean up brushwood around the pasture area and put it into piles for winter burning. Besides getting the cows fed early in the morning and milking and separating the milk, I had to churn the cream once a week into butter. Mrs. O'Brien made the best butter I ever tasted and sold it to a convent in Ottawa at twenty cents a pound. Mr. O'Brien supplied wood to the convent as well. After milking, the cows were turned out to pasture and had to be rounded up at night, fed, and milked again.

The country was mostly rolling terrain with lots of deep gullies that had small creeks running through them. There was a great deal of pine, maple and poplar trees as well as six-foot-high stumps all covered with charcoal, the result of a fire many years before. Below the charcoal line, the wood was good enough for kindling. Mr. O'Brien and I would clear the land and pull out these stumps. Many times we had to use powder to blast them loose. Then I would attach the team of horses with a logging chain and haul away.

We would fell trees in the winter for next year's supply and more for sale in Ottawa. When it was all piled behind the house, the O'Briens would arrange a woodcutting bee, when a group of neighbours and friends came over to help saw the wood, using a power saw. There were all kinds of bees: ploughing, clearing land, thrashing; and when a new person arrived in the area to farm, everyone would get together and have a building bee for him. This included digging a well and setting up a small house and stable for his stock and horses. Some of these bees lasted a week. The women would prepare the food and helped with the cooking and serving of the meals. People seemed to care more about one another in those days.

My first winter on the farm was rough. My English clothing was not warm enough. I had to have warmer underwear and winter coats for work since I was outdoors most of the time. My wages were two dollars a month which was sent to the Ottawa home for safekeeping. I couldn't touch it until I was eighteen years old, and so I never had two cents I could call my own.

Another thing that was lacking was education. Although I was supposed to go to school, I only went for a few weeks. When the inspectors came to see me to check if I was attending school and how I was getting on, I was told to lie and tell them I was doing well and was warmly dressed for winter.

Those few brief weeks of education were an experience. Miss Flossy Jessop, the teacher, was very kind and understanding. She had to teach all grades up to eight, and we were placed in small groups according to our level. With all the different studies, it must have been very difficult for her.

On the second day of class, I was asked to stand up and read aloud. The students all had a good laugh, not only at my English accent, but my reading speed. However, I felt a little better when one of the bigger boys got up to read, and he had a hard time of it. He sounded as if he didn't get too much practice.

I managed to get along with all the students except one. I got in one good fight when this boy called me a bloody bloke. It was the first time I had ever been called that, and I got angry. He said it again, and I punched him in the nose. I never saw anyone bleed so much. I must have broken a blood vessel. I felt terrible. Unknown to us, the teacher had seen and heard the whole thing, and after she doctored him up, she reprimanded me and added in a soft voice, "That boy has a bad tongue."

The next morning the boy's big brother drove him to school, and when he tied up the horses, he shouted: "Where's that little English lad?"

My heart sank. I expected a beating, but he ran over to me, shook my hand and said that his brother had a bad mouth. "I think, maybe, you did him some good," he said.

He made us shake hands and took off, and after that I was known as "Mick O'Brien's young lad".

Shortly after this I was taken out of school and never left the farm except for the odd time to go to church on Sunday. The Roman Catholic church was eight miles away in a village located in the central lower part of a hugh land basin. Once you reached the rim you could see for miles. The most spectacular view was on Sundays during the winter. All the different types of sleighs converged from miles around on the church down the gradual slope. From east, west, north and south they came, the sleighbells ringing in different keys and pitches and the people's voices wafting on the wind. It reminded me of a picture book of early pioneer days.

The church itself was unusual. The first time I went with the O'Briens, I couldn't believe my eyes when we stepped inside. In those days, women wore large hats with long ostrich feathers. They were every possible colour, and there were so many you couldn't see the altar. The ladies were dressed up in tight-waisted dresses with "fluffed-up shoulders" and button boots. I had been used to nuns' habits from my early years on and then farm clothes, so this was a sight indeed.

The congregation consisted of French Canadians and Irish Canadians. The priest would preach in two languages. When he started in English, the French would stand up and go out for a smoke. When he finished, the Irish would leave for a chat and cigarette, and the French would return. Sunday was a busy day for the congregation. Very few people had phones then, and a lot of business was transacted outside during these language breaks.

The first year I had managed to struggle through all the chores expected of me and perhaps more than should have been demanded. The second winter I was given responsibility for all the chores on the farm, because Mr. O'Brien was hauling wood to sell in Ottawa and left very early in the morning. He didn't get back until ten or eleven at night. I would get up at five a.m., feed the horses and put up a bundle of hay and bag of oats on the load of wood. I would clean the horses, harness them to the loaded sleigh and take them to the well for a drink of water. By that time, Mr. O'Brien had his breakfast, and he climbed onto the seat and drove off. I worked all day and had to wait until he returned to take care of the horses and sleigh. Many times I didn't get to bed until long after midnight.

The next day we would load the sleigh again with a cord and a half of wood while the horses rested. Mr. O'Brien hauled wood three times a week on alternate days depending on the condition of the roads. It wasn't long before I became capable of performing all the mediocre jobs without supervision.

Mr. O'Brien had to keep a certain stretch of road open all winter, and after every storm and very often at night, we would go out and roll the snow. There were no ploughs in those days, and we used a field roller to tamp down the snow. This road-clearing work was Mr. O'Brien's means of paying his taxes. Most of the farmers near the main road did this type of work.

One of the most demanding jobs in the winter months was taking the cows out to the waterhole in the creek every day. It was half a mile away, and I had to cut a hole at least two feet in diameter, hurry back to get the cows moving out of the barn, run ahead back to the creek and open up the hole again for it froze very quickly. In very cold weather, the cows would take a quick drink and hurry off back to the warm barn. All this was time-consuming.

This kind of work was beginning to affect me physically and emotionally. I became very lonesome and depressed and wrote to the Home in Ottawa. Mr. O'Brien was a hard man to work for, and I was terribly unhappy. Late in the spring word came through from Ottawa to have me returned. I was taken to the station the next day. Mr. O'Brien bought my ticket and left. I remained there waiting for the train. In a little while a man came over and introduced himself as Mr. Borden and began talking to me. He asked where I was going and I told him a bit about myself. He asked if I would like to work on his farm, but I told him the nuns were meeting me at the Ottawa station.

"Don't worry. I'll fix that," he said. He returned my ticket to the stationmaster, and we got into his buggy and went to his farm.

It was a nice place. The highway passed through it as well as a fairly large and deep river which cut across the middle of his land. He was a good man and treated me like a brother. I enjoyed working for him. He took me to the village to meet his father, mother and two sisters. They were all so kind to me, I felt like one of the family. Then Mr. Borden took his two sisters and me for a swim. I didn't have any trunks so the girls took a flower sack, cut off the corners, tied the top around my waist, and I had my first swim.

I guess it was the change in the atmosphere, but I really liked working there. The cattle would pasture across the river and I would get across sitting on the back of the bull as it swam over. He was a nice animal and liked me. He had a yoke around his neck and a ring through his nose with an attached chain, and I would lead him around like a pet. One day while I was crossing the highway on his back, an American tourist took our picture. I often wondered what happened to that photograph. I would have liked a copy of it.

I was there only three days when the police came to ask for me. They told Mr. Borden it was against the rules of the Home to put a Catholic boy in a non-Catholic home. Mr. Borden said he knew the Catholic priest in the village and would get special permission to keep me. The priest was vey nice and said he would intercede for Mr. Borden. My employer promised he would send me to church every Sunday, and he even paid the top price for a pew at the front of the church just for me. Imagine my surprise the first Sunday I went to church to be met by the priest and escorted to my very own pew!

However, two days later, the police came with orders from Ottawa to send me back to the Home. So Mr. Borden hitched up his buggy and drove all the way to Ottawa to talk to the nuns. He told them what he thought of their regulations and how disappointed he was in them. But they wouldn't budge. He gave me some money, the first I had ever had in my pocket since coming to Canada and shook hands with me. He told me to come and see him anytime I was free.

He was the only farmer who really showed affection and cared for me. And just because of religious differences, I wasn't permitted to stay with him. It was a terrible shame...religion first and a child's welfare and need for love, second.

I was kept at the Home for a few days and then sent to a French-Canadian family in Lancaster. They had a boy of six and a girl of four. The farm had 100 acres of level land and was more modern than the other two places I had been. It even had running water in the cattlebarn. There were about fourteen cows, a bull, two horses, pigs, geese and chickens, and the farmer had a Model T Ford. I was promised room and board, my clothes and four dollars a month. My bed was a bunk-type with a straw mattress that took getting used to.

We were about six miles from the Catholic church, and I could only get there once in a great while. With Mr. Borden I would have been there every Sunday.

The family bought me a new suit with pants just below the knees and knee-high socks that came up over the bottom of the pants. I was so glad to be rid of my English clothes. I learned to speak French pretty well. I was already fourteen and a half years old, and again I was back in the same old routine I had had before with no change, no breaks. I had no play, no school, and no sports . . . just drudgery, but at least conditions were better than at the O'Brien farm.

While I was working here, I met an older man who had come to Canada years before as a child immigrant. He must have been about forty, but he looked so tired and so much older than his age that I felt sorry for him. The first time he saw me ploughing he remarked that I was kind of small to be using a two-furrow plough. My feet were bare; my boots were too small and I didn't have any others. The man was amazed at the work I was doing for he had never used any kind of horse-drawn farm implement. He was just a cow and stable man. He would cross two farms just to come and talk to me. I would see him sitting behind the barn smoking his pipe and just staring straight ahead. He looked so unkempt; I never saw him in clean, neat clothes. From that time on the one thought in my mind was to get off the farms. I didn't want to end up like him. He was still on the same farm where he had been placed as a child.

And so, I decided to get back to Ottawa although I liked the French-Canadian farmer. The nuns already had me booked for another farm, but I refused to go and threatened to run away. This changed their minds, and I was sent to the Ottawa Golf Club as a bellhop. From then on I was on my own. Any money I earned was mine. I bought my own clothes and paid my own room and board where it was not provided. This was one of my biggest joys—working for myself and keeping my own money.

My first brush with a celebrity while working at the club provided a touch of amusement. We had had a bad snow storm. Although the main highway was open, the 300 yards to the club house were blocked. As bellhops, we had to meet all cars at the highway and carry the guests' bags to the club house, which was a hotel as well as a club. Guests often stayed for a week or more.

A taxi pulled up, and I carried two suitcases for a gentleman who appeared to be very important. I placed the bags in his room, and he gave me a ten-cent tip. When I came downstairs, the other bellhops were grinning. They told me the man was Sir Henry Thornton, director and head of the Canadian National Railway.

"Now you know Sir Henry as well as we do," said a bellhop. "We knew he was coming and put you in line ahead of the rest of us."

I never forgot that incident, and we all had a laugh over it.

I was at the club only a few months and requested something else. The nuns found a job for me at the Ottawa Protestant Hospital. In the morning I worked in the drug department on general cleanup and on medicine refill for the wards. In the afternoon, I was kept busy in the laboratory, doing all kinds of odd jobs. I enjoyed it, but somehow became very ill. Perhaps I picked up something there. We had just moved from the old hospital to the New Ottawa Civic Hospital, and I had been working in the laboratory all day. I went off on sick leave, but it was a long time before I recovered from my illness. The Home placed me with an Ottawa family because I was still shaky. I didn't do much work, just puttered around, and the hospital paid my room and board.

During this period, I would go to the Home on Sundays. There were many of us child immigrants there and we had get-togethers, sing-songs and parties arranged for us. It was the only amusement most of us had. There were quite a few like myself who refused to go back to farm work. The nuns found jobs for them in Ottawa. Three or four worked on an Ottawa newspaper as typesetters and some were telegram-delivery boys on bicycles. Many of the girls were working as housemaids all over the city.

I remember one girl whose name was Smith. She had been returned to the Home after working for a French-Canadian family for years. She had forgotten how to speak English. By then I spoke a little French, and she told me she had been on this farm since she was ten or eleven years old. She hadn't heard a word of English in seven years. I can believe it for I was getting to the stage where I was speaking half and half, and I had only been with the French-Canadian farm family for twenty months.

There was one girl I met at St. George's Home who came to a sad end. She was such a lovely girl and had been working for a dentist in Ottawa. About 1923 or 1924 I saw her picture in a Chicago weekly with the heading "Beautiful British Immigrant Girl Commits Suicide". The reason given was despondency. I can well believe it. However, I didn't see anything about it in the Canadian papers. There must have been more cases that were never publicized.

One day while I was still recuperating, I saw a huge sign outside Union Station. Men and women were wanted to harvest wheat crops out west. I went to the hospital and was given permission to go. My job would be held for me at the hospital when I returned. However, I never went back. I stayed out on the prairies for almost two years.

THE PRAIRIE YEARS

It was 1924, and I went to the Ottawa train station and bought a return ticket to the west for $15. I was probably the youngest there — only sixteen and a half years old. There were hundreds of men of all ages and some women as well who were to cook for the harvesters. The women were given the four coaches up front, and the men filled the last 25 or 26 cars. There were many other trains that left Ottawa after we did, loaded with harvesters bound for the west.

Once aboard, I chummed up with a young chap about my age. The conductor put us near two big men, a Scot and an Irishman. He asked them to keep an eye on us so we didn't get into any trouble. On one occasion, these two men chased away a couple of drunks who were trying to get us to drink with them.

With all the drinking going on, the train became very noisy and rowdy. Fights broke out, and we heard there had been a couple of stabbings. One coach was really wrecked the second day out as a result of the brawling. There must have been a telegraph sent ahead for help because the RCMP came aboard soon after and stayed until order had been established. Once things quietened down and were back to normal, the officers left.

Although no meals were served along the way, there were thirty-minute stops several times a day in cities or towns so we could run off and get something to eat. The railway had tables loaded with food set up on the platforms, and we paid for whatever we took. It was well-organized and continued this way until Winnipeg, where we were taken off and told to report to desks marked in alphabetical order. In this way we were directed to farms in various places and given extra tickets to proceed directly there.

It was hot and once we were back on the train and on our way, the heat increased. Some of the men went on top of the train, trying to cool off on the roof. We heard that several had been swept off when the train entered a tunnel.

At one point we were delayed by a hotbox, caused by friction overheating the wheels. It was mid-afternoon on an exceptionally hot day. About 300 yards from where we had stopped was a beautiful lake. The men asked the trainman if they had enough time to run over and take a swim. He said okay, and many took off, undressed and jumped in. They were barely in the water when the train whistle hooted and the engine started up. The men went splashing frantically through the shallows, grabbed their clothes and raced bare-foot and naked for the cars. The train was already moving at a good speed. A few made it aboard, many others were left behind, and a couple were hurt when they lost their balance trying to swing onto the moving train. It never slowed or stopped.

I remember some of the men stealing a cow somewhere along the route where we stopped. They tied it to the last car with a rope. By the time it was noticed, all that was left of that poor animal was a pair of horns on the end of the rope. I only hope that the men on the trains that followed ours didn't indulge in such vile acts of cruelty.

About an hour after the lake incident, we pulled into the railway yards off the main line for quite a while. Perhaps it was the hotbox again or maybe orders had been given to wait for the men who had been left behind. The heat had not abated, and we had run out of drinking water for all the coaches. The men spotted a well with a pump in front of a small house across the track. A number went over and asked the lady of the house for water. She came out with two pretty daughters, about seventeen and eighteen years old, and the girls carried buckets with mugs. As each girl handed out a mug of water, the men gave her a thank-you kiss. The kisses began lasting longer and longer, and finally the mother became very angry. She ran to the house for a broom and pounded a man off one daughter and then smacked another away. The funny part about this was the girls seemed to be enjoying the whole thing. Suddenly papa came out with a club, and he chased the men out of his front yard and back to the tracks. He took the water buckets back, and that put an end to the thank-you kisses. Considering that 300 to 400 men had been supplied with water as well as fringe benefits, everyone was happy, except of course, the girls' parents.

Again we were on our way and at 2:30 a.m. the train finally arrived at Redland, where my chum and I had been placed. The hotel and cafe were locked. There wasn't a soul around, and it began to rain. We had nowhere to sleep and very little money. We decided to walk the track to Rockyford, the next station, eight miles away. It hadn't rained there, and we were put to work immediately. The farmers had been waiting at the station to pick up the harvesters, and we worked for five days.

Then came the rains again, and the farmers took us to the station and told us they could not keep us in rainy weather. That was when my friend took off to Calgary. I decided to stay and found a job at the local hotel. I worked for ten days and thought I would head farther west. There was a better chance to get threshing jobs because the crops grew in later the farther west you went. But there was more wet weather, so I stopped in Calgary, stayed overnight and found a job on the railroad.

A new line was being built, and I became a teamster. I had to fall into line behind a huge grader that was drawn by thirty horses. Once it started a cut, it didn't stop. We teamsters kept pace beside it, and as the earth came through the slide door on its side, we loaded up and galloped off while the next wagon behind took up its position for a load. I had to circle around, dump my load and then fall into line again. It was monotonous work. We had to keep at it for ten hours a day and had to look after our horses as well. This meant getting up early, feeding the animals and at night we would have to do the same before we could get to sleep ourselves.

I did this for five days and had to quit because our only water supply came from a nearby slough which was impure. I got very ill drinking this alkaline water. I never made a cent from this back-breaking work because I had to pay my fare from Calgary to the job site from my wages. If I had been able to stick at it for a month, my fare would have been paid.

So I left and walked to Hanna, the nearest town. On my way, I cut across a field where a farmer was cutting wheat with a binder. I asked if he needed any help and I was hired and put to work stooking. While I worked I would sing and hum a song the nuns had taught us back in England and which we sang in the Home in Ottawa. I suppose it was meant to glorify farm life. It probably was a dream that kept a good number of lads down on the farm. We didn't realize how unrealistic it was then, and to this day when I sing it to myself, I smile ironically, certainly not with joy.

The Farmer's Boy

The sun went down beyond yon hills
Across yon dreary moor
When weary and lame, a boy there came
Up to the farmer's door
May I ask you, if any there be
That will give me employ?
To plough and sow, to reap and mow
And to be a farmer's boy

(Repeat last four lines)

And if that thou won't me employ
One thing I have to ask
Will you shelter me, till break of day
From this cold wintry blast?
At break of day I'll trudge away
Elsewhere to seek employ
To plough and sow, to reap and mow
And to be a farmer's boy

My father's dead, my mother's left
With her five children small
And what is worse for mother still
I'm the eldest of them all
Though little I be, I fear not work
If thou wilt me employ
To plough and sow, to reap and mow
And be a farmer's boy

In course of time, he grew a man
The good old farmer died
And left the boy the farm now has
And his daughter for his bride
The boy that was, the farm now has
He thinks and smiles with joy
Of the lucky day he came that way
For to be a farmer's boy

I stayed with him until all his crop was threshed and then went along with the owner of the threshing machines to get some other farmers' crops done. Then I spent the winter hauling wheat to the grain elevators for Mr. Lee Doyle of Hanna who supplied the wagons or the sleighs in winter. It was a cold job. In the spring I helped him put in his crop and then hired out to other neighbours who needed help. There were some who had no money to pay me, and that was how I acquired three saddle horses, a saddle and a rifle. I was paid in trade.

Mr. Doyle would board my horses while I worked elsewhere. After I had harvested his crop that summer, I sold one of the horses and took off for Calgary about 100 miles away. I rode one horse and strapped my suitcases to the other one's back. I stopped off at farms for food and water, and although I was willing to pay, people refused to accept my money. I slept outside with the horses and I remember these three days as the happiest of the five years I had spent in Canada.

When I reached Calgary, I went to the livery stable to put up my horses for the night. The man who looked after the stable asked me to have a cup of coffee, looked after my horses and then returned to tell me one of them had a saddle blister. He had already phoned the veterinarian to drain it. It wasn't serious, but the horses needed a few days' rest. It was getting late in the fall. I had intended riding over the Rockies, my idea of the thrill of a lifetime, but the stableman said he could get buyers for the horses if I wanted to sell them.

I agreed and offered him one-third of whatever he could get. The following day a couple of schoolteachers bought the horses. I was pleased to see the animals owned by teachers who needed them to get to and from the country schools where they taught.

We shook hands, I took my money and headed for the station where I boarded a train for Vancouver. I had enough money to last for a while. But work was very hard to find in Vancouver, and soon my money ran out. And so, I made a decision. I went down to the recruiting office, and on November 20, 1926, I joined the Canadian Army—Princess Patricia's Light Infantry.

THE ARMY LIFE

It was the best decision I could have made. I got involved in sports again, as in my earlier years, and in a short time, I was on the rugby team, football, water polo, baseball and boxing teams. Then the army opened up educational courses, and I went back to school to make up for all the years I had missed while working on the farms as a teenager. I went to classes two afternoons a week and at night. I had a lot of catching up to do, but I managed to get through.

When I was nineteen years old and stationed at Esquimalt, B.C., I wrote to the Home in Ottawa and requested the money I had earned on the farms. It was held for us until we were eighteen years of age. In my request I instructed the nuns to keep the price of a ton of coal for the Home as a donation.

They sent me a thank-you note along with a cheque for $70. This was what I had earned for two years and eight months of backbreaking work as a child immigrant.

I stayed on at the camp for a while as an instructor, teaching there and at two other army camps. I remained in the service for 28 years, 3 with the infantry and 25 with the Royal Canadian Engineers. I ended up as a sergeant-major and was foreman of works at Vernon Military Camp when I was pensioned. The last job I did was change the army camp to a summer camp for cadets.

Looking back over my years as a soldier, I think I did accomplish a good deal. I even managed to get married, raise a son and daughter and become a grandfather.

My wife died in 1972. We had been living on Vancouver Island and shortly after her death I disposed of everything and moved to Brandon. My son invited me to visit Yellowknife, N.W.T. and I ended by settling there.

THE RETURN

In 1977, I flew back to England and met quite a few relatives I still had over there. I saw my sister for the first time since we had been separated 64 years earlier. I had been five years old, and here she was in her eighties. She passed on not long after that.

Although I had kept in touch with my mother, I never saw her after she left for India and she died in 1949 or 1950. I met some grand-nephews and grand-nieces and some sisters-in-law and then booked passage back on the Queen Elizabeth II. That smooth, luxurious voyage crossing the Atlantic made me think of the storm-tossed trip as a child immigrant crammed in steerage so many years before.

Many times I reminisced about the past and I can honestly say that I was never happy being a British child immigrant. Except in Western Canada, we were ridiculed wherever we went. I don't think we were all that bad. Most of us said very little. After we lost our English accents, there were fewer problems. Learning to speak French certainly helped me lose my accent much sooner. What was worse than the ridicule, however, was the fact we were victims of society. We were exploited and abused, and there was a definite lack of understanding and proper supervision by those in authority. I'm not bitter now that it is all over, but there were times when I was terribly unhappy.

My life improved tremendously once those early years of farming were over, and my life in Canada was great. I often thought that Britain and Canada should have united to make some arrangement to send all those children still alive on a free trip back to England. I am very sure many of us did earn it.

To this day, my children do not know about my early years in Canada as a child immigrant. There was a stigma attached to being a "Home Boy". As much as I wanted to tell them, I could never speak about it. Perhaps this account of my life will help them understand.

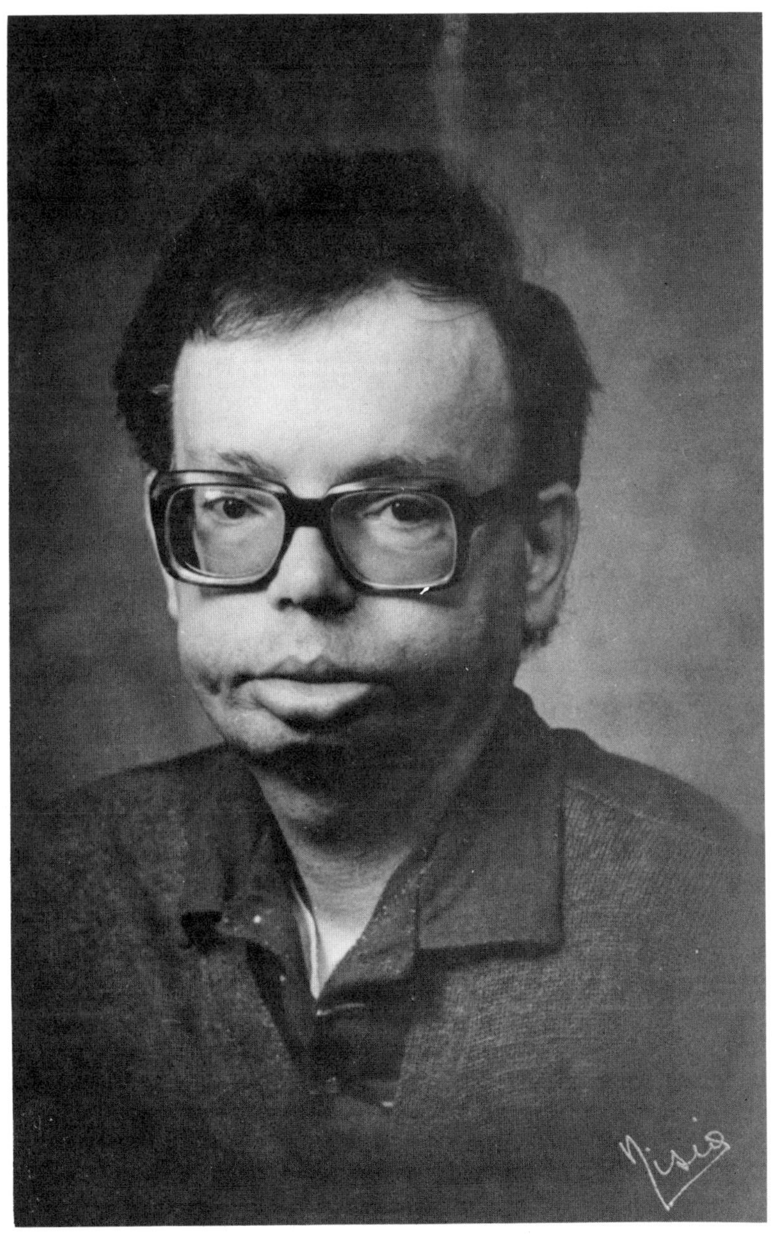

C.D. Minni

DOLLAR FEVER*
THE DIARY OF A PORTUGUESE PIONEER
by C. D. Minni

March 15th, 1954

We have been at sea four days now, out of Lisbon, and tomorrow disembark at Halifax. We are, I believe, among the first Portuguese in history to enter Canada.

Today, in anticipation of landing, Pedro, Estevan and myself tried to exchange the remainder of our *escudos* into Canadian money, but we were allowed only ten dollars each, for there are restrictions. So I spent some aboard—on a haircut, a tip to the steward and this notebook. For me the pen is heavier than a shovel; I left school at the age of ten to work on the farm. But I have a need to record my feelings; I do not know why. Perhaps it is not knowing what we will find in this mysterious country of Canada.

The *Hellas* is a Greek liner. Its home port is Athens and it has stopped at Trieste and Naples—so the steward tells me—and there are various nationalities on board, Greeks, Italians, Austrians and a few Americans. Except for the Americans most are emigrants. Yes, I would say this is an emigrant ship. From Halifax, I'm told, it will go to New York.

Most of the Portuguese aboard are from the Continent and are going to Connecticut. The ones who will disembark at Halifax are from the Azores. We number thirty. Pedro, Estevan and myself are from the same village on Sao Miguel. We share the same cabin and hope we can remain together after landing. Estevan has been seasick much of the time; he has trouble keeping food down and has lost two kilos.

I, fortunately, have no problem but am always a little hungry. The food is strange—too sweet, but I force myself, and the wine is both good and plentiful. We had, too, a supply of bread, fruit and hard boiled eggs that we bought in Lisbon; this lasted us for the first two days.

Ah, here comes the steward now with our thermos of milk and coffee and some biscuits. I tip with the last of my *escudos* and he thanks me. I better take these to Estevan but will write again tomorrow.

March 16th,

Land! Today, we sight land. After breakfast everyone is on deck. The wind snaps at scarves, jackets and women's skirts. One man has binoculars. Pedro has gone down to tell Estevan. Perhaps the news will cheer him.

*From a work-in-progress, *Details from the Canadian Mosaic*, printed by permission of the author.

Like myself, my companions know nothing of Canada. It is not a country to which Portuguese go, if you do not count the Atlantic fishing fleet, but the one fisherman we met on the Continent was able to tell us nothing. I think of the paintings of forests, mountains and snow on the walls of the Canadian Embassy where we obtained our visa, and I have new doubts about the wisdom of our choice. Perhaps the elders of the village were right. I can still hear them muttering, "Young fools. Young fools."

I think the man with binoculars sees something now. Yes!

I've been reading the little green book our government has prepared for emigrants. The quote on the cover warns: *Imigrar e travar uma grande luta,* to emigrate is to put up a big fight. But on Sao Miguel . . .

The man's excitement is contagious. Passengers are collecting around him.

. . . on Sao Miguel many have no other choice. Farms are small; jobs are scarce. Most can hope to better their conditions only by leaving. No, it was not the idea of migrating which the elders thought foolish, but the choice of place. If we had chosen Brazil, where many families have relatives, or even France perhaps . . . but Canada? Who did we know there?

The man is passing his binoculars around. I check my watch. It is two o'clock, Lisbon time.

My father asked the same questions as the elders. But the country needs agricultural workers and I am a farmer's son. It said so in the newspaper advertisement. I showed him the clipping.

In the end, he agreed. "Let us not part with bad feeling," he said. He wanted to come to the Continent, but I thought it best we said our good-byes on Sao Miguel. It was a painful departure. My mother wept. My father clasped me to his chest. The families of Pedro and Estevan were at the dock, too. We were all embraced, kissed, crushed—until the boat whistled. I had a moment of doubt; perhaps my father was right. In Lisbon I had no such feelings. I was already far from home.

A gull is circling above us now. The land is a pencil line on the horizon.

The ship's horn is deafening. We are moving towards . . . Yes, I've just thanked the man for using his binoculars. We are moving into harbour. A tug is coming towards us. It has begun to drizzle and the wind is chilly. Passengers are leaving to collect their baggage. I must go too.

March 18th,

On the CPR train, going to a place called Leamington. Outside, the landscape is bleak—farms, telephone wires, bare trees, a distant church steeple; the snow has not yet melted. On Sao Miguel, when I left, trees were in bloom.

We have been traveling for two days already. I did not realize before the extent of this country and, as the official who met us in Halifax explained, there is much more to the West. He was an old grey-haired man with a gold tooth. He spoke a little Portuguese, having spent some time in Rio de Janeiro, he said, and he saw us safely through customs. I had little to declare: a heavy coat, woollens, a shaving razor and thirty-one dollars.

If it was not apparent to us before, we know now; we Portuguese are different from other immigrants who disembarked with us. They have fixed destinations and often family waiting; a few have even been met at the ship. Like the Greek girl. Or I should say young woman; she is about twenty. On the ship she had long black braids and a native costume. Meeting her again in the train's restaurant car, I scarcely recognize her. She has cut her braids, has had a permanent and has traded her costume for a dress and a white sweater. Already she is like a Canadian.

We, instead, have been divided into groups, at random like so much baggage, and have been tagged with lapel colours: orange for Quebec, red for Ontario and blue for British Columbia. Estevan received orange. Pedro and I red. So we are not to remain together after all. On the train however, we devise a way of communicating. All of us will write home and the families will trade our separate addresses.

Because we made the trip from Halifax to Montreal at night, I remember nothing. The cold was bitter in Montreal, where we parted from Estevan and five others from Terceira Island; my ears almost froze. I felt sorry for Estevan. They say even the river freezes in that place.

March 27th

What a difference! Here in Leamington it is spring; the country is green.

Arriving, we stayed at the YMCA, which I understand is a Christian place, until our owners came to collect their baggage — us. I am bitter about that day; never was I so humiliated.

Still with our red tags, we gathered in the gymnasium and stood in a line along the wall while the farmers inspected us. Like slaves at a market, I thought. I could almost hear some of them think as they walked back and forth in front of us. "This one is big and strong. He'll work hard." Or: "This one is too fat, probably eats too much."

One farmer stopped in front of me. I expected him to open my mouth and examine my teeth, as one does with horses. Instead he pointed at me and motioned me to follow. At the door, he was given the necessary papers. His truck was outside; he threw my suitcase into the back and we climbed into the cab.

He pointed to himself.

"Ron Granger. You?"

"Bento Miquel Goncalves da Madeira."

"That's a mouthful."

"No onnerstan."

"Done any farming?"

"No onnerstan."

"You know, agriculture."

I nodded.

"Good, good, We'll get along just fine."

Driving through town, I felt like a stranger. On Sao Miguel, houses are of stone with tile roofs and vine-hung balconies, here they are made of wood with picket fences. They seem like toys. Outside the town, I saw a farmer on a tractor; it is the first tractor I have seen. We passed horses and cows.

Granger turned into a gravel road and stopped in front of a brown stucco house. He made a sweep with his hand: pasture, cows, barns, a silo and acres of fields for cultivation. He seemed to indicate that it was a small dairy farm, but on Sao Miguel an estate of such a size belonged only to the rich.

His wife had heard the truck drive up and met us on the porch. She was a fat woman, thick blond hair tied into a pigtail with a ribbon. Her face was flushed. She spoke some words of welcome and led the way inside. The aroma of fresh bread filled the house. For a moment I felt I had entered my own home, expecting to find my mother baking. In a way I cannot explain this bit of familiarity made me happy.

I am to sleep in a small room off the porch, where I am writing this, and share meals with the family. My contract is for a year, after which I am free to go where I like.

May 31st

Over two months have passed since my arrival here and during this time I have learned what the green booklet means by *Imigrar e travar uma grande luta.* I am lonely and homesick. I find the work hard, the food strange.

I was excited to receive a letter from Pedro. I have read it over many times. Pedro is happy, almost a part of the family. The farmer's wife sits with him at the kitchen table and teaches him English for an hour each day. Her husband drives him to the post office and to the bank and has shown him how to open a savings account. Pedro is enthusiastic about Canada.

It is different for me. My resentment, which began at the slave market, has grown steadily, and now I do not think I will last the year of my contract.

My problems are multiplied by the fact that Granger and his wife are constantly quarrelling, even in front of me, knowing that I understand nothing. My first week here Granger was pruning some fruit trees at the side of the house while his wife, watching from the porch, disagreed about which branches to cut. Angry, Granger finally climbed down from the ladder and threw his tools at my feet. I had in fact pruned trees before on Sao Miguel — it is an art of sorts, and was eager to please, hoping to find a friend in this woman. Instead, her praise only seemed to increase Granger's hostility, as if somehow I had taken sides with her against him. He began calling me the Porky, which I think means pig. I find the name an insult.

Granger keeps forty cows and has acres on which he grows corn for winter fodder. I do not know how to use his modern equipment, and he does not have the patience to teach me. So, when he began his spring plowing, he put me instead to driving his tractor because I had driven a truck in the army. For two days I plowed his fields and then the transmission broke. When he realized the damage, I thought he might strike me. I avoided him during the next week. Passing the garage on the way to milking the cows, I could see Granger surrounded by parts and grease, and when he saw me he swore.

He soon found a way to punish me by deciding that the barns needed cleaning. Each morning I load the truck with manure, using only a wheelbarrow and a shovel. In places the manure is two feet thick and caked like concrete. The chore takes all morning. Afternoons, we drive into town with the manure and sell it to gardeners by the square yard. I clamber to the back of the truck and heave the shit over fences with a pitchfork while Granger sits in the cab and smokes. He does not help and we do not talk. I have learned almost no English, but these trips to town have taught me my way around. I think I can find my way alone to the bus station, if necessary.

July 15th

At night I lie on the sweat-damp sheets in this small rented room, unable to sleep, listening to cats fight in the alley. The neon lights of a restaurant reflect on my ceiling, green, red, green. Somewhere a radio is playing. God, it's hot.

But I am glad to have run off.

That morning I waited until I heard no sounds from the kitchen. When I looked, the breakfast dishes were still in the sink and Granger's black cat was sleeping on a chair. The keys to the truck, which I had stolen, were in my pocket. I walked out the back door. Coming round the house, Granger saw me with my suitcase. "Hey!" I ran for the truck. The engine whined and I remembered the weak battery. "Porky!" The engine sputtered, then caught. I heard a metallic clatter. When I looked in the rear view mirror, I saw Granger in a cloud of dust, waving his arms, milk cans rolling on the ground.

In town, I parked the truck in the business district where it would be found and walked the rest of the way to the bus station. I had a month's wages in cash, Granger having kept the first two for my boat fare, and I peeled a ten from the rubber band before approaching the ticket booth. "Toronto," I said. "What clock?" The girl held up two fingers. I sat on a bench, waiting and expecting Granger to walk in at any moment with a policeman. Not until the bus came and I was on it did I begin to relax.

In Toronto, I wandered the streets with my suitcase, unable to ask for directions, order a sandwich or rent a room. Sitting in a park, watching children on a swing, I felt like an alien from another planet. To whom could I turn? Not to the authorities. Was there a Portuguese consulate in this city? Could I find it? I picked up my suitcase and began to walk, looking for a hotel.

Outside a building where a band was playing, a crowd had gathered. I hovered at the edge of the crowd, listening to the music, and was about to leave when I noticed a sign, Salvation Army. Something stirred in my memory. Leamington, at the Christian place we were staying, people like these had brought us little gifts of food. When I tried to enter the building, one of the men in uniform placed a hand on my shoulder. I did not understand what he said, but he seemed to want me not to go inside. Just then some young women came out, and boys began whistling. I guessed they were prostitutes, and this was a place they frequented.

"YMCA," I said, and kept repeating, "YMCA," until he motioned for me to follow.

He spoke to another man, and this second person took me by car to the YMCA, where I was given a room. At least I have a bed, I thought.

In this huge city a man can lose himself. In case Granger is looking for me, but maybe not.

Can I be deported for not fulfilling my contract? I have mixed feelings about this. If my father were here now, I'd kiss his feet and beg forgiveness, but I cannot go back to Sao Miguel a failure and face the derision of the village elders. Even now I can still hear their scorn, "Young fools. Young fools." When I go back, it will be as a success and this means that I must find a job.

There is a Catholic Church nearby and through the priest I've met an Italian called Vincenzo who is foreman of a road crew. He has promised me something.

August 10th

There are five of us on Vincenzo's crew. We repair potholes for the City Works Department and this week are tarring a whole new neighbourhood. When the tar arrives, we spread it with shovels and hoes. The heat is terrible. We throw off shirts. I feel like being in an inferno, sweat pouring from every gland. Already I am as bronzed as the others. But the pay is good; mentally, I convert the dollars into *escudos* and feel wealthy.

I am grateful to Vincenzo. I owe him more than this job. He has been my first real friend in Canada; he has taught me how to open a bank account, rent a room, buy an alarm clock and order pie and coffee.

"But you won't learn much English on this job," he warned me the first day. "Not from this crew." And he introduced me to Nikos and Gustav and Amedeo and Hans.

But I feel I belong with this gang; they understand.

Weekends are bad. I am alone. Saturdays, I take the bus downtown and watch people carry the city in their shopping bags. I buy fish and fry it on a hotplate in my room, keeping the window open because the landlord complains about the smell. Sunday, I go to the Catholic Church; the Mass in Latin reminds me of home, and sometimes I meet Vincenzo there, with his wife and his twin daughters, the girls each with a ribbon like a white butterfly in their dark hair. I envy him. Afternoons, I take the ferry to the Island. I stroll the beach, watch children swim and buy an ice cream cone.

"You should go to school," Vincenzo suggested another time. We were eating our lunch, sitting on the curb in the shade of a tree. The fresh blacktop shimmered in the sun.

"Or get a girlfriend," Nikos said.

They all grinned.

I told them I had not come to go to school but to make dollars so that I could return to Sao Miguel a rich man.

Vincenzo, unwrapping a green pepper sandwich from his lunch-bucket, explained I had a disease that he called dollar fever. "It is an addiction, like a narcotic."

Gustav was passing around a pack of cigarettes; he struck a match on his boot. Puffing smoke, he said, "Ha, vee all has had this disease."

The others nodded.

"I have a friend," Nikos said, "who worked twelve hours a day and saved every penny to return to Greece. Five years it took him, and when he went back to his native village, he realized that Canada had become the dream. Now, he is here again, working in Sudbury."

It was a common story, Hans agreed; they all knew someone like that.

Perhaps, but on payday I deposited the entire cheque in the bank, in my Sao Miguel account.

September 12th

I was laid off today. Vincenzo says one can get insurance, but I have not worked long enough to qualify. I must find other work.

October 1st

I have received letters from Estevan and Pedro. Both were surprised to learn how much I was earning on the road crew. Our letters are being traded on Sao Miguel, too, and several men have caught the virus from me. I may start a dollar fever epidemic.

October 5th

I wash cars. It is cold, wet work.

October 12th

Today it is snowing—goose-feather flakes, and children skate in the park, where the pool is frozen. I have bought some warm clothing, withdrawing money from my Sao Miguel account.

On Sunday I saw Vincenzo at church. He told me it will be spring before I can return to my old job.

November 1st

I have found a new job washing dishes in a restaurant. At least I am inside where it is warm and I receive meals free.

December 17th

Christmas here begins in November. It is a worship of Mammon. Downtown is all coloured lights. They have a huge tree. Stores are overflowing and carol music plays from the walls. Children sit on the knee of a white-bearded man in a red suit—he is called Santa Claus—and ask for more than their parents can afford. Everywhere cash registers ring up. The dollar is God.

I know now that dollar fever is endemic to this country; people carry the virus in their blood. If an immigrant is infected more severely, it is because he has not been exposed before so has no immunity. Like the Indians who died of the European's smallpox.

Today, I bought a spruce branch, which I taped to my window, though I have no coloured lights for decoration. It cost me twenty-five cents. I also sent fifty dollars home as a gift to my mother. My letters to her are always cheerful. I know she is sad at my distance from her.

December 27th

I spent Christmas Eve at the restaurant, standing at the sink up to my elbows in suds, while the radio played carols. Dishes, cups, glasses, trays and cutlery continued to pile up as fast as I could wash them. We were short-handed; no one wanted to come in and the few waitresses scurrying about were in bad tempers.

At nine, the cook left. At ten, the restaurant closed, and by eleven I had finished cleaning the grill. On the way home I attended Midnight Mass. The church was overflowing. Outside, it was snowing, the flakes falling like frozen moths against the street lamp.

Christmas Day, I woke at noon. I had told the boss, yes, I would come to work—Boxing Day, too. It was better than spending the holidays alone.

January 10th, 1955

I woke this morning to the roar of a plow clearing the street; it had snowed again during the night.

It was my day off. I did my laundry in the bathtub and hung it to dry by a rope I have placed there. Later, I wrote letters to my parents, to Pedro and to Estevan, and went out to post them.

February 12th

I am tired of winter, of staying indoors, of washing dishes.

March 15th

Is it only a year since I began this diary? It seems much longer.

Soon Pedro and Estevan will have completed their contracts on the farm and will join me here in Toronto. Pedro has persuaded us to go north this summer to work in the mines or the forest where the pay is good and one can do overtime. He is a mechanic by trade and wants to make enough to buy into a garage.

August 13th

I take up this diary again after many months. When Pedro and Estevan joined me in May, I no longer felt the need to record my feelings. I was with friends. Pedro who had learned much English acted as interpreter for all of us. Things were easier. And then, afterwards, I did not want to think about Estevan's accident. Writing to his parents was hard enough.

We went north, as hoped, to work in the forest, planting trees. The company planted two saplings for each tree logged and summers it hired transient workers for the purpose: students, immigrants, Indians.

Pedro hung the sack of young trees from his waist. "Temporary work," he said, meaning the garage in his future. Perhaps the thought lightened the weight of the saplings as we swarmed over the hills like ants, at intervals striking with a mattock, packing the earth round the sapling with our boots, then moving on.

We stayed together, usually, but that day Estevan was in the truck ahead of us as we returned to camp. We were tired. It had been a sultry day; the mosquitos were fierce. My back hurt. Perhaps the driver did not see the deer until it jumped in front of him. The truck skidded, spun and careened off the embankment. Three men were killed.

I walked beside the stretcher as they carried Estevan to the company's ambulance. He was bleeding from one ear.

"My mother," he whispered. "I have killed her."

It was forty miles to the nearest town with a hospital. Estevan died in the ambulance. The doctor told us he was hurt inside.

Pedro and I quit a few days later and took the train here to Sudbury, but they are not hiring at INCO just now. Pedro, of course, has a trade, but he cannot get journeyman's papers without Canadian experience and he cannot get experience without papers. He feels frustrated.

Tomorrow we leave for Flin Flon to try our luck there.

August 21st

The train speeds along an ocean-like expanse of golden prairie. As I stand at the aft rail of the caboose, two rails gleam absolutely straight behind me until they merge into one silver wire on the blue horizon. Below my feet, a continent is rolling away.

Again, I am impressed by the size of this country. I have travelled such a great distance that I feel like Ulysses, lost.

There was no work in Flin Flon. So we are going to British Columbia. Some of our friends from the boat are there, though mostly scattered by now, working mines or logging camps. Only three remain where they were sent, to work in the orchards near Kelowna. One is in Kitimat, a new town they are building in the forest for the purpose of smelting aluminum. He writes that they need workers.

August 23rd

I was too late to get a glimpse of the Rockies before going to bed, but early this morning I woke to find that we had passed Calgary in the night and were now running up a fairly steep incline, with a river hurrying down from the mountains alongside our track. Above us were jagged peaks crowned with snow even at this time of year.

August 25th

It is good to be with other Portuguese again. We have so much to talk about. Our three Kelowna friends — two are brothers — are already sprouting roots in this valley; they have pooled their savings, taken a big mortgage and bought this orchard. They plan to grow peaches, apples, pears and plums. Trees here are so heavy with ripening fruit that branches need supports from breaking.

The Okanagan is a beautiful valley, a cornucopia land. I am tempted to remain. I can be happy here, but Pedro wants to go on to Kitimat. So we shall stay only long enough to help our friends with the harvest.

Epilogue, 1981

Benny, my neighbour, has given me his diary to do with, he says, as I want. He is a great fan of mine; he reads all my stories. We sit on his patio under a grapevine trellis and he reaches up to pick a bunch of grapes. He says that they are not sweet enough to make wine but are good as table fruit.

He draws up a lawn chair. At forty-nine, he is a bronzed man with thin greying hair. I tell him I've read his diary.

"Is there more to it?"

"No," he says. "When I went to Kitimat, I left it behind in a suitcase with the Kelowna friends. Not that I was in Kitimat long. Our letters, you see, were traded back home, and soon we learned that someone else was making more money. So we'd quit and go there, too. But I never forgot this valley, the fruit so heavy on the trees." He made a sweep with one hand towards his orchards.

"And Sao Miguel?"

He laughs. "I did go back several years later — to get married."

I tell him that I want to translate his diary. He seems pleased.

"Those who come now have it easy. But for us, the pioneers —." He sighs. "You know, I still have the green booklet with the warning on the cover: **"Imigrar e travar uma grande luta."**

Mayer Romano and family

IT'S A SWEET LIFE

From an interview with Mayer Romano

You feel like a kid again, with your nose pressed up against the window. Don't let the chrome and glass fool you. Inside are all the delights, and more, of an old-fashioned candy store.

Chocolate Santas march around hand-molded candy sleds filled with giftwrapped packets. Hollow Christmas bells are stuffed and overflowing with sweets. Wrapped in glistening foil and crinkly cellophane of every imaginable hue, the gift boxes hint at all kinds of surprises inside.

Behind a display case inside the store is a little man with greying hair. Glasses perched midway down his nose, he is bending over a small tray of natural fruit covered with chocolate he has arranged on crisp paper frills. He straightens and grins.

"Bonjour," and he hands you one of his goodies. "Tiens, goutez-le. C'est bon!"

He looks like a happy elf, his face crinkled in a wide smile as he watches you bite into the chocolate. Rum trickles down your chin, and he reaches quickly to hand you a tissue.

"What do you think?" he asks. "Is it good?"

When you roll your eyes heavenward, your mouth too full to answer, he beams and rubs his hands together. The response has made his day.

He gives you another. It's fresh, he reassures you. He just made it early this morning. You're hooked! You only came in to look and you end up buying two pounds of handmade chocolates.

His name is Mayer Romano, and he owns the Chantilly Confiserie, on the second floor of Decarie Square in Montreal. Born in Lebanon, he came to Canada in 1975.

Starting as a labourer at the age of thirteen in a garage and later a printing plant, he finally found a long-term job in a chocolate factory in Beirut.

"I worked there for thirty-three years. The factory changed hands four times, and each time I stayed on. I was mechanically minded and I knew the way the machines worked. My boss gave me a lot of responsibility.

"Do you know I can't even write properly? I never finished school, but I learned a lot about mechanics, machinery and mixing. Everything stayed in my head. I could remember stock, merchandise, everything."

He grins as he tells the story of a German engineer who was sent along with a shipment of machinery from Germany to make flowers out of chocolate.

"He stayed for two months and couldn't figure it out. He used to go out for a good time and never did anything. I put it together myself, figured out the whole thing and had it working. And I didn't have a degree in engineering," he smiles proudly.

He worked his way up to general manager of the large plant. In 1962 he opened his own candy factory.

"Life was good until the civil war between Moslems and Christians made life unbearable. I was afraid my family would be killed. When the fighting broke out, different groups occupied sectors of the city. At the beginning my factory was in the Falangists' area, but when the Palestinians attacked and captured the sector, all property came under their control."

When the battle escalated, Romano moved his family to their summer house in the mountains outside Beirut. Almost every day he came down to check on the factory to make certain it had not been bombed, burned or broken into.

"But to get into that sector, I now had to get a special permit at Palestinian headquarters," he explains. "My son Henry accompanied me when I went with other businessmen like myself for the permit. We were herded into a room and savagely beaten for no reason whatsoever. When we were released, we considered ourselves lucky to have escaped with our lives.

"Our house was looted as well. Our neighbours had a hand in that, too. Friendship meant nothing. There was no point in staying and so my other son made arrangements for us to go to Paris and apply for entry to Canada from there.

"My factory, merchandise and home were confiscated. I lost everything — thirty years of hard work gone. It all disappeared . . . over $150,000 of my life, but we were lucky to get out of there with the whole family alive." He shrugs. "C'est la vie . . . non . . . c'est la guerre."

A customer has just walked in. She chooses her own selection of chocolates from the display case.

"Best chocolates in town," she says as she smiles at Mr. Romano. "I can't believe you make them all yourself. What else do you make?"

A sheepish look flits across his features. "Les enfants . . . children," he answers. "I have a dozen . . . nine boys and three girls!"

The woman laughs. "I hope they are as good as your sweets."

"Do you know," he continues after she has left, "how lucky I am to be here in this country where there is peace, doing what I enjoy?"

He pauses to fill a small paper bag with milk-chocolates for a teenager. He hands her a sample of fruit and nut mixture to taste. She smiles, thanks him and as she walks out of the store, her hand is already reaching into the bag.

Romano pauses to refill some trays of chocolates in the showcase and rearranges a display on a shelf.

"My son came here in 1967, worked for the Pascal Company and became a manager. He encouraged the whole family to emigrate, and he got all the papers and forms we needed and filled them out. He sent everything to Paris and told us what we had to do. The whole family came out together.

"I'm 65 years old," he says. "When I arrived here, I was offered a job at minimum wage at Laura Secord, a chocolate and candy company. I wanted a contract, and they refused. The pay was terrible for a master candymaker like me. I was unemployed for a year and a half.

With no work in sight and his age a detriment to employment, he became very depressed and wanted to return to Lebanon, war and all.

"My children worked and supported me and my wife. My oldest son got a loan for me and helped me open this store."

Arriving at Decarie Square at three or four in the morning, he works fifteen hours a day. Everything is handmade. He does his cutting, mixing and dipping manually. In Beirut, his family all worked in the factory with him, he says. Now they don't want to. The children come occasionally to help out behind the counter, serving customers.

It bothers him, he confesses. He wants one of them to carry on his work. The thought of the business falling into the hands of strangers is frightening.

"I'm not young. I could die tomorrow, and then what would happen to everything?" he asks.

He waves his hand toward the glass shelves which are stocked with giftware, china and crystal ready to be filled with chocolates and wrapped for individual orders.

He provides the sweets for christenings, weddings, showers and all kinds of parties and festive occasions, he says proudly. Behind the counter are stacks of empty boxes in varying sizes, rolls of shiny foil paper and colored ribbons. He makes his own decorations and does the giftwrapping as well.

"My chocolates and fruits are all natural," he explains. "There are no additives, chemicals or synthetic ingredients. I use very little sugar. Everything is pure quality . . . the best."

He grins as he punches up a sale on the cash register. Business has been slow. The shopping centre is only partially filled with stores, and there aren't enough people attracted to the square. His best day is Sunday when the afternoon theatre crowd fills the second floor area near his shop, he says. He is open and busy from 12:30 p.m. to 6:00 p.m.

People begin to trickle in. Suddenly there are half a dozen in the store. He moves quickly, a smile on his face, trying to serve everyone.

A customer says: "This is the first time I'm here. Can I try something?"

He offers her a sample. Her face lights up.

"Fantastic! Can you make up an assortment for me . . . the large box, please?" she asks.

He is delighted.

You know she'll be back for more. The Chantilly chocolate habit is difficult to kick.

EDITOR'S NOTE: Henry has just joined his father in the candy business.

Herma Brecht et al

TWO WORLDS

From interviews with Herman Brecht who emigrated to Canada from Germany in 1950

We have a saying in German about immigrants that translates so: "The first generation is dead, the second generation has the misery and the third generation has the bread."

Immigrants like me have to work hard to put roots into this country. The second generation have already their roots here. They don't have to fight for a place in it like we did. Like most immigrants, I live between two worlds. I still have bonds to my old country, but I have stronger ones to this new country.

I know life is hard, but you have to take it the way it comes. I'm not saying it doesn't affect my feelings, especially when my kids take things for granted. It makes me mad sometimes, but they didn't have to fight for everything the way I did. I earned everything myself. No one gave me anything.

* * *

For me life has been hardships and wandering from the time I was born in a cattlecar stopped on a railway siding in Piestersitz-on-Elbe, a town about three kilometers from Wittenberg, Germany. My mother, along with hundreds of deportees from Speyer, near Karlsruhe, was waiting to be relocated in Saxony.

When the French occupied Speyer after World War I, my parents' home was confiscated. Because my father had been in the Frei Korps as a soldier, the new government deported the family. My father was still in the army but my mother, who was nine months pregnant, was picked up and shipped out with many others.

Shortly after my birth, the entire train load was put into barracks in Piestersitz before being scattered across Saxony. There wasn't enough food for everyone, so my mother took me to Bavaria and left me with her parents.

I didn't even know I had parents until I was twelve years old when she came back to get me. I didn't want to go. I screamed and fought like a wild animal . . . I didn't want to live with a stranger, but I had to go. Only then did I discover that I had a brother, three years younger than me. My parents were just moving from Piestersitz to Berlin, and I was placed in a State School in the capital.

Because I had lived in a country area, I was far behind in my studies. Also, my accent was different, and I swore a lot. The kids spoke high German, and when I opened my mouth to talk, they laughed at me and bullied me. So I beat them up and got a bad name. I was a tough kid.

After eight years of school, I was sent to a polytechnical or trade school for four years to learn a profession. I became a toolmaker.

Because Germany, like most European countries, has compulsory military service, I didn't have to look for a job. The service was for a three-year period, and in 1938, I was drafted automatically into the army. I was eighteen years old.

There were two hundred and fifty of us in one group, and we were sent to work on government projects around the country. We lived in barracks in camps, and for our labour received twenty-five pfenning, worth six cents a day, believe it or not. We were like a para-military force even if we were workers and we had the same regulations as the army.

It was a bad period economically. We were dispatched to drain the swamps in the Memel River area bordering the Baltic States. We built dams and pumped water out of the bogs to make the land suitable for farming.

If you remember, there was a land corridor from Germany to an area behind Danzig that still belonged to us. Danzig* had become a free city after World War I. At that time, the land corridor was owned by Poland.

Political problems between Germany and Poland and Czechoslovakia were already creating a state of tension in Europe. The Poles refused to let any military transports through the corridor.

We were sent through in trains with all the windows closed and covered. There was no way anyone could see in or out. If the Poles had known we were soldiers, they would have stopped the trains. Once we arrived, we had to stay there right on the border, and we were automatically inducted into the regular army. The Nazis didn't want us back in Germany; they wanted to keep us there in case something happened.

I was three kilometres behind the Polish-German border when the war suddenly broke out early in the morning. We were told the Poles had attacked the Germans. As a soldier, you don't know what is going

*Danzig was seized shortly after Poland was invaded on September 1, 1939.

on. You get orders and you go in there and fight. Whatever they tell you, you believe.*

The border station was already being shelled, grenades were being tossed all around us, and we didn't know who started it or who was shooting at whom. We were stuck there, and when we were ordered to break over the border, we marched into Poland.

Shortly after, I was wounded; nothing serious — a Polish soldier shoved a bayonet into my hand and up past my wrist — and once it healed I was back on active duty.

On April 9, 1940 I was dropped with other units by parachute in Oslo, Norway and then again at Narvik. Once Norway and Denmark** were occupied, we returned to Germany, and soon after, entire units were shipped out to fight on the Russian front.

That's where I got it . . . four shots in my left leg. The medicos patched me up temporarily in the field hospital, and then I was sent back to Germany where I was to undergo four operations on my leg. They gave me the Iron Cross. Why? Well, I went out under fire and saved a poor guy out on the field who got shot, and I pulled him back behind the lines. That's how I got the four bullets in my leg.

What else could I do? I didn't expect an award for it. When things in life get you down . . . you see so much pain and misery around you — soldiers badly hurt, men dying — you want to give up and you think, what's the use, in the end it will get you, too . . . it didn't make any difference if it happened then or later. I didn't care any more when I went out after the poor guy, so I wasn't afraid of the danger. I didn't think of it.

The trip back to Germany was a horror. My leg was in a cast, and along with me in the cattlecar were many other soldiers who had been wounded, many seriously.

Think of a stove, like a Coleman, in the centre of the car and the temperature is fifty degrees below zero. You don't know those Russian winters. Those lying in front of the stove were sweating and the others at the back, far away from the heat, were freezing. You could hear the moans, the crying and the pain. Around me guys were dying one after the other, and as fast as they died, others grabbed their blankets to keep from freezing. The blankets were full of lice, and the buggers got into my cast and nearly ate me alive.

*Germany invaded Poland on September 1, 1939 at 5:45 a.m., simultaneously on four fronts.

**Denmark and Norway were invaded on the same day, April 9, 1940.

When the train stopped at a station I asked a nurse if she could get me something long to scratch inside the cast, and she brought me a stay from a lady's corset. I shoved it in and I scratched so hard I bled, and the more I bled, the more the lice went at me. I got my hands on a bottle of schnapps, and I poured it down into my cast. It burnt like hell, but I got the buggers drunk, and they were quiet for a little while.

When the nurses finally got me into a bathtub in the hospital, cast and all, all the lice floated to the top of the water and drowned. What a sight! I laughed so much.

I was in the hospital in Germany for almost a year. I wasn't fit to go back to the front, but I and others in the same situation had to work, no loafing, so we were discharged and given jobs in armament factories. I was hard at work at one of these in the Bodensee area near the Swiss border when the American bombers began their raids. There was one bad raid I remember when the Allies came over during the day to bomb the aircraft plants. The sky was black with planes. About 144 were shot down that day.

We were mobilized again and put into defense corps to man anti-aircraft guns against the Allied planes. We also chased pilots who had been shot down and were trying to get over the Swiss border.

In 1944, I was transferred to the Ruhr Valley. I was in a reserve unit. There I worked in factories and on farms, wherever help was needed. Because I was a toolmaker, I made machine gun parts, small arms, etc. in the plants.

Late one night, the army came without warning and picked us all up in trucks. We didn't know where they were taking us and we knew better than to ask. Those who managed to doze off woke up to find themselves in Holland. There we were without guns or other weapons and we had to march. Because of my leg, I couldn't walk so good.

I was assigned to an anti-aircraft battery near Arnheim. Of course, the High Command knew, but we ordinary soldiers didn't, that the English and Americans were going to attack across the Rhine near Arnheim.* We were there two or three weeks before it happened.

A group of us were manning an anti-aircraft gun, and not far from our battery a glider was shot down. We ran over to see if there was any

*Shortly after September 17, 1944, a British airborne division, which included soldiers from the Commonwealth, took Arnheim. The Germans called up reserves, surrounded the British and forced them to abandon Arnheim between September 25 and 26.

food or supplies we could salvage from the wreckage. There were always survival kits in planes with all kinds of things. We were surprised to find that the pilot was still alive. The glider was a mess. We pulled him out and saw that he had shrapnel in his legs. I carried him over to our position and when he came to, we talked to him for quite awhile until the medicos came around and picked him up. He told us he was a Canadian. Anyway, he was taken to a hospital and then put into a POW camp along with all the others who were captured. After the war they were released.

When the battle had started it was hell. Remember the film, *A Bridge Too Far?* That was Arnheim. The real thing was much worse. When our soldiers retook the town, we were pulled back to the Elbe River and again put to work in factories producing tools and ammunition.

By then the Russians were already on the eastern German front. It was the spring of '44.

Once again, we were pulled out, loaded on trucks and sent to Berlin, but only for a short time. The Russians broke through over the Oder River. We had to get out of Berlin fast to avoid them and we fled to Leipzig, east to Prague and down to Munich to get away from the enemy units.

But it was no use. We were captured by the Americans and taken to Dachau.* It was May, 1945.

Thousands of us were dumped into a large, open field and were kept there with no food or water for two weeks. Stationed at each corner of the field was a tank, and if any of us tried to break through, we were shot. Whoever dropped dead was hauled out. The field was a sea of mud. We shit and peed there. It smelled awful, and disease hit everyone. Men went crazy, nuts and attacked others. They died like flies. A trailer truck went around every morning, picking up the dead. The men were dying for a cigarette. There was nothing, so they pulled up the grass, if they could find some, and smoked it. If a light was seen by the guards, they shot at it.

Finally they handed us over to the Russians at the border, and marched us out to cattlecars headed for Moscow and then Siberia.

I spent one winter in Siberia. It was pure hell. We ate everything that moved. I couldn't take it, and I escaped, hiding by day and running by night. It took me two and a half years to get to Finland. I was in a hospital there and then went to Sweden.

*Dachau was the site of one of the most infamous of the death camps set up by the Nazis to exterminate Jews, gypsies, etc.

When I got back to Germany in 1948, I weighed 98 pounds. I'm a big man, no? All I weighed was 98 pounds. I was a total physical and emotional wreck.

It is very difficult to talk about those years to anybody. I have buried them in my mind and I don't want to talk about them anymore. You have no idea . . . you don't know how cruel men can be. If you have never lived through it, you can never know.

I had to kill people . . . no, it's not that simple . . . it's unbelievably difficult to live through it, and to live with it as a burden on your mind for the rest of your life. You haven't seen anything like it, so you don't know how terrible it was. I don't think I will ever be able to talk about it and I don't think any man would be interested in hearing about the savagery and brutality that happened over there. No one would believe it.

I saw men eating men. I killed because I had to just to keep from being killed. But I never did anything so bad that I couldn't live with it. I never killed for fun, for sport, never unnecessarily...only when I had no choice and would have been killed myself. It was them or me, so there was no question in my mind whether I should have done it or not. I would have killed for a piece of bread. Hunger makes men do unspeakable things. I don't want to judge myself and I don't want anyone else to judge me.

I have seen things you couldn't imagine that men could do to one another. I can understand the feelings of hate and revenge...I can understand it, but it doesn't mean that I wanted to be a part of it. To eat, to survive, to live, you have two choices. You kill or you get killed...and you learn to live off the land.

You've got to have the will to survive and you have to do terrible things. If I sound brutal, I can't help it. I don't trust any man, not then, not now, and that's the only way I survived. No matter what, you can't read men's minds. A guy could say to your face, "Brother, I would never do a thing like that," and when the time came, he would sell you down the river for a lousy ruble. I never, never took a chance.

You have to understand that in this period there were millions of people on the move, displaced from their lands of origin. Everyone was fleeing, everyone wanted to save himself . . . to get away from something. They would do anything to stay alive, like me.

I wasn't alone, but I wasn't with a group. I never trusted a group. You leave yourself open to stupidity. I was with a woman, a Polish woman, whom I met in the Russian camp. She had a tough time, too.

While we were escaping together, we got caught up with the partisans in Northern Russia. They took us prisoner. We ran with them for a certain time because we had no choice. We had to kill or be killed. I realized after some time that we couldn't get away from them . . . they wouldn't let us go. We knew too much, and they would kill us because we were a danger to them.

The army was always chasing them because they attacked villages and stole anything they could, food, drink, supplies, and all we did was run, run, run, days on end, non-stop. We were still prisoners.

It was up around the Lena River area, the very northernmost part of Russia. The good thing about it was the farther north you got, the easier it was to travel because everything was frozen. You could get across rivers and lakes that are impassable in the summertime.

We learned to dig holes in the snow and sleep in these snowholes. This kept us warm. All the survival tactics we picked up were invaluable. Many of those who escaped never made it; many that did went crazy or ended up losing hands and feet from the cold. Some got to China by going south and, I heard later, some made it to India by crossing Hindustan.

I finally reached Finland and had to cross over into Sweden to get back to Germany. I couldn't go to Germany directly from Finland. You see, the Finns had an agreement with the Russians that anyone they picked up crossing the border was to be returned to the Russian side. When the patrols saw the tracks of those who had crossed, they demanded their return, and the Finns gave them back if they caught them.

You had to travel far inland not to fall into the hands of the border people who return escapees, but once you are far inland, you don't belong in this category anymore.

The Polish woman didn't cross with me. She never made it. She got shot by the Russians, but she was responsible for me surviving. They were following us and she sacrificed herself for me because she pulled them away from our tracks. I could have shot at them, but I would have been killed too.

She saved my life many times. I didn't speak Russian so well, and she spoke it like a native. When I couldn't walk because of my bad leg, she even carried me on her back. In those circumstances, what is between a man and a woman you cannot say with words. She had such hard times, too. We only trusted each other.

When I finally got back, I went to Bavaria to find my grandparents. I stayed a short while and got a job in the Kugelfisher and Werkzeugmacher factories that made ball bearings. It wasn't easy trying to keep food in my stomach. All fifty marks bought was a loaf of bread.

Then, like many others, I got into the black market business. You have to after a war or you don't survive. The Americans were stealing from their own supplies and selling it to Germans, who in turn sold it to their people. A lot of stuff was left behind when units went back to America, and we lifted that and sold it.

There was a club in the town, and the girls went there to dance with the soldiers. Once, when I was there and had just left the club, two soldiers came up to me and asked what time it was. I had a nice watch I had bought on the black market. They wanted me to take it off and give it to them. They were both drunk and got violent. I wouldn't give up my watch, so I hit them and knocked them both out. If I hadn't done it they would have robbed and killed me, and if I had been caught beating them up, I would have been killed anyway. I had no choice. That had happened before with others like me who got involved with the military. We were always the losers.

I went home, and an old schoolmate came to my house and told me to disappear. They were looking for me . . . so I walked fifty kilometres to Bavaria. I had another ex-soldier with me and we decided to go to the French occupied zone. We had heard they hired people to work at rebuilding the country, so we swam across the Rhine. Unfortunately there was still some barbed wire in the water from the war, and I got a good bloody scratch when I came up against it.

We arrived in Speyer. I had family there, my father's brothers. I didn't know them personally, and I realized when I saw them there was no way I could expect any help from them.

So we continued on to Kaiserlautern, which had been occupied by France. There was an employment bureau there, and the French government was hiring people to do clearing and rebuilding on the French side.

You have to understand conditions during that period. Every German front was occupied by another country. There was Belgium on the northwest, England on the north, France from the south, the Americans were in Bavaria and other western sections, including half of Berlin, and Russia was on the east holding the eastern part of Berlin.

The French were the only ones who would give Germans a chance to get a passport. No other country would. They hated us. The French were looking for soldiers for the Foreign Legion but I had had enough of the military. It wasn't for me. They were also looking for people to work in a chemical plant. You had to sign up for a one-year contract. There were all kinds of Europeans and North Africans working there. There was a German prisoner-of-war camp near the plant, and even the prisoners worked there.

I was there for the year, and when the contract was finished, I was what they called "un travailleur libre" and I could take any job with any French company that paid me according to my trade. So I took a job with twelve other guys to build a power plant for a construction company that built chemical and power plants all over Europe and Africa. I did the pipe fitting and welding.

They sent us all over. I worked in Central Africa, Fort Lamy, French Equitorial Africa . . . I think it is Chad now. Then I was sent to Tunisia to work on pipelines, then back to Alsace to rebuild an oil refinery.

In the group of Germans working there, I met another German who had been a prisoner of war in Canada. He had been with Rommel in North Africa, was captured and taken across the ocean to a camp in the West. I had already decided not to stay in France because there was so much hatred against anyone German. I and others got into fights and had plenty of problems. I decided I wanted to go to Chile. I already had a visa and passport from the French, but this ex-soldier talked so much about Canada. He told me that he had worked on a farm out west as a prisoner of war. The lady's husband was away fighting and she ran the farm, and he ran the lady and the farm. He kept talking about the country, all the food there was to eat and how good he had had it, so I thought seriously about going there.

I didn't speak English and what French I had picked up wasn't so good either. This guy spoke perfect English. His name was Ernie.

So off we went to Paris to the Canadian Consulate, and an immigration officer told us a pack of lies. He said Canada needed tradesmen, and that we could earn three times what we were getting in France. I believed the immigration officer, but it was different when we got over here.

You see, every time we had worked in Africa, we had six months in France since the head office was in Paris. I earned good money in France because I worked in construction and got free room and board. We worked forty-eight hours a week, got our expenses paid and still had $350 a month. That was a lot of money then.

So Ernie and I got our visa, bought tickets, took a plane in Paris and landed in Montreal. We took a taxi to Dominion Square because we didn't know the city and didn't know where to go. Ernie went off somewhere.

Here I was finally in Canada and I was sitting on a bench looking all around me at the people and the buildings. I didn't know anyone and had nowhere to go. An older woman came up to me and started talking to me in French, but I couldn't understand her. She sat down on the far side of the bench. I couldn't answer. I didn't know how to handle myself in this situation, and then suddenly she started screaming at me. I didn't know what was happening.

People gathered and were standing around watching us. The next thing I knew, a policeman arrived. It was my first day in Canada. I didn't know what to do, so I pulled out my passport and tried to explain that I had just arrived a few hours before. He talked to the woman. I don't know what he said to her, and then he took me down to the police station. They found a translator who explained what had happened. The woman was an alcoholic and was asking me for money for a bottle. She thought I was making a fool of her and that I was pretending not to understand her.

The police sent me to the Salvation Army, and I got a room there. I started looking for work, and that was when I realized that things were different from what the guy in Paris had told me and what I saw here. I had only a couple of hundred dollars and I went down to an employment agency and saw lines of people looking for a job. There were lots of immigrants in the line, and when I saw this, I got a very pessimistic view of things. Winter was coming. I needed a job.

Some guy in the line told me there was work in Toronto. So a couple of us took the train over there, and there were lineups for jobs there, too. I felt even stranger and more alone, because I couldn't speak English. I did speak some French, Parisian French, but of course, it wasn't useful in Toronto. No one could understand me.

We couldn't afford to stay in hotels so we hung around on the streets, and at night we sneaked in to sleep at the Union train station. The guards would come around and kick us out. When they left, we would sneak back in and sleep a little more. There was a whole bunch of us in there. It was the only place that was warm. It was winter already and cold. We couldn't stay outside. Even though we were woken up a few times during the night by the guards, we didn't mind.

I spent two weeks in Toronto, looking for work. It was depressing. My boss in France had said I could have my job back anytime . . . he had been very satisfied with my work. I was beginning to think seriously about going back to Europe.

All those people standing in lines for jobs . . . all of us were in the same boat . . . it was hard to take, so when I heard someone say there was a chance of getting work in Northern Quebec, I decided to go back. The recruiting was going on in Quebec City, so that's where I went.

The Immigration Department had a large, extremely long building on the pier in the harbour. It was part of the wheat storage silos. We were put up there by the government. That building held 10,000 people . . . like barracks, full of cots.

I did some work, shoveled snow in the town, did odd jobs and kept looking. When I saw some people building oil storage tanks, I figured with my welding experience there might be some work for me. So I asked a French guy working there who the foreman was, and he pointed to a little shack where there was an English guy. When I explained, and it was hard to do with my English, that I was looking for work, he asked me if I could weld.

I looked at the machine he showed me, and he told me to take it and make a couple of passes. The welding machines here are not the same as the ones I used in Europe, and I was scared to try it, but the man who had used it before had left it on the right setting. So I started welding and bluffed my way through it. The foreman told me to come to work the next day, and I had a job.

Because the head office was in Fort Erie*, and the pay cheques came from there, I had to work a week and wait a week for my money. But when the immigration people found out I had a job, they kicked me out of the building. I had nowhere to sleep and no money. I would have to wait two weeks to get paid. When I told the foreman what happened, he let me sleep in the shack.

I worked at the job for four weeks for $1.75 an hour and when I got my money, I nearly dropped dead. It was $75 a week and no tax deductions.

It wasn't long before the job was finished, but in the meantime I heard from other guys that someone was coming who hired people for work on a power dam project on Lake St. John at Chute de Diable above Chicoutimi on the Peribonca River.

Along with me, forty-five people from the immigration group were hired. We worked seventy hours a week and received $1.35 an hour, time and a half after fifty hours. Room and board were free, and we got lots of food. It was clear money, and I did all kinds of work there.

A strange thing happened while I was working there. I hurt my hand, very minor, and I went over to the medical shack to get it looked at. I was talking to the medic who fixed me up and he recognized my accent and said he had been in the war and in Germany.

"Where?" I asked.

"I was shot down at Arnheim."

"What were you flying?"

"A glider."

I took a good look at him and nearly fell over. It was the pilot I had pulled out of the wreckage and carried over to our installation. Well, we started talking and he told me what happened to him after we had

*Now Thunder Bay.

parted, and we were great friends from that time on. But can you imagine finding him there after seven years or so?

Finally the job was finished. The Aluminum Company of Canada had been doing a lot of the construction on the dam, and when the word got around that a welder was needed for another job, I applied. They told me to go to Montreal to a trade school and take a test because I needed a certificate. When the guy at the school saw how good I was and there was nothing he could teach me, he gave me the certificate after three days.

I was supposed to go back, but in the meantime I looked around Montreal to see if anything else was available. Now that I had a little money in my pockets and more confidence in my English, I could pick and choose. I looked through the papers and saw an ad that said the American Army Engineering Corps was looking for welders for the Goose Bay area. I applied and got the job for a period of six months.

I did all kinds of work, and because I could speak French, I became the translator. There were at least 12,000 people employed there and there were a lot of French people from Quebec and France. The boss had a pickup truck and I used to ride around with him when he had to talk to the guys. He was an American and didn't speak any French.

The most exciting thing about this period was finding my two younger brothers there. I didn't even know they had emigrated to Canada. When I was still in France I had heard from my mother that my younger brother was in a prisoner-of-war camp in southern France. My youngest brother had studied to be a toolmaker and lived in the eastern section of Berlin. The Russians wanted to draft him into the Volks army. That's like the Home Guard. So he picked up and ran away and came to Canada. Imagine finding him there that way, and he told me that my other brother was there, too. What a reunion we had!

Six months later, Jim Brady, the boss, told me the company was looking for a welder on North Baffin Island and the area, where a number of building sites were in progress. Radar stations were being put up. I think it was a part of the DEW* line because the American Army Engineering Corps were doing it. It was supposed to be top secret. We had to be cleared and given special security cards. This was in 1951.

I thought I would make good money, even more than I was making here, and it was a seven-day-a-week job. By then my English had im-

*Started in the early 1950s, the Distant Early Warning (DEW) line went into official operation in 1957. Canadian and U.S. air defences operated under integrated control to detect any enemy aircraft penetrating northern Canadian airspace.

proved so I could speak to anyone. It was a matter of dollars and sense.

I had learned the value of money and I went after jobs that paid well. I realized that if I worked for forty hours in the city, I couldn't save anything because the cost of living was so high. But on these northern jobs, my room and board were paid, I could work overtime, and there was no place I could go out, run around and waste money. I didn't have to pay transportation to work. Here I was, already thirty years old and except for a couple of hundred dollars, I had nothing. I wanted to make something of myself, get settled, start a regular life . . . no more running and wandering from country to country.

So I took the job and was sent up to Site 32 on Resolution Island, just south of Baffin Island. I was there for two and a half years, and the pay was $2.35 to $2.85 an hour. Every year it increased. There were six of us from the original group, and the others came from all over the Maritimes: Nova Scotia, New Brunswick and Cape Breton Island.

We left Halifax with a convoy of thirty-six ships and ice-breakers, but there was such a bad storm that we were unable to land on the island and had to turn back. When the storm subsided we sailed again for Resolution Island and when we arrived, it was bare rock, mountains and desolation.

We started the site from nothing. The convoy had been loaded with everything you could think of for the campsite we were going to build. There were landing boats full of stuff — clothing, PX supplies, blankets, food, beer, booze, construction supplies, survival gear, books — you name it. We were given chips to pay for this . . . no money.

We built a campsite, a landing pier on the water, a ramp for the boats and a radar station on top of the mountain near the site. There was so much to do, and we worked more than seventy hours a week.

The first winter, supplies were dropped by parachute because we didn't have a landing strip. It was impossible to build one in the mountains, so in the winter, we used the frozen lake as a landing field and in the summer, seaplanes landed on the lake. However, by the last year, we made a small gravel airstrip for small planes, very small.

We had a stupid accident happen as a result of a parachute drop. We saw the heavy crates coming down, and one of them was moving too fast. I knew there was something wrong with the parachute and I yelled and some of the others did, too: "Hit the dirt! Get away, it's coming too fast!"

A bunch of us scattered in all directions. There was this big, six-foot-three-inch Newfie by the name of Patrick who was standing near a couple of trucks. He stood up to take a look and didn't move fast enough. The crate dropped like a stone on top of him and smashed his hip and leg. We thought he was dead, but one of us noticed he was still breathing. We gave him a shot of morphine and tetanus as well and radioed for help. The pain must have been terrible.

A helicopter flew him out the next day to Nova Scotia. I got a Christmas card from him while he was in the hospital, but with that kind of injury, I don't think he would have been able to walk again, poor guy.

In the summer there were 150 to 180 men on the site, but in the winter most were shipped out and only maintenance people, who looked after the machinery, stayed. It was just too cold and unbearable, and many couldn't take it.

The two and a half years I spent there was a real adventure. The winters were the worst, but I kept myself busy. I made friends with the Inuit in the area and two of them, Henry and Bobby, became my companions. Both had been educated in the missionary school. Henry was older, and his English was pretty good. Bobby wasn't as good at it. But even though they had studied in the white man's schools, they both kept to the old Inuit traditions. One of these was offering your wife as an act of hospitality. This is an old custom. But don't ask me if I accepted his offer.

With my friends I hunted polar bears and trapped foxes. I even made my own traps. Those bears were a nuisance. They were always hanging around the camp looking for food in the dump where we threw the garbage. When they became a danger to the men, we had to go out and shoot them. But even that was a problem. We couldn't keep them from walking around, but there was only one rifle in the whole camp.

You think that's strange, only one gun on the site? The reason for it was that many of the Americans, both officers and soldiers who came up there, didn't respect the wildlife. They would shoot at anything that walked. They were always shooting at the polar bears, and this one particular time, they killed some, skinned them and buried the carcasses. They hung the skins up to dry in the camp.

They didn't know that there is a certain way of handling skins . . . they have to be prepared and tanned. The skins hanging there attracted all kinds of flies and insects. First the hides were crawling with flies and then it was a mass of maggots. They stank! We had to take the skins down and bury them in the dump, but even that was no good. So we poured gasoline on them and burned them.

What a waste that was! The Inuit would have used the meat and skins to live. Nothing would have been wasted. Well, the word must have gotten around because the RCMP found out and they sent an officer over to talk to the American officer in charge. They posted regulations, and it became a law that the killing had to stop. This was still Canadian territory and the Americans were there by permission of the Canadian government. The Americans were permitted to keep their guns, but we were allowed to have only one gun in our camp. Every once in a while the Americans would break the law and shoot something. If no one squealed, they got away with it, but anything killed had to be given to the Inuit for food.

Our rifle could only be used in extreme emergencies. That meant we couldn't kill for sport, only for defense and to make sure this was followed, the officer in charge sealed the rifle with lead.

Can you imagine someone being chased or mauled by a bear, screaming for help, and one of us has to go running for the gun, and unplug the bore so the gun can be used?

I remember the first Christmas. Most of us got drunk, and one of the guys who had too much went out to pee not far from the bunkhouse. There was a polar bear right in front of the door, and it reared up, smacked the guy and knocked him over. The man was screaming like crazy, blood was running down his face, and we all ran out, one of us lugging the gun. He unplugged it and shot the bear, but can you imagine what would have happened if it had been half a mile away from the camp and we couldn't get there so quickly? The guy would have been dead.

And every time we killed something, we had to make a written report. The head of the project would send someone over to take the details in person, look at the kill, and then he'd seal the gun up with lead again. It was the camp joke.

The only way we could stop a bear when the gun wasn't available was to take rocks or sticks and throw them. Sometimes we lit the sticks and threw the flaming wood at the bears to frighten them away. Polar bears are stubborn. Once they find a food dump, they'll come back no matter what you do. They aren't afraid of anything, especially when they are hungry.

We were there to do a job, but the bears weren't interested in our work. They had no consideration for us, and without proper arms, we had no choice. Whenever they wandered too close in the camp, everybody dropped everything and ran. We got lots of exercise.

Our bunkhouse was a tent with a wall of plywood all around the base. It had a proper door, front and back, and was heated by an army regulation, large Coleman-type stove. We didn't have inside plumbing . . . that was in another building with the showers. There were just four bunks, one for each of us and some storage space for our things.

Well, one of the guys opened the door to take a fast pee. It had to be fast or you froze something. He saw a bear right outside the door and he panicked. He ran back in and forgot to latch the door. The bear followed him in and started sniffing around. Three of us pulled ourselves up on our bunks as far as we could go, and one of the men near the back opened the emergency door to make a quick getaway.

The stove was right in the middle of the bunk, and while the bear was smelling everything in front of it and getting too close to us, it backed into the stove and burnt its ass. It let out a howl, turned and shot out the back door at top speed. One of us ran to lock the door and another went for the front door in case the bear doubled back.

That was a real close call, but what could we do? Even if we had the gun, it would have been impossible to use it in such a small area. One of us could have been killed, maybe more if the bear wasn't shot and killed outright. There's nothing worse than a wounded polar bear.

I guess the word didn't get around, because the bears continued to bother us. There was one that was hanging around and seemed to be limping. We didn't know that one of the American officers had shot and wounded it in the paw. As I said before, a wounded bear is the most dangerous thing there is. It goes crazy. Because this was a construction site with men everywhere and there was no control over their movements, running for protection was next to impossible with the gun situation the way it was.

As soon as I realized what had happened, I got my two Inuit friends, Bobby and Henry, and we decided to go after the bear to kill it before it got one of the men. We couldn't take a chance.

The bear seemed to know we were tracking it. It crossed the ice to the open water, slipped in and started swimming across to an island. The guys had a boat and a two-tack motor, you know, the putt-putt kind, and we launched it in that frigid water and went after the bear. Besides Bobby, Henry and myself, there were two others with us, both Canadians.

We spotted the bear lying on a small rocky ledge on the island and had to manoeuver the boat very carefully because the currents were tricky and kept sweeping the boat aside.

The wind was blowing in the bear's direction because it must have smelled us first and then seen us. It dived off the ledge and instead of trying to escape, it headed straight for the boat.

When you see a polar bear swimming in the water, all you see is its head which is very small compared to the size of its body. We had the camp rifle, and Bobby and Henry each had a gun, and we all aimed and fired at the animal. The seas were so rough that the boat kept dipping and bucking, and we missed. The bear dove under as the shots smacked around it, but it kept coming and suddenly it bobbed up right beside us and with one whack of its paw, broke the rudder right off the boat.

It was attacking us!

I was sure the next thing it would do would be to get under the boat and overturn it. I had heard from the Inuit that these bears are sneaky and vengeful when they are wounded. They'll get you, no matter what.

Had the boat flipped, we would have been dumped into that freezing sea and would have been dead within a minute. Nothing survives longer than that in those temperatures.

As the rudder snapped, Bobby was thrown to the bottom of the boat, but he still had the rifle in his hands. He put the muzzle against the bear's head which was just a foot away from him, separated only by the side of the boat. He fired and killed it. The bullet tore right through its head.

The body, caught in the current, began drifting away. We had no steering with the rudder gone, the current was impossible to fight, so we had to steer with the oars we had in the boat. It took us hours to catch up to the body. We had to go after it because Inuit never abandon a kill, not just for the meat, but the fur. It's their existence, their survival.

We finally caught up with the animal, tied the rope we had with us around its body and tried to pull it into the boat. I never realized how heavy one of these bears are and how difficult it is to get a dead weight like this into a boat in heaving seas.

All five of us pulled, two of us counter-balancing on the other side. The rifles had been stacked together and were leaning against the edge of the boat. As we yanked as hard as we could, the body suddenly fell in over the side. It was so heavy it slammed up against the rifles and broke the butts of all three guns right off.

Here we were with this hulk in the boat, rifles gone, no rudder to steer, in frigid seas with a bad current pulling us farther away from camp. We battled the water for hours, and we kept thanking our lucky stars that the bear hadn't fallen on the oars and smashed them, too. By the time we finally got back to the campsite, we were nearly frozen, exhausted, and it was dark. We had only the lights of the camp to guide us, and the temperature had dropped even more.

The Inuit skinned the bear immediately. The only thing they discarded was the liver. It's so rich in Vitamin A and D that it is toxic and can kill you. It's sure death to use it for food. I got the head and I still have the skull as a trophy.

Now it's different with a seal. When one is caught and skinned, the liver is removed and cut into small pieces. You can slip it down raw. I've seen that done many times. It is still hot when it is eaten and is a delicacy, the same as raw fish. There's nothing better than biting into the back of a freshly caught, small salmon. It's the best eating there is. I know because I had it lots of times with Bobby and Henry.

About this time we were heading for our second Christmas on the island, and the worst thing happened.

We ran out of beer!

The first year, the Americans had brought up a warehouse of beer and schnapps, and we could get two kinds of beer every day, and four on Sundays. Sometimes we saved it up and threw a party. Everyone got drunk.

But this was a real emergency, and we had to do something.

Our cook, who was Yugoslavian, had all kinds of canned food and fruit . . . not just little tins, but the gallon size. We had cherries, peaches and bags of dried raisins. Because I was an experienced toolmaker and welder, I decided to set up a still and make a brew.

We had a boilerhouse that provided the hot water, and the bathrooms, toilets and showers were attached to it. It was nice and warm in there which was what we needed for the brewing—controlled temperature. We opened the tins, tossed in the raisins and mixed the fruit. I took a big stainless steel pot, put sugar and yeast into it, and on the top I welded a pipe into it and made a copper coil. I passed the coil through another pot that had ice in it to condense the alcohol that comes out.

Inside of a week, oh boy, you could smell it in there and depending on which way the wind was blowing, you could smell it outside, too. The Americans knew what we were up to, but nobody squealed. The only officer there must have had a pretty good idea, but he didn't say a thing. He was pretty desperate himself and needed something to drink real bad.

Do you know something about alcohol? You have to keep the heat up and watch before it boils. The first run is never any good and has to be run through again. The temperature has to be just right and kept constant or you ruin it.

Can you imagine about twenty-seven of us standing there crowded into that small room behind the toilets, practically on top of each other with our tongues hanging out, each one with a cup in his hand, waiting for the fluid to come out of the pipe?

"It's no good," I kept telling them, "wait, it will make you sick. The first run is bad. Let me run it through again." But it was very hard on them. They drank it. By the second run, I had the heat controlled properly and I got practically pure alcohol.

Most of the guys had nothing to drink for months . . . you couldn't bring in supplies from the outside in the winter . . . and by midnight, everyone was dead drunk, lying around everywhere on the floor. There were only two guys sober, me and the cook, and we had to carry all the men out to their bunkhouses, dump them on their beds, clean up the mess . . . but I tell you, oh boy, that second run was really good stuff. It made the holiday.

Like anything else, there were good things and bad things, and most of the bad things were the results of stupidity. One of these I could never forget because it shouldn't have happened.

The Chicago Bridge Company built oil tanks, and sent three men up to the island — three men who were supposed to be experts — to build an oil tank at the bottom of the mountain. The tank was built in sections, or rings, and as each ring was welded, the next ring went on top of it, five rings in all. It looked like a giant oil drum with the ridges. A small opening at the bottom allowed a man to crawl in and out of it to work on the inside.

Because of our location with the mountain behind us, the wind blowing in from the sea was very strong here. I realized that the top ring would get the most pressure and that the hollow interior didn't provide enough resistance to the wind.

I told the guys working on the tank to attach guide lines from the top all around the rim, tie the lines to big stakes and pound them into the ground in a circle around the tank to keep it from blowing away.

They wouldn't listen to me. They knew it all.

The top ring hadn't been welded completely, just fastened in some places. The wind must have picked up and was blowing into a gale. The three men were working inside on the bottom of the tank when suddenly the top ring with the scaffolds attached to it, collapsed. Sheets of metal, twenty by eight feet, just blew apart and fell into the tank on top of the men. Other sections were being whipped back and forth by the wind as they hung there attached by a few feet of welded metal.

It was too dangerous for us to try to get in through the bottom hole. We had to get cranes to lift the pieces off from the top before we could get inside to the men. Two of them had been killed instantly and the third seriously injured. He died the next day. A helicopter flew in to take the bodies out.

It shouldn't have happened. If the guide lines had been attached, three men would be alive today.

Except for things like that, for me those years were good. It was like a healing. The country was unbelievably beautiful. The mountains are stark rock faces where nothing grows, like monuments sticking up against the sky. The landscape is desolate and bare. The sky is the bluest blue you ever saw, no clouds at all. The sea, a darker blue, could turn gray in less than an hour when a sudden storm came up. You could get a snowstorm in the summer, and an hour later it would be gone. The glare and the shadows on the snow reflected so much you could go blind. We had to wear snow glasses with slits in them.

As you went farther north toward the Pole, the night and day disappeared into grayness. You have twenty-four hours of daylight sun in the summer and then night for six months. So when summer comes, everything pops out fast. In the valleys where the ice runs off the mountains, you would find beautiful flowers growing . . . white, yellow, blue. Little creeks formed and rivulets where there was nothing before. Suddenly there would be grass valleys folding one into the other.

I could stand there and watch the swarms of mosquitos, black flies, bumblebees and birds swooping down to feed on the insects. Wheeling in the sky or sitting in the bushes were flocks of other birds and ravens. They always returned with the spring.

You could see herds of caribou wandering around. The animal life was unbelievable. They weren't afraid to come up to me and eat from my hand. As long as I didn't make a sudden move and kept perfectly still, they came to me. The foxes were running around and would come and sniff my clothes and my hands. Now the bears are another story. If they're hungry, and they're always hungry, they'll eat you. the only time you're safe is after they have eaten. Then they go to sleep and don't wake up until they're ready to eat again.

There were no real trees. There were stunted, crippled birch trees and scrub, one or two feet high, and bushes. Some grew cranberries and others blueberries. Whenever I looked around there was something beautiful and different to see.

Toward the sea the view changes. The shore ice breaks up in May and June, and the wind and tide move the ice in and out, back and forth, so the scenery is always changing, never boring. The ice blocks everything so you can't move, and giant icebergs get left over, stuck and hanging around in the scrap ice.

You could see the current slamming waves against the rocks, white-capped, blue-gray waves, and when the sun was hardly over the horizon, the blue would fade into a dozen shades of gray.

On a clear night you could see the Northern Lights. You know it was the result of the wind from the sun and the earth's magnetic field above the Pole. It was the most beautiful thing I have ever seen, the colours flashing and sparkling across the sky. There is nothing in the cities to compare to this, nothing. I could stand there and look up, and feel small, insignificant, as if I were nothing. I tell you the country made me feel special because I was walking where man had never walked before and hadn't had a chance to spoil anything.

We were isolated and cut off in the winter. You could go crazy up there with nothing to do . . . some did and had to be shipped out. With the convoy had come a library of books and games to keep us busy during the long winter. There was everything from the Bible to detective stories. I think I read them all, every book. If the weather was bad, and we couldn't work, we got paid anyway, so we just lay around. I took a dictionary, looked up the words I didn't know, and kept reading. That's how I learned English, all by myself up there, so I wouldn't go crazy.

When the ice broke up in the spring, the seaplanes flew in to land on the lake and deliver machinery parts, gasoline, the special oils we needed, food, other supplies, etc. We had built a floating platform the first summer we were there. It was made of empty barrels with a frame around them, and we towed this float to a nearby bay and anchored it there. Here the seaplanes landed, unloaded, and we put the supplies on landing craft and brought it back to the camp.

You have to imagine what it looked like then. There were so many icebergs this time of the year, drifting in the water. They weighed thousands, no, millions of tons, some of them stuck there, almost anchored in the water.

There was this one big berg that was different. It looked like a dome and had a tunnel-like opening in it. Every time I drove there with Johnny Whittiker, we'd stop and take a look at it. Johnny was a farmer's son from England. He wanted to make enough to go back and buy himself a farm.

He handled the outboard motor on the boat, and as we went by the iceberg one day, Johnny said, "Let's have a look in there."

He shut off the motor and using the rudder and oars, we

manoeuvred the boat right into the passage. It was fantastic! The sun was shining and filtered right through the ice of the berg. It caught the light so it looked like a million diamonds sparkling. There was a glow I have never seen in my life . . . blue, blue . . . such a colour!

I looked up and inside on the ceiling of this tunnel was a great big crack. The ripples were slapping against the side of the boat, and this crack was right above us. It made me nervous, and I said to Johnny, "Let's get out of here. You never know when that crack will go."

We turned the boat around with the oars, and I said, "Don't start the motor."

"There's nothing wrong, nothing to worry about, what the hell!" he said, and he pulled the cord of the motor before I could stop him. He opened the throttle of the motor all the way, all 70-horse power, and the boat shot out of the tunnel in the ice. The shock waves caused by the vibration of the motor split the damn iceberg in two. We were barely out of the hole and running full blast. When the berg split and hit the water, it created a tidal wave that came after us. We got swamped, and there was a good two feet of water in the boat. We were bailing with our hands. We were lucky the boat didn't swamp completely or we could have been drowned in that freezing water.

When we got back to camp, I said to him, "You son-of-a-bitch . . . never, never again I go out with you!"

For him it was just a joke. He laughed all the way home to the camp. He was enjoying every minute of it. It didn't matter to him that we could have been killed, either by the ice falling on us, or freezing to death in the water in less than a minute.

That crazy Johnny had another funny habit. He was always wandering around with a paint can, painting something, anything, just to leave his mark on it. Once he climbed up on the cliff's rock face and painted his name on it. He was nuts. You never knew what he was going to do next.

One day Johnny wandered off with his paint can. Without warning a sudden storm hit the area, and when he didn't return, we knew he was in big trouble.

I had bought a pup, half dog, half wolf, from an Inuit and I called her Skinjer. She was wild. No one was allowed near her but me. She would let me scratch her belly and feed her. Anyone else that went near her would have been ripped to pieces.

Well, I took Skinjer, put her on a fifty-foot nylon rope and with about six guys went out into the cold to look for Whittiker. I had given Skinjer Whittiker's jacket to smell, and the dog took off over the snow at full speed with the rest of us dragging along behind.

We found Johnny all right, found him half-frozen in the snow. Somewhere along the way, he had either thrown away or lost his lousy paint can. He must have been looking for another mountain to autograph. Gott, was he nuts!

Oh ya, we had all kinds of strange guys there. One of the men who ran the store was an alcoholic. Believe it or not, his father was an MP. The family was pretty embarrassed by his drinking, so he was shipped up to Resolution Island and given the store to handle. He'd be wandering around at night in a drunken stupor, and someone always had to round him up and get him back into his bunk.

One night he mixed up a real strong brew of alcohol and shaving lotion and drank it. He went violent crazy, got his hands on an axe and had to be subdued. We radioed for help, and a helicopter was sent in to pick him up. They put a straightjacket on him and shipped him out. We never knew what happened to him.

Another guy, a French-Canadian, was the best damn mechanic you ever saw. We called him Shorty. He could fix anything. He was so polite and so kind, he'd do anything for you, but he was afraid of water. He had the bunk next to mine and in the two years he was there, he never changed his underwear. He smelled. I never saw him shower or bathe. When he left at the end of the job, he took off his underwear and stood them up in the corner against the wall. They were so stiff, they stayed there upright. They could have walked away.

When the weather was good and the work was done, I went hunting with Bobby and Henry and his wife. Both men were married, but Bobby's wife was expecting and couldn't go. She also had to stay and look after Henry's two kids and she and Bobby had a couple of their own.

You have to understand the role of women in Inuit society to know why the men always take a woman along when they go hunting. These women do more work than you could ever imagine, much more than white women do. The men's work is to hunt and look after their hunting equipment, their boats, bringing in the kill; but the skinning, cleaning and preparing the animal is woman's work.

You know how they prepare furs? The women stretch it on a board and scrape it with a primitive knife that looked like a wide wedge of a pie with a wooden handle on it. Because they have no tanning fluid, they soak it in their own urine, and when it's dry, they wash it and then chew and chew it with their teeth to make it soft. By the time an Inuit woman is thirty, she has no teeth left. They are worn down to the gums. Ya, it is a very hard life for them.

As well as selling furs to the Hudson Bay Company, the Inuit sold some of their work. They made beautiful things with walrus tusks and soapstone. The company had a monopoly, so it took as much as it could get out of the natives. It took a pile of furs almost a yard high just to buy a rifle.

The factor would check the skins carefully, and if there was even a tiny flaw, he would cut the price in half. It was like that then, and I don't know if it is better now.

I guess you can't condemn them . . . the company. They were a group of adventurers who were out to make money, and they naturally took advantage of their position with the fur trade monopoly. There was no competition, so the company sold the natives what they thought was good for them and took the most they could get out of them.

One of the times I was out hunting with Bobby and Henry, we got a big walrus. We cut it up. loaded it on the sleigh and fed the dogs with scraps of meat from the carcass. From one of the tusks, Bobby made a cribbage board with all the pegs and holes, even a compartment to hold the pegs . . . very beautiful and fine work. I have it to this day.

There was one day we weren't so lucky. Bobby's wife was back at the Inuit camp, looking after all the children. Henry's wife was with us. We had already prepared a snowhouse, you know, an igloo. Looking for walrus or seal, we were jumping from ice-floe to ice-floe. The wind and the current move the floes so they are never in the same place for long.

Bobby jumped to another one, and he slipped and fell into the water. The current pushed the other floe, and I saw the ice was moving together. I grabbed him by the top of his parka and pulled as hard as I could. As I dragged him onto the ice, the floes crunched together. Another second and he would have been killed, crushed between tons of ice. He wouldn't have had a chance to escape.

Accidents like that happen very often in the way of life these people have. It is almost a daily thing for men to die this way in the hunt. They live for fishing and hunting, and the risks are very great.

We got Bobby back to the snowhouse. The soapstone lamp was full of oil, and we stripped him and hung his clothes around the lighted lamp to dry. If we hadn't he would have been frozen solid and died of exposure and pneumonia. We all shared our clothes with him, something from each of us—Henry, his wife, myself—while we waited for his things to dry in the warmth of the igloo. Only when everything was dry could he leave.

Well, Bobby was so grateful to me for saving his life that he wanted to be my bloodbrother. We each made a small cut on our wrists and putting them together, intermingled our blood. It may sound primitive, but it is a good feeling to know you have done something good and been accepted by one of the real Canadians of our country.

Because I was and felt like one of them, we depended on each other for many things.

When Bobby's wife went into labour, there was a serious problem. There was a storm . . . the weather was terrible, and the doctor couldn't get in either by plane or dogteam. Bobby's wife was a tiny little thing, and the baby couldn't be born. Not only that, she had never seen a white man before and was terrified. She never came along on the hunts with us because of her condition.

Bobby asked me for help. How could I say no! I told him I could fix up a guy with a minor injury, but what did I know about delivering babies? Nothing. So I radioed for help almost four hundred miles away to the Frobisher Bay hospital, and the doctor gave me instructions, step by step.

She was in so much pain and so frightened, and we didn't have any anaesthetic, so I took a bottle of whiskey and poured it into her . . . got her so drunk I almost knocked her out. I was just as scared as she was, scared I would do more damage than good. With Bobby helping me, we finally got the baby out. It was a boy.

I cut the cord, got the afterbirth out, everything. She was so badly torn because the baby was too big, and we didn't even have forceps to make it easier. A week later when the storm stopped, the doctor flew in from Frobisher Bay in a helicopter and sewed her up. She was okay.

Before I left the north, Bobby wrote the Inuit alphabet on birch bark for me, and I still have it somewhere. He made me some soapstone carvings as well — kayaks, animals, an Inuit hunter — I kept them all.

When the job on the site was finally finished and the American engineers were going back to the United States, they did something that made me feel so helpless and so angry that I almost cried. The convoy had brought up so many supplies and more were flown in while I was there. What was left could have been distributed among the natives or given to the men who had worked so hard to build the site, or they could have taken it back to the United States, but no . . . they piled it all up in one big heap and set it on fire — expensive parkas, blankets, sleeping bags, books, all kinds of costly equipment, food burning up in front of our eyes. There was stuff that was worth hundreds of thousands of dollars, no, more . . . maybe way over a million. That was a lot of money then.

This was the way they wasted the taxpayers' money. They burned it, and no one was allowed to touch anything, to salvage something. I couldn't believe they could do such a terrible thing. I never forgot it, and it still bothers me to this day.

I went back up north twice more after I got married in 1956. This time it was to Site 34 on Baffin Island where I worked for six months, still on the same project.

The third time I went back up north was to Great Whale River in the Hudson Bay area where there was a small station. What I found different there was the Inuit and Indian community who lived in separate camps and went their separate ways. A religious order from Austria had a school and church there, and they had to conduct services separately because the Cree and Inuit don't mix.

After this I put in a twelve-month period in Gander, Newfoundland, and a few years later I worked in Labrador City for fifteen months, and put in eleven months in an oil sands plant in Alberta four years ago. I've seen a lot of different parts of Canada, but I tell you this . . . if I hadn't met my wife and got married, I would have gone back up north and stayed there. For me, that's the real Canada, the north country, not the cities. I will never forget the years I spent up there . . . that's Canada!

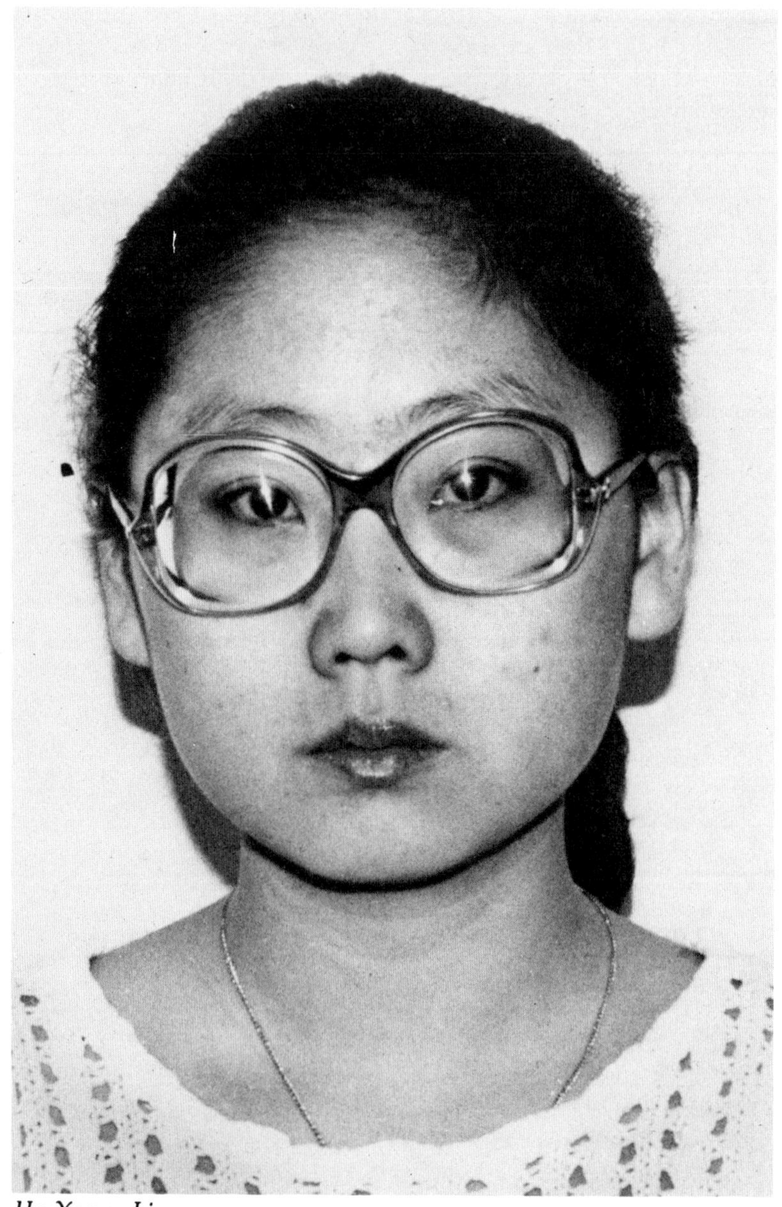

Un-Young Lim

MIRROR IMAGE

by Un-Young Lim

It is a hazy, summer morning in the city of Seoul, capital of South Korea. Inside the international airport the atmosphere is harried and noisy. A woman who has just passed through customs pauses, her eyes searching the crowd. She is not quite sure whom or what she is looking for, but a moment later she glimpses a face in a sea of people. It is her mirror image—the same, yet different. The two come together hesitantly, smiling shyly at one another. There is instant telepathic communication as the other thinks: "I would not have forgotten our rendez-vous. This is the place. Do you remember where we parted that day so long ago? Here at this very spot I watched you disappear into the clouds and I wondered when I would see you again." She moves her head slightly to one side and reflects a moment.

"You have changed a lot. Have I?"

Who are these two?

They are strangers, yet part of each other for they share the common denominator of the same beginning and thus have been able to recognize one another in the crowd. They are the two halves that diverged that day so long ago into two futures. The one who stayed behind looks into the other's eyes and says, "I possess the life you forfeited, the life you abandoned. You cannot have it back. You cannot return. Do you regret it?"

The other cries out in despair. "I had no choice. The decision was not mine to make. Please do not chastise me for something that was not my fault."

She cannot answer the question. How can you regret what you do not know?

In silence they make their way out of the airport. Outside they must part, diverge again. The other turns and in the blink of an eyelid is lost in the crowd.

Once she reaches her hotel room, she stares out the window. Perhaps her other self is still out there living out her life. Perhaps she never existed, except in the never-never land of ifs.

She sighs and turns away from the window. Tomorrow she will go back and visit the old places, although she already knows what she will find. It won't be as large as it seemed in her childish vision. Different people will be living out the same routines. She will go to a place where once she carved her secret mark with a knife. Even as a child she had felt the need to leave some imprint of herself to prove she had once existed. Perhaps another child had crouched there and thought about the person who had scratched the star into the wood. She will wander in and out of the places that had been a part of her, places that had helped create her.

But after tomorrow, she resolves she will not go again for she will grow larger and places grow smaller until finally they will cease to exist altogether.

That night she lies on her bed under the weight of the oppressive summer heat, trying to think and rethink the past into the present. Because she is looking at her life from the viewpoint of twelve years before, it proves difficult to recall herself as she once was. She is trying to go back in time, to remember her way of thinking, trying to shed all the things she now takes for granted. Back, back to the beginning she goes, deeper into herself in the dark hotel room while the sounds of traffic blend with the discordant strains of her mind. She is trying to return to that state of mind when her universe was half-formed and only partly discernible.

Korea is a small country, living in the double shadow cast by two giants, China and Japan. But to her it was everthing she knew of the world. Her world was herself, and everything revolved around her because she only knew what she herself witnessed. Then came her family, other people, cars, roads and buildings. The city was big enough to surpass her comprehension of the concept of place, time and distance. However, she accepted what the world was and had an expectation of what it would be in the future. The notion that the future could be different from the present was alien to her childish mind.

She understood when people spoke because first there were ideas which came into her mind, then words, which were merely audible ideas. How can a child understand that language is only a medium and not an extension of ideas themselves?

There had been a war. After dinner, the grownups would gather and tell of their experiences, sometimes with a relish she found ghoulish and at other times, pathetic. But there were also those who sat and said nothing, those whose eyes told more of anguish and torment than words could ever have expressed. If a picture is worth a thousand words, does not silence bespeak an infinity?

She saw war as a thing that killed people. Death was something that caused people to vanish from sight. But if you did see them, they were still and cold to the touch. Death and war seemed so far away, but when she heard the grownups speaking, she imagined she saw the two spectres hovering in the room, kept alive by the memories which made people what they were and brought them where they were.

Her mother often told her stories about those years when she was a schoolgirl under the Japanese occupation. She spoke about the end of the Second World War and the coming of the American heroes. After that came another war—civil war. Her mother had been through air raids, had seen relatives searching for remains in piles of corpses laid out on the playground where she had once played. Her mother and her family became refugees retreating from an enemy that was her own countrymen. Her father had been in the army during the war. He was one of those who did not speak of the past.

She knew all this as historical fact and fitted it into the puzzle of her universe, but there was so much she did not comprehend. She could only accept it blindly and dumbly.

Although her childhood years were times of relative peace, there were hard times for many people around her. She had been born in 1963, ten years after the Korean conflict, and that war had been the result of years of foreign occupation and civil struggle. The country was slowly trying to rebuild itself. She had only vague memories of Seoul, the huge city in which they had lived. She remembered the different houses, parks, her school and the little places of childhood that form the setting of a child's secret life. When she was little they had lived in different houses and in rented rooms with many neighbors and so they never felt isolated.

Their first home was a traditional structure composed of connecting rooms built around a square central courtyard, which contained a well covered with a wooden board. There was also a green cistern in which rainwater was collected and stored. When she was younger, the water was carried from the cistern to the kitchen in bamboo gourds. As she grew older, these were exchanged for brightly colored plastic ones.

Sometimes she would imagine what the courtyard must have been like before—perhaps a wealthy merchant who sold silks and spices had built it for one of his concubines. He must have commissioned a rock garden with little winding paths and a lotus pond with goldfish lazily flicking in the still waters. In the spring the ladies holding parasols would stroll under the apple blossoms, guarding their complexions against the sunlight. Perhaps it was a fool's paradise, but it was a paradise all the same.

Now many families inhabited the house, and the children ran around the courtyard, making the walls ring with their laughter in the long summer twilights. Her brother would catch dragonflies and put them on string leashes. They had all the elusive charm of captured magic about to escape.

There was the day when her brother entered middle school and came home wearing a uniform. His head was shaved. Of course, they made fun of him, and inside she felt white anger and shame. How vulnerable he looked!

There was a man in their neighborhood who used to make the rounds to fix pots and pans. They called him "The Tin Man", and the children were terrified of him because he had a bloody eye which seemed to have a will of its own. He terrorized the children, enjoying the effect his wandering eye caused.

The passing of the year was marked by the time of the monsoons and the time of the snow frosts. The monsoon meant walking through streets with shoes squelching in muddy water and uplifted faces washed clean by the warm rain. And when the first snow fell, the children would wake up early to rush outside and gather up enough snow for snowballs before the sun melted it all. Because it was so exotic and so foreign, the snow brought with it an excitement and perhaps a foreshadowing of the land they soon would be going to.

There came the day she told the teacher her family was leaving the country and she would no longer be coming to school. The teacher made her stand on a chair to say farewell to the class and tell the others about the country to which she was immigrating.

"Canada is a land like America, but I do not know why it is called by a different name," she said. "Everything in this land is upside-down, backwards and opposite to what it is here. It is a land where everybody has yellow ruffled curtains at kitchen windows and every Sunday people walk to church holding hands."

(This was from an illustration she had seen in one of her mother's books.)

The teacher was very proud of her, for leaving was an accomplishment greater than anything she could have achieved alone. Now the thought leaves a bitter taste in her mouth like the aftertaste of medicine.

It was on a night a few weeks before departure that they awakened in the pre-dawn to the shrill sounds of alarm sirens and the monotonous tread of army boots in the nearby alley. Her father had already gone to the new land to prepare the way for the family's arrival.

The siren was the alarm which signified the invasion of the country by North Korean troops. The fear had always been there like the nightmares she had of Communist spies and what they did to people.

She had heard these stories from the adults. In that moment listening to the fury of sounds, she knew fear and recognized her mother's fear growing and taking shape on her face in the darkness of the room. She almost felt she could open the door and touch that awesome thing called war, and its face would be terrible. It was not a real invasion, of course, only a surprise military drill, but the memory of that night remained for a long time. Some days it lived underneath her bed or inside her closet, but always the fear emerged with the coming of darkness.

Leaving was a paradox—a dying and a rebirth. Was it an action or an inaction? There was the unwillingness to carry on their lives in despair and the willingness to start a new life in hope. How was it that they could come to live out their lives on the other side of the world, exiled from their identity and their past? In the process they had to abandon the selves they might have become.

On the day of departure, their faces wore both sorrow and joviality. Her grandmother, huddled in the corner of the room, was weeping hot, slow tears. Suddenly she seemed very small and old.

"Grandmother!" she cried. "Though twice removed from your womb, yet still born of you, I ask why do you weep? We shall return from the far-off land paved with gold. Our pockets will be filled with jewels which grow on trees there. It will all be as if nothing happened, as if no time had come between to separate us like a velvet curtain after the final act."

She did not know it then, but that was what it was—the final act. There would be no returning. The new land welcomes, but it also transforms.

The airplane's snout is painted black like the beak of a giant bird about to carry them off to a fairy-tale world. They walk up the steps and are swallowed in its depths. For the next few days, it becomes a womb, a place from which they will emerge with the eyes of the newborn, wailing aloud with fear and dismay as they take their first shocking breaths of foreign air.

They are suspended within their cocoon, between two lives, past and future, memory and hope. They look at each other's faces. Who are we, they ask? What are we to become? What does the future demand of us?

The journey goes on and on—an endless series of planes and terminals. Stewardesses smile ceaselessly and incomprehensibly. Is this to be their new existence, forever doomed to sit strapped in chairs, bumped and tossed about like homeless seedlings? There is no night or day as they pursue the sun eastward.

Fog hovers over Vancouver when they land, and their first glimpse of Canada is obscured by the drifting strands of mist. It looks as if they have arrived in a new world that is partially formed like the swirl of cosmic dust on the verge of coalescing into a galaxy.

Waiting at the airport for the next flight, she sees a man and woman embracing. Embarrassed, she turns her head. They seem shameless, oblivious to the people staring. In Korea, it is not so long ago that a woman showing her ankle would have been considered scandalous. People would never be so bold there. It is just another proof of the topsy-turvy new world.

Canada is not the place a seven-year-old girl has pictured. Her imagination, prejudices and stereotyped images colour the scene. Korea has been the land of the black-haired, black-eyed people, and logic dictates that Canada should be a country of blonde, blue-eyed ice-maidens like those in picture books. Who else could survive in such a climate? But no, there are many people with muddy-brown hair and no-colour eyes. If Canada is not a land of contradictions, but instead a land of maybes, shrugs and in-betweens, then the surprise is that people do not walk upside down, unaware they are on the bottom side of the world and in danger of falling off.

Perhaps this is all a dream or nightmare. She closes her eyes, squeezing them tightly shut to block out the insanity surrounding her. She wishes deperately she could return to Korea and its familiar security.

Finally the journey has ended, and they have arrived at a place they will call home. It is a fishing village of about 3,000 people located on the northernmost tip of Newfoundland. Compared to Seoul, a city of six million or so, the difference is shocking. Where have all the people gone? Has the rest of the world disappeared?

They are the first Orientals the villagers have seen although there is a resemblance to the Inuit. Why do people look at her so strangely? Their eyebrows are knitted in concentration as if she somehow has destroyed the ordinary scheme of things. Is it because her eyebrows slant upward where theirs slant down, she thinks? Or perhaps her tongue bends in different ways to produce sounds they cannot duplicate. Surely that is the answer. They fear the incomprehensible the same way I hate and fear them. We laugh at jokes that are a string of unintelligible sounds to them. They are afraid. That is why they hoot and poke me in the back with hard fingernails as I come home from school. My back is held stiff and upright against their derision. My back bears the burden of my pride.

People ask her where Korea is. She doesn't know and can't tell them. How to explain?

"Korea is a land of my beginnings, my centre from which my world expanded."

How could a place exist one moment, surround her entire existence and disappear the next? Is it possible she had not existed before? Perhaps Korea did not exist just as these people had not existed for her before she arrived? Her past was destroyed by their ignorance of it. What awesome power to be able to destroy a past!

How can she explain?

"Korea is the place that was—yesterday, last week, last year. Korea is the known, my waking life, my past. You, this place and the present are my dream and nightmare. Do you, can you, realize that?"

But slowly, so slowly that she does not notice the change, Korea becomes the dream, and this new existence, the reality. Through routine, a past builds up in the new place, and accumulates like sand on a delta. It somehow becomes connected to the present. And so comes the conclusion that this must be real, the here and now, and not some hallucination.

It is November 1, 1970, the night of their second day in their new home. Her father is at work, and only the four, mother and three children, are at home. Suddenly, there is a knock at the door. They look at one another and wonder who it can be. How will they handle it since none of them knows English? The presence on the other side of the door waits, and custom demands they open the door.

And who is it but some belated Halloweeners with stockings pulled over their heads? Their sacks drag on the ground. Of course, the family does not know of this Western tradition. Their reaction is fright and puzzlement.

What kind of burglars would come brazenly knocking on someone's door, they think? Is there some kind of protocol involved in the behavior of would-be thieves, which requires them to announce their arrival so politely? The family is puzzled because these stocking-faced children seem as bewildered as they are. For the eternity of a moment they stand there, mouths agape, staring at one another, both at a loss as to what is expected. The trick-or-treaters begin fidgeting and are embarrassed in the same way as invited guests who must eat and run. How do they say good-bye when there has been no hello? Finally the children leave as silently as they have come. The atmosphere that has been stretched taught as a drumskin in the family's lungs is now expelled in a sigh of relief.

After the humour of the situation is explained much later by their father, the event becomes the ultimate symbol, the demarcation point in her mind. Literally and figuratively, by opening the door, she has met the other side of the world standing on the doormat.

Back in the hotel room, she stands in the pre-dawn light beside the window. Her journey into memory is finished. She has remembered many things she has not thought of for many years—things that seemed important in the darkness and that now recede with the coming of day. They leave a lingering trace like portents in a dream. Now she crosses to stand before the dresser mirror and solemnly regards her reflection. She remembers a long afternoon spent playing with a friend who has come to stand with her in front of a mirror.

Suddenly, the oneness she has felt while playing is split asunder, and with a pang she realizes the physical differences that separate them can never be erased. It is as if the mirror reflects the internal as well as the external. Will it crack under the strain?

She remembers the times when her two selves, her two worlds overlapped despite her efforts to keep them apart. They have always seemed to be at war with one another, and she has been unable to be herself without the sensation of trespassing on forbidden territory. There is the feeling of being caught in some shameful act when someone or something betrays the secret of her double life to others. For an instant she recalls the odd looks her Western friends sometimes cast her way when she has let slip some aspect of her other self. It seems as if they are looking at a Janus-like creature which only half belongs to their world and so cannot be trusted.

Now she draws a line down the mirror with an Autumn-Berry coloured lipstick, splitting her image in two. She whispers a magic incantation to herself.

"Step to the right or step to the left . . . forward or backward, but you will never know which is which."

She half-smiles, and a tear spills down her cheek.

"Or perhaps, because there is no choice, I should remain exactly where I am — in the middle."

Andy Melamed

QUEBEC: A HAVEN OF PEACE

by Andy Melamed

If we go back far enough all of us come from immigrant stock, ever since Adam and Eve left Eden. My parents left their homes and families during World War I: my father to avoid conscription into the Czar's army; my mother to get an education that was not offered in her village near Kiev, Russia.

They came to the United States, met at college and both became pharmacists. My father was conscripted into the U.S. army at the end of the war. They were married shortly after, and bought a drugstore in a working-class neighbourhood in Philadelphia.

We survived the Depression of the 1930s and then came World War II. I was nineteen when I enlisted in the Air Corps, and by the time I came home from the war, forty-two months later, I had begun to question many things I had formerly accepted on faith. In a war against racism, I had been in a segregated army and had seen Japanese-Americans stripped of their property and interned in camps like prisoners, accused of no crimes. German and Italian Americans were spared this fate, as they were in Canada. Overseas, in Normandy, I had seen blood plasma in the hospitals "segregated" by race as well as by bloodtype. I met well-educated Germans, cultured, gentle people, who explained their compliance to Nazism either by invoking ignorance of what had happened, or impotence to do anything about it. I asked myself what I would have done in their place.

With the start of the "Cold War", many of these concerns sharpened and were clarified when I returned to university under the G.I. Bill, first in the U.S., and then in France at the Sorbonne.

By the time I returned home and settled down, the Korean War had begun, and McCarthyism was in full bloom. The witch hunts sent artists and writers to jail and executed the Rosenbergs for espionage during peacetime. The C.I.A. became a household acronym, meddling in the internal affairs of Guatemala, Iran and dozens of Third World countries. The breaking point for me came with the full-scale intervention of the U.S. in Vietnam, the bombing of innocent populations, the indiscriminate use of napalm, pellet bombs and other horrors aimed at terrorizing an impoverished nation into submission. Like Hitler's Germany, the U.S. invoked the Communist menace to suppress legitimate aspirations for national independence, begun during the Japanese occupation, continued under the French invasion, and after Dien Bien Phu against the Americans and their succession of puppets.

By 1965 when the bombings began, and the war was extended to North Vietnam, I knew that the lessons I had learned in Europe were forcing me to search my conscience. Unlike the Germans, I knew what my country was doing. Unlike them, I had been able to participate in demonstrations against the war. Like them, I was unable to alter the murderous war which my homeland had launched against millions of innocent women, children and the elderly; against guerrillas who were fighting to liberate their country from foreign domination, just as American guerrillas had done two centuries ago against British rule.

It had taken a shamefully long time for my conscience to respond to such excesses of U.S. power as the C.I.A. directed Bay of Pigs invasion of Cuba which failed; the Cuban missile crisis and the maintenance of the U.S. Naval Base at Guantanamo despite Cuban protests at the continued occupation of its territory; the invasion of the Dominican Republic by U.S. Marines to overthrow a newly elected government which was pledged to restore democracy to that poor country after decades of dictatorship under Trujillo, one of the staunchest defenders of U.S. privilege there; and literally dozens of U.S. armed and sponsored militay coups in Latin-America (Bolivia, Brazil, Uruguay, etc).

Under ordinary circumstances I would have discussed my problems of conscience with my wife and our three children. Instead I posed it to them as my problem, as the only way to regain my mental health by moving to a country where I would not feel like a murderer because my taxes and my country were burning and maiming the innocent in a land 10,000 miles away. I was prepared to leave my loved ones if they chose to remain in the U.S. I gave my wife the choice of where she would prefer to move if she would come with me and leave the killer nation that was my native land. We tried Mexico first, but it was impossible for a foreigner to get a job there unless invited by the Mexican government. That was in the summer of 1965, and it was to be the last vacation we would spend together as a family. It was a happy time and it helped us decide that we would leave the U.S. as a family.

In the fall I had interviews for jobs in Montreal and Toronto. I had been to a planning congress in Montreal in 1955, and was impressed by the vitality of the city. Ten years later, it was even more exciting with the exuberance of Expo '67 already bubbling, the new Metro well under way, and the ferment of the quiet revolution creating a heady brew politically. By early 1966 the Montreal City Planning Department offered me a job. My wife Lanie was completing her M.A. at the University of Pennsylvania, and we decided to wait until summer to move.

Our ignorance of things Canadian was almost total. Schools in the U.S. somehow forget that Canada exists, and the newspapers reflect this myopic view of the staid, northern neighbour which is larger, less flamboyant or aggressive, and rarely newsworthy on a global scale. Our images of Quebec were of the Dionne quints (later we discovered they were born in Ontario), wayside crosses in an essentially rural province and the Canadiens. We had also heard about the excesses of Duplessis' Padlock Law, and we knew that most of the people of "La Belle Province" spoke French.

The most difficult part of uprooting a family is the loss of contact with friends and family. It takes time to make new friends, and in our case, we left all our relatives behind. We took our time coming to Canada, stopping to visit friends on the way. It made the journey easier and the trip more pleasant. It also gave the children more time to adjust to the idea that this was not just another vacation where we would return to the same house that we had lived in for eleven years.

We had crossed borders with the children before. This one was more involved than the others. We were applying for landed-immigrant status, had more questions to answer, more documents to produce, an interview with the Immigration Officer, made arrangements for moving our belongings, etc. We were lucky compared to other immigrant families.

I had a job waiting for me in Montreal. We spoke one of the official languages (I spoke both, thanks to the years I had spent in France during the war and at graduate school). We were affluent compared to most immigrant families who came to Canada fleeing poverty, oppression or both. And we were Americans, among the first of the flow of intellectuals coming to Canada, which has long had the problem of losing many of its most talented people to the better pay and wider choice of jobs in the U.S.

As we crossed the St. Lawrence River into Montreal, I felt a strange elation, as if I were freed from an enormous burden of guilt. My two sons would not have to fear military conscription (they were ten and twelve years old then). My tax money would not be spent on killing and destroying people and crops. I would be spared many hours of useless arguments with friends who were not as convinced as I was of the brutality of that senseless war.

It had been a lovely day. We swam in Lake Champlain and picnicked on the beach. By the time we entered the city the sun had set, and as we drove through working-class districts adjoining the heavy industrial areas along the Lachine Canal, the children asked if this was where we were going to live. We had lived in a section of Philadelphia which resembled these older sections of Montreal, and the children had become more uneasy there as the tensions mounted. The violence in the neighbourhoods of Philadelphia echoed the example set by the government in Vietnam, and by the police in the poor wards of the city.

Our children had been spared the gang fights that swirled through the streets, but they were witness to some of them. Robbery and assault had touched enough of our neighbours to make one afraid., We were virtually untouched by these manifestations of frustration and anger. We were forever reporting our bicycles lost or stolen, but were able to replace them at police viewings of bicycles recovered in the streets where we could claim the ones we lost.

Despite these negative images of the old neighbourhood, we had many warm memories of mutual help and collective living: the babysitting co-op; the community association; the co-op nursery school; the new elementary school that we had fought for and gotten; the clean-up campaigns; the fight to save the neighbourhood from demolition; zoning battles; community fairs; sledding parties; UNICEF collections on Hallowe'en; our own housing rehabilitation company, all of them racially integrated activities. They were happy times, but the mood had been changing. By the time we left, Lanie and the children had become uneasy and afraid of the neighbourhood.

It was this fear that motivated their concern as we drove through the older sections of Montreal. We arrived at the apartment which old friends had lent us while they were away in the country that hot summer of 1966. Our children made instant friends with the children next door, as we did with their parents.

In the midst of a heat wave in late June, we left the city and drove east to Cape Breton for a two-week camping holiday with our two younger children. For the first time we began to get the flavour of Canada and Canadians. There is none of the arrogance of the Americans in the back country of Quebec and the Maritimes. Tourism is much less developed, and camping is more varied and congenial. One can find luxurious campsites with hot water and laundromats, and one can find spartan sites carved into the woods.

Shediac in New Brunswick was a key experience for us. The campsites surrounded a series of playing areas for all tastes and ages. Whole families of campers were participating with enthusiasm. We joined a volleyball game with no difficulty, and for two hours or more played together with total strangers. There was not a single harsh word nor criticism during this time. There were no arguments in line calls or rules. Each person seemed to feel responsible toward the others. It was such a contrast to the win-at-all-costs mentality that dominates sports in the U.S. We learn that the greatest coaches believe that "Nice guys finish last" (Leo Durocher), and that "Winning isn't the only thing, it's *everything*" (Vince Lombardi). Destroy the quarterback and your team will have a better chance to win. Violence is as American as apple pie. Although Canadian hockey is known for its violence, this too may have been imported during the period when there were only two Canadian cities represented in the six-team National Hockey League.

We spent several days at Sight Point Camp in Cape Breton. The owner, a friend of ours, has led a campaign against the provincial government, which wants to push a modern highway through that wild coastal setting. There is a strong commitment among the residents to retain their traditions. Nova Scotia has been better at accomplishing this than Smallwood's Newfoundland, where thousands of residents of the outports were forcibly relocated in the name of progress. We were lucky to be able to share a lobster feast on the beach at Sight Point with the campers and the lobster fisherman on the staff who had emptied his traps for the summer. The sight of hot butter dripping down the chins of the campers as they ate their lobsters, cracking the shells against the cliffs at the beach, is still vivid in my memory.

We had also experienced the warmth and the welcome of villagers in Mabou at their weekly square dance, complete with live music and caller. The traditions in the rural areas of Canada are certainly in danger of extinction, given the omnipresence of TV; however, they are much more alive than in the U.S.

We were also impressed by the unselfconscious acceptance of language differences in the scattered francophone communities we passed through. This may have been more superficial than real. However, we didn't feel the kind of crackling hostility that pervades the ethnic islands in the U.S. and erupts periodically into race war. Canada does not, fortunately, have that long tradition of military intervention into the internal affairs of countries dominated by Americans. We do not foster race hatred in training our soldiers, as the U.S. Marine Corps did in bayonet training where the recruit was told to attack "the gooks", a racist epithet for Asiatics. This is a major difference between racism in Canada and in the U.S.A., except for occasional lapses (Internment of the Japanese Canadians from west-coast cities during the last war, following the U.S. example). Every country has its racists and bigots. But Canada's tradition does not include slavery, and does include giving asylum to fleeing slaves as the last stop on several "underground railways" prior to the Civil War, and to draft resisters during the Vietnam War, among many other political refugees. The record could be better (depending upon how servile the particular foreign minister was to U.S. pressures), but it is generally creditable.

We returned to Montreal relaxed and reassured. The process of finding a place to live, of adjusting to a new job, of finding things to do during the summer took all the energy we could muster. The children adjusted painlessly to their new lives. Summer sports are the same in Canada as in the U.S. Lanie took her time finding new interests to replace the ones she had left, and concentrated on househunting. She must have done a good job because we are still living in the same place sixteen years later.

My job was another story. I was the second American to be named to a position of responsibility at the Montreal City Planning Department within a period of three months. There was considerable hostility toward me on the part of the young Quebecois professionals who had been passed over in offering the job to an anglophone. My French was rusty, and I started out on the wrong foot by writing my first reports in English, even though my spoken French was good enough to let me communicate with the members of the planning group for which I was responsible.

My superiors had assured me that I could write in either official language. I continued to use English until I realized that no one was reading my reports. Worse still, the assignments that I gave to the members of the team were, for all intents and purposes, being ignored. I found myself covering up for them and for me by doing the work myself. After a confrontation where I found myself having to justify my qualifications for the job and invoking the support of my superior to do so, I realized that I would have to make major changes in the way I was relating to the people in the planning group.

We held a meeting at which we shared our frustrations. They complained that the assignments made no sense to them. They knew that I was simply forwarding the assignments which had been given to me and they wanted to discuss the total workload, have some input into how it might be handled and the direction the work should take. My role would be transformed into that of "first among equals" rather than that of "boss". I agreed without hesitation and also pledged to start writing in French, on the condition that they would help me with this. They agreed.

The climate of work changed abruptly. Suddenly I had become a colleague instead of their superior. It was conceded that it made more sense for me to give the appearance of still being "boss" by representing the group at senior staff meetings. I would make reports to my group on what decisions had been taken by senior staff which might affect individual group members, and they would react by adopting a collective response to the cadres.

With the help of two capable and gentle secretaries, my written French began to improve rapidly. It was an extremely humbling experience to have my drafts returned full of red marks indicating mistakes, together with a perfectly literate final copy of what I had tried to produce. Gradually the number of red marks decreased.

My colleagues became increasingly supportive of my actions on behalf of the group and also began to respect the new approaches that I had brought with me on the basis of fifteen years of experience as a professional planner at city, regional and local levels. Montreal was in the throes of catching up to the growing pains of a rapidly expanding metropolitan region. There were several urban renewal plans in the works, a host of private projects in the wake of the artificial prosperity of Expo '67 and the public works improvement generated by it.

I found it increasingly difficult to keep silent on issues which I had faced in the U.S. where certain responses had been tried and failed. Canadian city planning still reflected its British origins and its American orientations. Montreal was still carrying out wholesale demolition of neighbourhoods inhabited by the poor and the powerless.

As a newly arrived "expert" on the scene, I hadn't dared tell my colleagues that the same type of projects on which they had been working, namely, the downtown expressways and La Petite Bourgogne renewal area for example, had created social havoc in cities throughout the U.S., and that such policies were no longer in force. It wasn't until the disastrous riots in the summer of 1967 in the States that I dared criticize the destructive effects of proposed public and private renewal projects. To do this I began to use the reports which the Planning Department had already issued, comparing what had been hoped for with what had actually occurred.

Victoriatown, a residential enclave demolished by the city in the 1960s, was supposedly a slum area, according to the official report prepared by the Planning Department. Yet this same report revealed that all of the social indicators were more favourable than those for the city as a whole. There was a higher proportion of home ownership, lower rents for more space, a lower rate of crime and juvenile delinquency, a better record of community health, and history of mutual aid between residents in improving the housing. The planners invoked the fact that the resident, poorer than the city average, paid lower taxes on their housing, and that the area's economic potential wasn't realized.

The real reason for razing the neighbourhood was that its location, at the entrance to Expo '67, was embarrassing to the city. It was replaced by a stadium, used for professional football games and occasional outdoor spectacles. A white elephant financially, it was sold for one dollar by the Federal government which had assumed responsibility for it. The vacant site is now used for industrial parking and for a hydro-electric substation. Its tax revenue for the city is less than it was for Victoriatown.

On the basis of this and other experiences, I began a systematic effort to oppose the neighbourhood demolition which had become a major symbol of progress for the municipal government, and a plague for the low-income residents who were evicted from their homes by this policy.

Meanwhile back on the home front, Lanie and the children were adapting easily to the new homeland. Although the children were shocked to hear that strapping was still possible in Canadian schools, none had seen it happen. Teachers were generally better than those they had known in the U.S., and the children enjoyed school and had many new friends and activities. Lanie decided to make the most of her uprooting by writing a book on folk-dancing that she had wanted to write for years. She also took on a weekly folk-dance group, continuing her long experience in teaching adults to relax and enjoy international dances. In addition, she learned to weave, profiting by the fact that traditional arts were more widely practiced in Quebec than in Philadelphia, where rural traditions had virtually disappeared.

The children learned to ice-skate and to ski almost immediately. This was new for them, and they took to winter sports like ducks to water. The parents straggled behind, but we shared many fine winter days with them before they became too good for us.

Then came Expo '67 and the deluge of friends and family who came to visit. During the six months of the Exposition, we welcomed ninety-six overnight guests and developed all kinds of ways of making them feel at home. At one point during the summer there were seventeen people sleeping at our house at one time. We had posted instructions on what to see at the Fair, where to eat, how to get tickets, what buses to take, how to use the washer, dryer and dishwasher etc. It was a marvellous celebration, and an ideal way to ease the shock of lost friendships which were renewed during those wonderful months. It was unique, too, because it was linked to the peace movement in many ways.

I still recall the "love-in" on St. Helen's island, organized by the Voice of Women. Lanie was a member. People were picnicking peacefully on the grass when suddenly a detachment of Mayor Drapeau's riot squad appeared, complete with hard hats and billy clubs. The policemen looked around them carefully, taking in the scene of this quiet gathering of people of all ages sitting on the grass. The billy clubs disappeared miraculously, and so did the riot police without a word. Policemen don't have to be "pigs". Most of the time they have to be ordered to behave badly. Not this time, however.

Since we had come to Canada for reasons of conscience, it was only normal for us to offer our home as refuge for draft-resisters and deserters from the U.S. Quebec's long tradition against military conscription, and the fact that Canada had no law requiring military service, meant that what we were doing was perfectly legal. Yet we had visits from the R.C.M.P., asking us for details about young conscripts who were staying with us. They admitted they were doing this as a favour to the F.B.I., and that we were not bound to furnish any information. Our young guests were in Canada legally, had committed no crime and were no threat to peace and security in Canada.

A number of the draft-resisters stayed in Canada after the war was over and became useful members of our society. We are still in touch with several of them. A number of our pacifist friends came to Canada as we did, saving their children from having to disobey a cruel law.

Looking back on those early years in this country, I realize that much of the excitement of Monteal and Toronto as cities comes from the variety of national traditions which their residents have brought with them. These microcosms of what the world might be like if the majority of the population could enjoy differences rather than feel threatened by them, offered us constant pleasure through our folklore interests. The Mariposa Folk Festival in Toronto and our own folk-dance and folk-singing experiences in Montreal were in marked contrast to what we had known in the States. When Mariposa announced its decision to become a "festival without superstars", the atmosphere on the Toronto islands changed miraculously to an even more gentle demonstration of how well people of widely different tastes and backgrounds could enjoy each other. Children and adults shared the same space cooperatively, without violence. The same feeling was generated at the non-commercial St. Jean Baptiste Day celebrations that replaced the department store floats and sexist parades that had led to riots in Montreal on election eve in 1968.

Our earliest memories of Montreal include the folk-dancing at Beaver Lake on Mount Royal, Dominion Square and Old Montreal; recorded Sunday concerts of classical music in Mount Royal Park; the babble of languages, the sights and smells on The Main; the exuberance of public demonstrations in support of our favourite causes (peace, human rights, self-determination, etc). Our children were no longer afraid of the city they lived in. Social tensions were handled in a more civilized way than in the society from which we had moved. The only area in which the level of violence equaled the one we had been used to in the U.S. was on the highways, nearly always involving aggressive male drivers.

All of the positive experiences were enriched by the variety of people who shared them with us. Because we found so many young Quebecers sharing and enjoying the cultural treasures of other ethnic and racial groups, we felt hopeful that such understanding might one day replace the hostility and suspicion that distorts national and international affairs in our crisis-ridden world. The key to such a change may be our ability to subdue the competitive aspect of our nature in favour of our cooperative tendencies.

At the same time as I was enjoying the ethnic diversity of the city, I was working to achieve social change.

My job at the Planning Department had made me increasingly aware of the links between problems of the environment and the strivings of people to achieve personal satisfaction and collective control of their urban space. The hierarchical decision-making structure of Montreal meant there was no role left for the citizen, except, perhaps, to vote every four years, and that the technocrats were responsible for justifying decisions which had already been made by the political pontiff of Montreal, and for carrying them out. This was not the role I chose to apply, and this upset people at the top.

The conflict began when the priest and elders at St. Elizabeth du Portugal Church in the working-class section of St. Henri, asked the city to purchase the garage-warehouse of a trucking firm that wanted to move. The church wanted the Housing Department to build public housing on the site to induce people to move back into the parish. My superiors had decided the area was more suitable for industrial use, and I was assigned to transmit this message to the church people, despite my protests that I did not agree with the decision.

At the meeting the local residents answered all of the Planning Department's reasons for not going along with their request, and asked to participate in decisions involving their neighbourhood. I transmitted their messages to my superiors, but was told that the decision was final: no new housing was to be built in the area, despite the new elementary school, church, park areas, credit union, and other facilities that served a stable residential population there.

On my own initiative, I prepared a sketch plan showing how the vacant lots could be integrated with the proposed site for housing in the area. I listed the value of public investments in community facilities there and sent these documents to the priest at St. Elizabeth Church, suggesting that he present them in person with his committee to the head of the Executive Committee at City Hall, without mentioning the source of the documents.

Two weeks later at a meeting, I was asked my opinion of a plan prepared by representatives of the parish. The head of the Executive Committee had personally asked for an answer. I saw the plan I had prepared on the table, surrounded by professionals from the department and the parish priest who winked at me. I indicated it made sense to carry out the plan, and others agreed, now that it seemed to be acceptable to those at the top. The decision was made to build public housing in the area, and since then, several projects have already been completed.

I learned that since I had been frustrated in dealing with my own superiors, the easiest way to work within a rigid bureaucracy in Quebec was to jump several levels and then work my way down to reach the people who would not listen to reason in the beginning. Shortly after, I was asked to work with a private developer and his architects on a project which would destroy low-rental apartments through a city-sponsored urban redevelopment project and replace them with high-rental units. I refused the assignment, preferring to consider the interests of the residents rather than those of the developer whose main goal was profit. I contacted the people who lived and worked in the area, told them about the project, and they in turn began organizing resistance to the city's plan. Because the city could not intervene to expropriate properties for the developer, he was forced to alter his plans. As a result, only a part of the area was demolished, and the remainder is being restored for the residents of the areas as cooperative housing. Government subsidies will keep the rents at a level most residents can afford.

Another city issue united the French-speaking and English-speaking communities in Point St. Charles when the Engineering Division was finalizing the proposed extension of Georges Vanier Boulevard through the working-class neighbourhood of the Point. When my efforts to convince my colleagues at the Planning Department that the project was disruptive, dangerous and unnecessary, failed, I went to the community and gave them enough information about the secret project the city had planned — to put a new bridge and boulevard through the middle of their neighbourhood.

A massive strategy was mounted, groups were formed and the resulting publicity made the city announce at a public meeting that it would drop the whole project and would accept other recommendations from the study groups. Most important was the transformation of the firehouse into a golden age centre and library for children and adults. By dropping the project, $5 million and 150 dwellings, occupied by low-income households, were saved.

This proves you can fight City Hall.

Despite my battles on the work front to achieve social change, I managed to keep an eye on the children's activities. They had no difficulty in adapting to their new lives in Quebec. Perhaps it was due to the fact that we had settled in an English-speaking area of the city. However, the year the children spent in French summer camps gave them the necessary lift toward functioning in French. This was particularly true for our youngest, who had the easiest time learning the language. She spent a full year at a francophone school, and could communicate in French. The boys never had that intensive experience and were less at ease.

The fact that I was spending my entire working life in a francophone milieu did not affect the language habits of the family. Lanie always asked me to speak French at home to encourage the children. I agreed if they would agree to read and watch the French media, to reinforce the learning experience. None of them was willing to make the effort, so the family remained essentially unilingual.

Several years later, our youngest found a job in a francophone area and managed to function fully in both languages. Of all the places I have ever visited, I have found more people here who are able to function without a trace of accent in either of the dominant languages in this cosmopolitan city. It is especially true of the native francophones, probably because of the overwhelming influence of American culture on the media in Quebec.

Although all three children have migrated to other cities in search of jobs or additional education, they still gravitate back to their home in Montreal and all of them have strong friendship links here.

Our mid-life role brought changes, challenges and new horizons. By 1976, Lanie's professional career had blossomed and it was as important as mine. She was a full-time teacher and administrator at Dawson College. When I discussed the possibility of leaving my job with the Planning Department to look for a teaching position, she encouraged me with no hesitation. After twenty-five years of traditional marriage in terms of roles, she was to become the principal breadwinner, and I would be working part-time as a university professor. Because I came home from work before she did, I was responsible for more of the household chores than before. But I was also freer to become more active in community work. While Lanie reduced her commitments to the peace movement and political activities, I accepted increased responsibilities in the areas of social change.

While none of this was due to the fact that we were immigrants to Canada, it is no less true that the role shifts were possible here, and might have been more difficult to realize had we been elsewhere.

I applied for teaching posts at several universities, and one of them came through in Montreal. For the past seven years I have been coordinator of the Urban Studies Program at Concordia, in addition to teaching several courses there.

With others who shared the same value system, I have tried to help students do more than just get the magical diploma. I try to convince them that mindless technology can do the work of the devil. The lyrics of a song about the German missile expert Werner von Braun illustrate this idea perfectly: " 'I just send them up, who cares where they come down; that's not my department,' says Werner Von Braun." His V-1 and V-2 missiles rained death and destruction on London during World War II. And what of the trained biologists who are developing germ-warfare to kill indiscriminately anyone designated as the "enemy"?

In my profession, we have been trained to bring order out of chaos in the neighbourhoods of the poor. This has meant the destruction of millions of housing units which provided shelter at affordable rents for the poorer members of our society. They have had to move and start the process all over again. The power-structure is embarrassed by poverty. It tries to replace that image by an image of well-being. This involves replacing or hiding the poor, and encouraging the building of expensive megastructures which house the rich or their offices, and which provide taxes to pay for the follies of the rich and powerful, and distractions for the poor and the powerless.

At this point, I can look back on the major turning point in my life: coming to Canada and more particularly to Quebec.

What I like about this country is that Canada has not invaded any other country but has sent peace-keeping forces all around the globe. Quebec has an even better tradition of long-time opposition to military conscription, in the Boer War and in World Wars I and II. Today Canada is one of the few countries in the world without conscription, and I am proud of both Canada and Quebec.

I do believe that there is room for change. The various governments are all involved in passing laws which are designed to improve our society. Each of us has a responsibility to work for constructive changes without victimizing anyone.

I am free to try and bring about such changes and to get together with others who are working toward similar goals. I am fulfilled in my own life and am not coerced into victimizing others.

For these gifts I am most grateful to the country of my adoption — a country I chose rather than one into which I was born — which has thus become doubly dear to me.

Tom Telfer

GOD'S COUNTRY
by Tom Telfer

My wife and I were born more than 7,000 miles apart, she in Western Canada and I in Scotland. We met in the 1930s — the Depression years — through my wife's elderly, retired Scottish uncle who decided to visit, for the last time, all his relatives who had emigrated to Canada over the years.

After arriving in Peace River and spending a short but pleasant visit, he suggested that his niece, his brother-in-law's only daughter, return to Scotland with him for a six-months' holiday. After much deliberation, the offer was accepted and my future wife, Chrissie, and her uncle arrived, in Scotland. A few months later, she and I met for the first time at a Masonic Whist Drive and Dance held in Kirkcaldy, Fife. We were partners at the same table of whist, won our game and still have the scorecards, dated May 4, 1936, as souvenirs of our meeting. We began dating and after a six-month engagement, we were married on June 25, 1937. In due course, our first daughter, Pat, arrived, and so did the war.

The six-month holiday my wife's uncle had envisaged stretched to fourteen years due to circumstances beyond our control. One of these was my five and a half years of army service. I volunteered, leaving Chrissie pregnant with our second child, Tommy, who was born a few months later. My wife's telegram announcing the birth was proudly pinned to the unit's canteen wall, and I received many congratulations and good wishes from my buddies.

Chrissie bravely carried on looking after the house and children, helped by our little Scottie dog, Dykie. He proved to be a valuable watchdog and companion during those trying times, faithful in his duty while I was away. Luckily, my family had been living in a small village, but it got its share of bomb scares during the conflict. Times were difficult and food strictly rationed.

Once in a while the local grocer would receive an extra treat for his customers. On one such memorable occasion, he got a case of twenty-four small cans of peaches. The word went around the village, and a queue started at 6:00 a.m. in the pouring rain for the 8:00 a.m. store opening. I was due to arrive on leave and my wife was near the front of the line and one of the lucky twenty-four to get her "one only" can. What a celebration!

At first I got regular and fairly frequent short leaves home, but as the war progressed and Britain's back was to the wall, my leaves became less frequent. Finally "D Day" arrived and I went over with the rest, not knowing if I would ever see my wife and children again. In fact, it was fourteen months before I did.

General Montgomery was our leader as head of the British Second Army, while the Canadian First Army was under the command of General Crerar. Both armies went in together on the left of the invasion, aiming for Bayeux and Caen. Bayeux fell on the second day of the invasion, but Caen, more heavily fortified, held out for a month before the Canadians took it.

In due course, the Allies battled through France, Belgium, Holland and finally on to Germany. After the war, the demobilization was carried out in an orderly and fair manner. The rule was "Longest in, soonest out" with extra points for married status and size of family. That motto seemed to apply equally to our great leader Churchill. In 1945, just a few weeks after Germany's surrender, the British nation, to its eternal shame, showed its ingratitude by throwing out one of the greatest leaders, geniuses and benefactors. The labour government swept into power and Churchill was swept out. Personally, I could never forgive my countrymen. Shakespeare wrote truthfully when he said: "Blow, blow thou winter wind,/Thou are not so unkind/As man's ingratitude."

Eventually I was demobilized. Strange as it might seem, Dykie, our Scottie, seemed to realize that his work was done and his master had returned. In coming to welcome me, he suddenly toppled forward and without warning, died. Poor old Dykie — his service was done.

After a happy and joyous reunion with my wife and family, I found myself back on Civvy Street. One happy result was our third child, Kathleen, held up for several years because of the war. We jokingly referred to her as "Hitler's child" because he was responsible for her being postponed so many years.

Times were not easy, rationing was still in effect and there were regulations for everything. In 1949 weekly rations consisted of:

Meat—3 oz.	Margarine—9 oz.	Bacon—3 oz.
Sugar—8 oz.	Lard—4oz.	Candy—5 1/2 oz.
Tea—2 oz.	Cheese—3 oz.	Eggs—2 when available.
Butter—4 oz.		

It raised doubts in the minds of the population as to whether we had won the war or lost it. The labour government was in control, and after I tried for three years to get ahead, I found that although I worked hard and diligently, the government was taxing my efforts so much they seemed to be reaping the benefits while I was stuck with the expenses. Of course, I was not alone. Millions were in similar circumstances.

Frustrated and discouraged with conditions, regulations and taxes in Britain, we wrote a letter to my wife's mother, now a widow, in Peace River, Alberta. Her reply was that in Canada "we'd never starve". She had a natural longing to be reunited with her long-absent daughter, to meet her son-in-law and the three grandchildren she had never seen. There and then, in the spring of 1949, we decided to leave my homeland.

We sailed from Liverpool on the *Empress of Canada* like boat people, hungry and feeling deprived for so many years. Three miles out, where British jurisdiction ended, the ship's canteen was opened revealing unending stocks of goodies — all unrationed. The daily menu was, to our unaccustomed eyes, Waldorf-Astoria class, and for the first time in years, we saw and tasted white bread. The harassing regulations, rationing, queues for food, frustrations and hardships were all left behind, and it was like emerging from darkness into light. We had seven, wonderful cruising days crossing the Atlantic and such happy memories.

At that time, the British government would only allow emigrants to take £250 out of the country, and so, happy, free and almost penniless, we arrived in "the promised land". On our arrival in Halifax, we were welcomed by a minister of our church, shown where our immigrant train was and handed a packet of cigarettes — gratefully received. Then we were on our way west, day after day, night after night, making me realize what a vast and beautiful country we had come to.

We had a happy and joyous reunion in Edmonton with Chrissie's mum and brother, Bobby. Although it ended our cross-Canada rail journey, we still had to get to Peace River. However, we had to wait over the weekend in Edmonton to board the Monday train north with a change at McLennan.

Work was scarce that spring in Peace River, but I was willing to try anything. Like many other Scotsmen before me, I got my foot into Canada's door via the Hudson's Bay Company, but unlike the early Hudson's Bay men, I wasn't sent out to a remote fur-trading post. I settled in the heart of Edmonton, in the Bay's Jasper Avenue store. Changing times: From trading posts to giant department stores.

My wife and family joined me in Edmonton, but Chrissie's heart was in her birthplace, Peace River, so within the year, we were back in "God's Country", and I was a part-time schoolbus driver and store clerk.

Soon after, with the help of a friendly banker, I started a small neighbourhood grocery store. It enabled me to support my family until they left the nest. My eldest daughter married and left for New Brunswick, 3,000 miles away. Our only son met with a hunting accident and was taken from us at the age of twenty. Our baby daughter (Hitler's child) got a job with the Alberta government telephone company. As our business was a family affair and circumstances had changed, we decided to close the store. Robert Burns' words came back to me about the best laid schemes of mice and men often going agley.

There followed a summer season as a forestry tower firewatcher, then three years with the Town of Peace River, mostly in their water treatment plant. Then, for ten years, I was employed at the Provincial Correctional Institute, first as a guard and in my sixties as a storeman, until I reached the mandatory age of retirement.

I had long since become a Canadian citizen, and my retirement has been contented and pleasurable. Both our daughters are happily married and we have six grandchildren.

On looking back over our lives since we came to Canada, we can truly say that we have never regretted our decision. We have been back to Scotland several times, but we are always happy to return to the mighty Peace River — God's Country.

William Martin

MEMORIES

by William Martin

"I'm biddin' you a long farewell,
My Mary—kind and true!
But I'll not forget you, darling,
In the land I'm goin' to;
They say there's bread and work for all,
And the sun shines always there—
But I'll not forget Old Ireland,
*Were it fifty times as fair!**

I am eighty-four years old now, but my memories are still vivid. I was born and raised in Northern Ireland, County Down, eleven miles east of Belfast, in a little town called Bangor situated on the sea front. We had been country people, and my father was a farm labourer. I was born in the reign of Queen Victoria, and when she died on January 22, 1901, I was barely three years old. I remember I was twelve years old when King Edward VII died on May 7, 1910.

Both my parents were Irish. There were seven children in the family, four girls and three boys. Three of my sisters and a brother died, but my oldest sister, who is eighty-six, is still living in Ireland in my grandparents' old house, while my youngest brother, now retired, lives in my parents' house.

My grandparents had a small farm and lived only a short distance from my home. I think I spent more time there than I did with my parents. I loved my maternal grandfather dearly. I was four when my grandmther died, but I still remember her lying dead in her coffin.

When I was fourteen years old, my father took me to see the *Titanic* the day she was launched from the Belfast shipyards. She was the largest ship that had ever been built, over 46,000 tons, a floating palace. There was nothing on the high seas to equal her, and she was said to be unsinkable. Many millionaires came across the ocean from the United States to take her maiden voyage to New York City, and most of them went down to a watery grave when the ship hit an iceberg about 1,600 miles northeast of New York. She sank two or three hours later, taking with her over 1,500 souls. That tragedy, the worst sea disaster ever, shocked the world. Who could have believed when I watched the launching how short her life span would be!

*"Lament of the Irish Emigrant" by Lady Dufferin. (1807-1867)

At this time before the war, Ireland was a peaceful country. The houses and homes rang with music and laughter, even if we were poor. There were no radios or television sets. We never heard what was going on beyond the sea and rarely saw a newspaper. They were for city people. Despite the poverty, the Irish were a happy people. The fields and meadows were green all year round. The wild primroses and daffodils grew in abundance, adorning the slopes and gardens. In the spring, the hawthorn was in bloom, and the wild honeysuckle and flower scents filled the air with perfume. The little birds in the glens and groves sang all day long, and Ireland was at peace with its people and nature.

We were a happy family and loved our parents, God rest their souls. After work, we had our favourite meeting places and we could go bicycle riding or play football in the fields. In the winter, we had barn dances. The young boys and girls came from far and near, and we always had lots of good accordion players. The Irish love singing, and their songs are known all over the world, all of them extolling their country and their devotion to their emerald isle.

Then, of course, we had special parade days, with bands and banners — pipe bands, flute bands, accordion and fife and drum bands. On these parade days, you could stand in one place for five hours before they all passed by.

All that changed with World War I and by the time it ended, the allies had suffered over 22,000,000 casualties. Of these more than 5,000,000 had died or were killed, almost 13,000,000 had been wounded and over 4,000,000 were prisoners or missing. The Central Powers' total casualties were a staggering 37,500,000 men. This figure did not include air and navy losses, civilian casualties or the death toll from influenza in 1918 and 1919.

Kitchener was Secretary of State for War at the time, and his picture glared down from every wall, billboard and fence in the country, his forefinger outstretched — "Your Country Needs You. Join Your Country's Army. God Save The King" or "Your Pals in the Trenches are Waiting to Shake Hands With You."

In the first month, 500,000 volunteered, and the recruitment rate ran at over 100,000 a month for eighteen months thereafter. I joined up in February, 1916 just before my eighteenth birthday. At the start, we drilled in civilian clothes until we were fitted with uniforms. We lived in canvas tents. The young men of Kitchener's army were not trained for the horrors of war. They were only school boys and knew nothing of the hell they would come up against. Many were saying the war would be over in three months, but little did they think it would last four years.

After a few months' training in Ireland, we were shipped to England to finish our training there. We were called the British Expeditionary Force (B.E.F.). It wasn't long before we were sent over to France.

The Battle of the Somme was preceded by seven days of heavy bombardment on an eighteen-mile front. On July 1, thirteen British divisions moved forward together, threading their way through the British barbed wire, and then inching in single file across no man's land. The Germans came out of their dugouts to man their machine guns, and the bullets mowed down the first line of our soldiers. The second line moved into position, and then it faltered and fell as the clattering guns took their terrible toll. The third and fourth lines of assault met the same fate.

By early afternoon, the pitifully few survivors were back in the trenches. On that fateful day in 1916, the British suffered 60,000 casualties, 20,000 in the first wave. The British tried frantically to regroup and July 14, at 3:25 a.m., 20,000 men attacked the Germans. More casualties were added to the already swollen list. The fighting dragged stubbornly forward to September 15, and now the autumn rains began to fall.

The front churned into a morass of mud, and everything bogged down in it. The last battle on November 13 came to a dismal end. The rains turned the Somme battlefields into a sea of viscous mud, where animals, men and gun carriages struggled and sank. Shell holes were filled with dead and dying, and the sight of broken and shattered bodies and limbs strewn about was made even more horrible by the stench of unburied corpses, both men and horses, rotting all around us. The men stood up in the trenches, their clothes sodden, horror stamped across their faces at the sight of the suffering and agony they were witnessing. In the Somme campaign alone, the Allied troops, mostly British, sustained almost 500,000 casualties; the Germans had about 450,000.

Severe shell shock broke my health, and my nerves gave way. I couldn't take any more, and I was taken out of the lines to an army hospital and then sent to another one in England. Most of my unit, the 13th Battalion, Royal Irish Rifles, was wiped out. We had seen action in Flanders and France, and those who survived were killed at Ypres a year later. Eleven of my school chums didn't come back. I spent four months in the hospital and finally was discharged from further active service in 1917 and sent home to Ireland.

The war years had brought some measure of prosperity to rich and poor alike. The country was flourishing, and because of the thousands of men away on active service, work was easier to find. Wages had risen and it seemed everyone was making money, especially the horse breeders.

The army was buying all the thoroughbred horses and paying large sums of money for them, at least £100 ($500). Because of my love for animals, it broke my heart to see these lovely horses sacrificed — sent out to the front to be cut down by German machine guns or blown to pieces by the artillery shells. It was bad enough that men were being killed, but the animals had had no part in it. I saw so many of these cavalry horses and their riders mowed down during the Battle of the Somme, and I returned to see these poor creatures being shipped out to their deaths. This senseless and meaningless slaughter of men and animals was something I could never forget.

The war ended November 11, 1918, and our boys, who had been taken prisoner by the Germans, were released and sent home. They weren't away from the killing for long. As early as 1916, the trouble flared up in Ireland. Many of the old regular Irish Constabulary were being shot down by the Irish Republican Army (IRA). One of the first incidents was Bloody Sunday, November 21, 1920 when seven officers, three ex-officers, two of the Constabulary and two civilians were killed. Between 1919 and 1921, this civil uprising was responsible for the death of almost 1,300 people, civilians, police and soldiers, with close to 900 casualties.

I went back to farming in 1919. The senseless killing bothered me. I'd seen enough of it in the war. For me the land was the only work I knew. It was a pleasure to work in the fields with the men and women, listening to them exchange jokes and to hear them singing the lilting Irish melodies.

But in 1921 civil war broke out in Ireland, and many of us ex-army men enlisted in the Royal Ulster Special Constabulary (R.U.S.C.). Most of us had come from battlefields in France, and because we had served before, we were again under war-time commanders. The men got their commissions back in the R.U.S.C. and we were posted to Newtownards Military Training Camp. The drill and discipline came easy as we had gone through all that before. However, we felt sorry for those young and raw recruits who had just enlisted. We were compelled to wear our battle ribbons to distinguish us from the new men. Because of our experience, we were soon posted to border patrol units between Northern Ireland and the Irish Free State.

We never saw any of the fighting in the streets of Belfast or Newry, but because marshal law was in effect, it was our duty to arrest anyone out after 10:00 p.m. curfew. All cars were stopped and searched for arms and ammunition. If we found any, the men were arrested and escorted back to army headquarters for questioning. We made house to house searches for arms, and anything found was confiscated. We uncovered rifles and guns by the thousands.

After three months on patrol, we were relieved by the New Patrol and transferred along with nine other men to guard the waterworks in the Mourne Mountains.

The IRA had attempted to blow up the powerhouses that supplied Belfast with water. We patrolled day and night, four men to each shift. Half remained in the barracks and replaced those who returned. As far as the eye could see was darkness across the entire valley. All lights had to be out by 10:00 p.m. and this was rigidly enforced.

We were there until the end of the trouble in Northern Ireland, and then many of the men joined the New Force, The Royal Irish Constabulary, after the other was disbanded. I didn't. I left in 1924, but work was hard to find. In winter two or three of us would go from farm to farm picking up jobs here and here, a few days in one place, and if we were lucky, a little longer at the big farms. In this way we were able to help our families. Some of us always had a job and we all contributed at home.

This went on until 1928 when I went to a lecture and lantern slide show at our old schoolhouse. They were showing pictures of Canada, and we were told about the many opportunities the country offered good farm labourers. Many emigrated that year, and I decided to do the same. I came across on a huge ship, *Letitia,* owned by the Anchor-Donaldson Line. It must have carried 3,000 passengers from England, Scotland and Ireland. I lost track of the days for I was so seasick, I couldn't leave the cabin. One night the ship sat out at sea off Newfoundland unable to move because of a mass of icebergs driftting before us. The thought of the Titanic flashed through my mind.

We landed at Quebec after a week at sea, and as soon as we cleared customs, we were put on trains for Toronto. I spent my first year in Canada on a farm. It was dull, dreary and lonesome work compared to Ireland, for the farms were small in my country and you could talk and socialize with your neighbours. Here in Canada, the smallest farm was 200 acres, and the farmsteads were scattered and so far apart that you never saw anyone. In the summer you could go for a long walk to visit your neighbours on the next farm, but in the winter you were snowed in and isolated. It made life miserable, and I was happy to return to Toronto.

I didn't realize it, but I came to Canada just at the start of the Depression. I couldn't have picked a worse time. A year later, 1929, the stock market crashed, and hundreds of thousands of people lost everything. Billions of dollars vanished into smoke, and many people committed suicide. Factories closed, and thousands of people roamed the streets in search of work, a bite to eat and somewhere to sleep. Many, like me, rummaged in garbage pails for a bun or a slice or two of stale bread. We lined up at different hostels for a bowl of watery soup and a slice of dry bread. One such place was the armory on University Avenue, run by a famous owner of racing horses, and the other place on Elizabeth street was run by a Jewish man. If not for them, we would have starved.

In the summer, we slept in parks on the grass or on park benches if we were lucky to get one. In winter, we crept into the old Union Station and slept on the floor. Many a time, I would pick a private garage and sneak inside to sleep in the car, but I had to make sure I was out early before the owner appeared.

The one good thing about those days was that people were different — kind and considerate — and everyone helped his neighbour. And I can remember when we poor, starving creatures were lined up on the street, waiting to get into the Sally Ann for a bit of something to eat. A bread wagon would stop, and the driver would actually clean out his wagon and give whatever he had to us hungry souls, may God bless him whoever he was.

In spite of the hard times, people were better. I never heard of a bank getting robbed or someone murdered. You could walk at any hour of the day or night and never heard tell of a girl or woman getting raped. In fact, the word was never mentioned, and to be honest, I wouldn't have known what it meant.

There were horse-drawn carriages then and very few cars. If you were lucky to own one, you didn't have any trouble finding a place to park like today. Clip-clopping down the street came the Eaton's, Simpson's and Silverwood Dairies' wagons and all the bread wagons. Even coal was delivered by horse.

In 1929, I met and fell in love with a beautiful Irish girl who had come from Fivemiletown in County Tyrone, Ireland. Emily Robinson was her name, and we were married in 1932.

By 1930, I was getting the odd job with Runnymede Nursery Landscaping, planting flower beds, laying new lawns and building rock gardens. The wages weren't much and no overtime, but then, a dollar was like a gold nugget. I never knew what it was like to worry. I was always happy and carefree, and with the few dollars I saved, I was able to get a nice room on Bathurst Street in a house owned by a lovely couple, Mr. and Mrs. Davies, who came from England and were very good to me.

I was never able to sit still, but was always on the go, looking for work. For many unable to find anything, it was heartbreaking. Men drifted in from all parts of the country to add to the ranks of the unemployed. There were men called hobos who rode the rails on freight cars. They never stayed long in one place. They'd find a bite to eat in the soup kitchens, look the place over, and if there was nothing, they'd move on to greener pastures. You didn't make much money, but things were cheaper then. You could get a full-course meal, bacon and eggs, tea and all the bread you could eat, for twenty-five cents. Some places charged fifteen. A haircut and shave was fifteen cents.

After we married, my wife stayed on at work so we could rent a flat and buy our furniture, and in 1933, we found a bed sitting-room, kitchen and bathroom for twelve dollars a month. Our daughter, Marion, was born on October 15, 1936.

In 1940 things started moving again. The war was on, young men were joining up everywhere, and the streets of Toronto were filled with men in uniforms. They were being called up for service, and by 1941 and 1942, with so many away on the warfronts, you could find a job of any kind, according to your skills.

I started as a truck driver with Toronto Fuels, perhaps the largest fuel company in Toronto. I remained there until 1951 when we rented a seven-room brick house with five acres out in the country. It was up near Sutton on the shores of Lake Simcoe. We had a lawn and grew lots of vegetables, sharing with the neighbours. I found work with a plumbing company owned by four brothers who were the nicest people I ever worked for.

In 1961 my daughter, Marion, and I sailed back to Ireland from Montreal and landed in Liverpool. We took a boat back to Belfast. It had been thirty-three years since I left in May 1928, and nothing was the same. Great changes had taken place; the tractor had replaced the horse, and it seemed everyone had a car. When I left my homeland, all I had seen were horse-drawn wagons and carriages, and now the modern age had caught up to Ireland.

We returned to Canada, and I lived in our home near Sutton for eighteen years with my wife. But age was catching up to us, and we were no longer able to carry on the amount of work required to keep the place in shape. Slowly I began to get rid of things — furniture we really didn't need, garden tools, whatever, and made plans to move. It nearly broke my heart to leave the place. We loved it so much. Our daughter found us a nice apartment in Toronto on Glen Echo Road near Yonge Street, and in 1969 we were back in the city.

I looked back over the years and thought of all the things I had done in this country. I was seventy-one years old and my life had been a busy one. I had helped raise barns, and assisted farmers during the harvest after my regular day's work was done; I had even gone out and stooked grain in the fields on Sunday to help out when there was no one else available. During the years I worked with the Holder Brothers Plumbing and Heating Company, I put in hundreds of septic tanks, sewage disposal beds and systems from the town of Keswick along the shores of Lake Simcoe, through Jackson Point as far as Beaverton.

I had never been in any trouble with the law and in fact, had never been inside a courthouse. I never participated in any strikes. It's true, I never made much money and never became rich, but I was always happy in my work. What good is money if you don't have the health to enjoy it?

I guess if I had had to do it all over again I still would have picked Canada to immigrate to. It has always been a country of opportunity for those who were willing to do their share. No other country in the world has done as much for its people as Canada. Look at the many benefits our Senior Citizens receive, and the pensions are increased four times a year as the cost of living goes up. Truly we should be most grateful to our government and the people involved in making it work.

We settled down in Toronto in our retirement years, but my wife was in poor health. Because she had never been back to Ireland since she left there in 1924, I wanted her to see her homeland again. And so, on May 3, 1970, we flew over and stayed with my sister, Mary, for a few weeks until we found a little cottage on the Bangor Road, two and a half miles out of town. By the time we had set it up and furnished it, it was July.

Shortly after, my wife took sick and a doctor was called. He had her sent by ambulance to Newtownards Hopital where she had surgery to remove her gall bladder. Two weeks later, she was transferred to a convalescent hospital in Bangor, a mile from where we lived. I could visit her three times daily. The doctor had let her come home, but a week or two later, I received a card saying I was to bring her in right away. She didn't seem to be getting better, and I would sit by her bedside.

One night the head nurse called me into the kitchen and told me she was sorry, but my wife had cancer of the liver, and it had spread to her pancreas. My knees buckled from the shock.

"Oh, don't tell me that," I whispered. "Is there no hope at all?"

"No, none whatever," she said.

When I asked how long she had, the nurse said about three weeks. I was heartbroken. She died on the morning of November 22, 1970. I had sat by her bed all night. She was laid to rest in the Bangor Cemetery a mile out of town. I sold everything and came back to live with my daughter, Marion in Toronto.

In 1972, I flew back to Ireland and had a headstone placed on her grave.

And often in those grand old woods
I'll sit and shut my eyes,
And my heart will travel back again
To the place where Mary lies.

Henry Dugas

THE NEED TO TEACH

by Henry Dugas

I was cold, really cold. I stood shivering under the marquee of the Royal Bank at the corner of Sherbrooke and Peel Streets in Montreal wearing khaki shorts, running shoes, a white canvas shirt and a light raincoat. All round me people hurried through the blinding snow in heavy overcoats, boots, mittens and ski caps, their heads bent against the cold wind.

It was March 24, 1965, and I had about $20 in my pocket. I was very tired and broke after a long BOAC flight fom Nairobi by way of a cold and rainy three-day stopover in London where I got my shoes drenched.

To this day whenever I pass by Sherbrooke and Peel, an instant involuntary reflex is triggered, and regardless of the weather, I feel the shivers again, just as I did that day of spring — my first day in Canada.

A little more than an hour after BOAC had deserted me at Dorval Airport, Murray Hill Limousine Service had taken me to the Laurentian Hotel, the end of the line — and nearly the end of my money. In the phone booth in the lobby I found the phone number of the school commission, telephoned, and then passed through Simpsons to purchase a coat of some sort.

As I boarded the Sherbrooke Street bus, I asked the driver what the fare was, without realizing I was using Kiswahili. (Don't all bus drivers speak Kiswahili?) I'm sure he was more distracted by my appearance than my language: my shoes were soaking wet and my bare legs showed beneath the hem of my raincoat with its tags dangling from the sleeves. He answered in French.

The bus was very crowded — as only Montreal buses can be crowded in winter. Passengers standing around the driver had to overhear the conversation — French answers to Kiswahili questions. The driver's Gallic good humor turned to dismay when I threw 2/60 EA in the coin box.

As I joined the other standees, all in heavy coats and galoshes, one lady, barely repressing a smile, asked in English where I had learned French.

Because most of Canada was experiencing such a dire shortage of teachers at the time, the commission needed me as much as I needed the job it offered: I was hired on the strength of my previous letter from Kenya and the simple statement that I did have a degree and was a qualified teacher.

After a memorable interview at the school commission, I returned to the centre of town to look for a cheap place to stay. I got a bargain for $5.50 a week.

That first evening in the dim, grey city dampened my spirits considerably, but I had liked most of what I had seen during the day. Though I was nearly exhausted and shivering with cold and fever, the excitement of a new and entirely different home kept me awake.

To change suddenly from the wide open spaces of East Africa to the narrow, closed confines of a Montreal turn-of-the-century stone facade borders on the traumatic.

Through narrow slits in the dormer window I saw only the glow of the street lights three storeys below on the cold street; I missed the Kenya night with its thousands of stars, singing insects and heavy fragrance of oleander, frangipani and coffee blossoms.

The room stifled me, closing in on me oppressively, but I knew I could never return to the reality of those pleasant sights and sounds. I resigned myself to wild shrieking of the blaring noises of the jungle around me, in the street below and in the throbbing hi-fi in the basement.

A routine established itself in a few weeks although I had never really been a creature of habit. One doesn't emigrate that easily.

Because I was entering Canada from a tropical country after having spent many more than two years there, I had to prove that I had no contagious diseases; proof meant a series of injections.

Among other things, Immigration demanded a series of injections.

The school commission demanded a series of injections.

I enrolled at the University of Montreal shortly after arriving and it demanded a series of injections.

In fact, they all demanded the same three injections.

None of the three groups would accept the injections I had received from the other two, though in one instance I received the same injection twice from the same agency in the same afternoon, one on each arm.

I had roamed the earth quite a bit by that time so adapting to new surroundings was not really all that difficult, but I was comforted in the thought that this would be the last time, though the memory of Kenya — Africa, in general — pained me.

In Kenya I had been teacher, then headmaster of a rather large high school for boys, a boarding school. Now I was at the bottom of the ladder again and in a completely different type of school, teaching a new type of student and working for a school board much larger than any I had ever worked for.

I don't think it's fair to compare one school with another; too many variables enter the consideration. Student attitudes, teacher abilities, administrators, school boards and all sorts of community influences make immeasurable differences.

Schools are different — maybe one is better than the other in that it might do its job more efficiently than another — but who can really judge? If all students could be handicapped the way golfers are, then perhaps we might make some judgment since schools turn out students.

In those areas where schools are an integral part of the community (as they were in Kenya fifteen years ago), they prepare young people for a place in the community. I am convinced that Kenya's success as an evolving nation is due in part to the strong influence of many of the teachers who worked in a system which had discipline and demanded much from the student.

Only years after when students have accepted their places in society — for better or worse — and brought what they started in school to some practical and meaningful end, do I think their schooling might be evaluated. But other influences, home and community, have to be considered.

In Montreal schools, as in any other system, the new teacher has to make a niche for himself. Ability to manage a class, knowledge of subject matter and organizational aptitude or their lack soon become apparent.

I could feel myself passing through a sort of inspection by the other teachers. Most of them were men with the same length of experience, and they knew their work well. They were kind, considerate and genuinely interested in what they were doing; they showed a more than polite interest in my background and in the way I was adapting to a new situation, and made the transition much easier for me.

In some staff rooms cliques weed out and select mercilessly; in others a lack of enthusiasm for an often thankless job can dissipate the energy of the new teacher quickly.

In Kenya I worked with interesting people from England, Canada, Australia, India, parts of Europe and other parts of Africa. That experience had to be one of the best ones while I was there.

The staff among whom I worked when I re-started life in Canada was also interesting — they were mostly sons of European immigrants who had become staunch Canadians while retaining close ties with their ethnic backgrounds.

Most pleasant was their tolerance. Tolerance among Canadians seems to be a reciprocal affair, at least such has been the situation among those with whom I have lived. There are exceptions, but they are few and far between. Of the places in which I have lived, Canada would have to rank first for the tolerance the individual here shows to others.

There were times I did see examples of prejudice here in Canada, and in Quebec, blind and unthinking hatred is sometimes expressed. However, I am convinced that the worth of the individual still ranks very high among the values the Canadian puts on himself and others. Often, in my experience, his actions speak much louder than his words.

I had seen so much of human prejudice that I came to Canada hoping that I would see little of it; my judgment was made while in Africa and based on the Canadians I had seen working in different parts of the country.

On coming to Canada my salary had suddenly quadrupled: I couldn't get over the sudden wealth.

In Kenya as headmaster one had five rooms, a cook and a houseboy, a garden and, in my case, one of the most breath-taking views of snow-capped Mount Kenya possible, for which luxury I paid nearly ten dollars a month; in Canada, for slightly more I had one room, did my own cooking and cleaning and could look out on snow-capped roofs and chimneys. If I wanted better, I needed cash — that North American curse that bestows its blessings on those who never have enough of it but who always struggle for more.

Because I had lived sparsely in Kenya, I managed to save in Canada. I had several advantages: single, I had nothing, literally, in the way of possessions, but I also had no real debts. I spent one dollar a week for a loaf of bread, a packet of cheese and a packet of sliced meat. I made a sandwich each day of two of the slices of bread, one of the slices of meat and a slice of cheese. I spent five dollars during the same period for supper and perhaps all of two dollars for breakfast.

On Saturdays and Sundays I studied all day and ate one meal.

I was taking home the princely sum of $195 every two weeks and most of it was saved. In Kenya on that salary I would have felt wealthy; in Canada I knew I had a long way to go, but the future was bright as long as I could stand the frugal living among so many who made quite a show of their wealth.

When I look back after several years, I feel sure that I see things exaggerated in one sense or the other — pessimistically or optimistically; maybe some of that past is rosier now that it's gone, but those lonely days and nights spent working on Chaucer, Marlowe, Keats, Conrad, Greene and others and studying French while correcting math papers, cooped up like never before, often turned into hours of silent musing: Had I done the right thing in coming to Canada?

Most of the men in my age bracket (35) with whom I worked, I felt, were way ahead of me. They were happily whacking away at mortgages they could see paid off in the not too dim and distant future. They had wives, and most of them had families. Sunday meant more to them than a noontime splurge in the local restaurant with other silent, single diners in a quiet room with the occasional noisy and happy family group.

I had chosen to leave Southern United States in the very early fifties because I saw an opportunity to aid those who needed the skills of a high school math teacher in Uganda (where I worked a while) and in Kenya. I worked in isolated areas away from the big cities of Kampala and Nairobi.

When native teachers became more plentiful, non-African teachers knew they would eventually take over the teaching posts. In Kenya the Africanization processes in the educational system worked from the top down; organizations like Teachers for East Africa (TEA) and the Peace Corps stopped sending out the academically oriented teacher in favor of the "shop" teacher whom the evolving countries needed.

I had hoped eventually to leave education and then stay on as a white farmer perched on one of the many fertile hillsides of Kenya to assume the lifestyle comparable to that of so many farmers around Nanyuki or in the White Highlands.

Their life was simple, gracious and appealing. The European community lived well. The lot of the African was constantly improving, and many of them were moving into the business world in Nairobi.

Coffee, dairy products, wheat, sisal and meat could be raised commercally on large acreages just begging for someone to farm them. The opportunity was golden, shining in this verdant land of indescribable beauty, just waiting to be exploited. Young men's dreams are made of such stuff.

Young Africans were migrating to the bright lights and desk jobs of Nairobi; once educated they lost all desire to use the jembe or the panga (hoe or knife used by most Kikuyu farmers). Unfortunately the trend continued after independence, and Nairobi grew as the fertile, productive land of the country lay fallow.

When "uhuru" (independence) became a reality, the Kenyan, like everyone else, wanted to be master in his own house. Land ownership policies changed. Civil servants had to return to a Great Britain they hardly knew — in fact, some had never known. Settlers, remembering the radicalism of MauMau*, feared the worst and fled to Rhodesia. "It can't happen there," they said, "because the white Rhodesian government is much stronger than the colonial government in Kenya."

Anyone living in Kenya three or four years before independence came should have known about it — even the ostriches running around in Tsavo digging and hiding their heads in the sand should have known about it.

I knew it was just a matter of time before we would have to leave or accept land reform laws. Trying to settle ten acres was impossible.

Rhodesia was out of the question. I felt sure that the situation there would worsen. They hadn't had their MauMau insurgence yet, but I knew it was just a matter of time before the fighting started.

I considered many possibilities. Australia had vast land and all sorts of opportunities for teachers in the sixties. The Australian government advertised in *The Times* of London and in other newspapers of international circulation.

Australia had much to offer and the enticement was great. Mombasa to Perth was less of a voyage than Nairobi to Toronto to Montreal, and the government seemed stable enough.

I made inquiries at consulates and travel agencies in Nairobi about countries in West Africa, South Africa and South America as well as about Canada.

Some of the countries needed immigrants and offered incentives. I didn't want to leave Kenya but I had to, so I typically put off the decision as long as I could.

I remember during that period often sitting down on a small hill or on the ukumbi (porch) looking at the slopes of Mount Kenya while the sun played master artist with the clouds, casting lights and shadows around the summit. The sight is impressive and not easily forgotten. It seemed that Jackson, Nelion, Bation and Lenana took turns in the sunlight as the main peak while the other three awaited their turn.

At such times childhood memories of New Orleans came into focus. In the classroom and in hundreds of books only the far away and the unusual could hold me. The thought that I had attained part of those dreams of the far away only to have it all taken away, was harsh.

As a child in the last year of my elementary schooling, we sat in the classroom one hot Friday afternoon in May when nothing could distract us from thoughts of the coming summer vacation. It was a reading lesson and we were reading a story about mountain climbing.

*A violent and bloody insurrection in the early 1950s by Kikuyu tribesmen to rid themselves of foreign rule.

The boy who was reading continued, "When someone asked me why I climbed the mountain, I always said because it was there."

Two or three of the girls in the class giggled, and the one or two boys who were following the reader laughed. So did the teacher.

It suddenly struck me that there couldn't possibly be a better reason to climb a mountain. I wanted to object to the laughter that some expressed at the idea, but I knew I was a minority of one; such situations have never been pleasant, no matter how often they arrive.

I thought about the climbing of mountains and of building foundations under castles in air. The more I thought of them, the more I liked the idea.

Unfortunately, most of my castles have been mounds of sand washed away by changing tides and most of the mountains have eroded with the awakening from a dream.

I knew while trying to decide where to immigrate that something solid and lasting would have to appear on the horizon somewhere.

When I thought of some of the west Indian Islands and the beauty and challenge they offered, I had to consider the instability of some of their governments and the fact that more people left than settled there.

As much as I did not want to face the fact, but would rather continue to dream and wander, I knew I would have to settle.

In those days one rarely heard of domestic squabbles in Canada. The country made no pretentious claims of grandeur — no chauvanistic military background or heroes — and a policy of welcoming outcasts from other countries all appealed. The Canadian missionaries, school teachers and other skilled workers I had met in Kenya, all took life in stride. And they all did a good job. Even in Africa their tolerance for others singled them out. They had no axes to grind and they worked well with the Africans.

I had chosen Africa in my early days because I thought I had something to offer; I eventually settled in Kenya because it welcomed foreigners. In Nairobi one found Italian mechanics, south African merchants, Indian shopkeepers, English government officials and traders, and members of different tribes all working together, but the colour bar was strong and rigidly observed while the British were in control. With MauMau it crumbled, but was still there. And then, sometimes, the groups had disagreements among themselves.

MauMau made everyone aware that things were changing, and they would never return to what they had once been. Other African countries were undergoing the same changes. Few of us realized how fast the changes would take place and how far they would go. Erstwhile members of the British Empire had paid a certain amount of lip-service to remaining in the Commonwealth, but the phrase became almost meaningless as independence became a reality.

I considered South Africa very seriously. The country is very stable. It is settled and well-run. The African worker receives much higher wages there than anywhere else in Africa.

The economy is almost self-sufficient. But their treatment of the Indian and the African is harsh and repressive. One has to admire the industry, self-reliance and cleanliness of the Boer and his descendants, but I could not see myself settling in an area where skin colour is so important.

I would like to think that I sat down and gazed into the African sunset on Mount Kenya and came to my final decision while pondering the beauties of nature and the equality of man, but money also had something to do with it.

Teachers' salaries in Canada generally surpassed those of all of the other countries that I had considered. I might have settled for less but Canada also had all the other advantages that I considered important at the time.

In the Outspan Hotel in Hyeri I picked up a copy of one of the international magazines and saw an appealing ad published for Canadian Immigration.

A few small pictures showed the Rockies, the compulsory shot of the Mountie, a scene or two of Montreal or Toronto and a few of the Quebec countryside. The copy told of the life-style of the Canadian in the Maritime fishing villages, in the logging camps of the West and the life of the prairie farmer. The copy underplayed what they were selling and caught my interest. I remember they used the word "invigorating" in describing the climate.

Many different plans of action passed through my mind once the choice seemed to be Canada. It would not be that easy because I would certainly leave much more in Africa than I could take out of it.

I wrote to the school comission in Montreal and another in Toronto. As it became evident that the ticket to Toronto would be more difficult to manage, I continued the correspondence with the Montreal School Commission and their affirmative replies encouraged me.

As I knew I could travel on ten minutes' notice, I sat back and waited for the axe to fall.

After the first two years, life in Montreal eased considerably; the old anxieties and fears were switched for a whole new set as they were laid aside. I was accepted at school by staff and students and I felt I was doing something worthwhile in the classroom.

A master's degree became a distinct possibility, and frugal living had begun to pay off. I met a French-Canadian who shared my ideas and who also had experience working in Africa. She was also willing to attempt to raise a family with me.

We married and moved into a larger apartment — real luxury after the downtown attic I had become accustomed to. Because Monique had also been living rather frugally, we suddenly had a little money to spend.

We spent our honeymoon in St. Lucia in the West Indies and nearly changed our whole future when one afternoon on a walk we came across a school on a hill-top overlooking the Caribbean. The headmaster happened along just then and after a few minutes' conversation mentioned he needed a French teacher and an English teacher. He even took us into his office to sign a contract. I keep the contract with other souvenirs.

When we returned, we purchased one of the popular VW Bugs and started to take week-end jaunts around the province in all directions. Sometimes we went straight north hoping to find the end of the road. As in Africa, turning off the main road to follow a side road to its end proved interesting and instructive. In Africa the side roads end in small villages, and then a path leads to another village where the path becomes smaller, but rarely does one find the end of the path. I feel sure that one could walk from the Atlantic to the Indian Ocean on African paths. What a trip what would be!

In Quebec, the roads did end — especially those going to the north, but they always joined with another road.

We enjoyed the small villages. We saw in them the life-style that later gave away to the North American influence of television.

Farming had appealed to me when I was in Africa. When I saw the ravages of the winter winds on the fields and considered the work of the dairy farmer in Quebec, life in the city became more interesting. Perhaps twenty years sooner I might have tried the land for my living, but my age and that rocky soil decided against it.

We also discovered the joys of winter sports. One can read and hear or talk about skiing, but there is really only one way to experience it. The rigors of winter disappeared to a large extent once we found how to put them to use.

We also began camping in the summer. Whole new worlds opened to us because there is so much to see in Canada. The Maritimes, with its unspoiled ocean views, had been one of our most pleasant camping sites.

In those days Canada really was a promised land for us. The political climate was more or less stable, and the Quiet Revolution didn't have the harsh ring that Separatism has. During Daniel Johnson's time I began to have second thoughts about Quebec, but nevertheless I finished my M.A. and became ambitious.

Although we had a small daughter and son, we applied for overseas service with Canadian International Development Agency but were refused because I was not yet a Canadian citizen.

We felt the disapointment because we had hoped to spend a few more years overseas before settling down with a good salary and job security here in Canada.

We had retained the dream of one day returning to some wilder country, but what we had to offer was less and less in demand.

However, the ambition was still there. Not content with the classroom job once I had an MA, I applied for a position as assistant principal and was accepted.

In Kenya, as headmaster, I taught four periods a day and used the rest of the school day to do the office work and take care of the many odds and ends needed.

The three hundred students lived at the school as boarders. They had to be fed, clothed and housed. Those were the "odds and ends" that took up most of the time when not actually teaching.

We had no telephone, so ordering food and clothing more often than not meant personal contact with many merchants in the area, most of them Indians. Beans, meat, vegetables and cereal had to be raised or purchased. Milk presented problems, but the growing boys needed it.

Schedules had to be worked out for the classes not only for the after-school activities but the Saturday work period and the Sunday rest periods. It all took time.

Teachers aided in the after-school activities and in the dormitory supervision. The headboy system used in the English schools in Kenya also made life a little less harried for the headmaster. A good headboy could handle most of the minor disciplinary infractions. In school, the Kenyan students worked well. Their education cost too much to be wasted. Sometimes in the dormitories and during work periods or rest periods they had to be straightened out.

The headmaster was very much in the life of the school and he could do much to make it a good school.

The headmaster in Kenya could also hire and fire his teachers. He also paid them, and he had the right to levy fines for tardiness or absenteeism.

In Montreal such methods are not acceptable.

Rather than fight the system, I buckled under and had a heart attack. A month in the hospital (where I realized the full blessings of government-sponsored medical care) and two months at home made it clear that the life of an administrator was not for me.

I rationalized that the only worthwhile activity in education was in the classroom and returned to it. Anyway, it was a hurt in more ways than one.

Monique and I turned our energies elsewhere and decided to do something about that house that we would have to buy. The frailty of my health indicated that the limitless horizons in front of me were narrowing. We spent some time looking for a house and then paid for most of it with the investments we had been making over the years. We felt good that the purchase did not deplete all our investments; we demonstrated much faith in our purchase because we bought it on the day Rene Levesque was elected.

When I signed the deed, I could feel that I had finally killed the wanderlust within me, or maybe that I had been untrue to some part of me. We had hesitated on several occasions before signing because both of us knew, though we never admitted it, that buying a house would be like tying an anchor around our necks. It was an admission that we were here to stay.

All my reading in Thoreau and other dreamers smashed against the rocks when we purchased our home — or at least was put in hiding somewhere for the present.

We had taken up sailing with an elan that we didn't realize we had. Another dream started to form in our collective mind as we sat in cockpits of rented boats on Lake Champlain, Lake Ontario and on my brother's boat in the Pacific. Perhaps we might one day leave it all, buy our own boat and do some serious cruising while living aboard.

We still talk about the cruising we're going to do one day — and we probably will do it. One has to have a dream, if any dreams are to come true. In the meantime we have discovered that purchasing a home has made many of our lesser dreams become realities.

One of the memorable steps to settling in Canada was becoming a Canadian citizen. When my five years as a landed immigrant were over, I studied the history of the country as outlined in the brochure and became a citizen.

The lack of violence, the fact that there are really no military heroes and that wonderful tolerance of the Canadian are among the most pleasant aspects of Canadian political life and history.

Obvious differences of opinion do exist; still the country does hang together. The pattern has been tested in Canadian history. There has been some shooting but nothing on the proportion that is taken for granted in some countries where differences of opinion are not respected.

Just as I had sometimes spent stolen moments in Africa daydreaming of an unknown future while admiring the four peaks of Mount Kenya, I do the same here while cross-country skiing or sailing.

The mountains here in Canada aren't as high as those in Kenya and perhaps they are deeper purple on a receding horizon, but they are there waiting for me — and others like me — to climb them.

Mary Rajtar Kolarik

I'D TRY AGAIN

From an interview with Mary Rajtar Kolarik

I came from a farm in northern Yugoslavia, but I was born in southern France. There was no work to be had in the 1930s in Yugoslavia, and poverty was a way of life. And so, my parents went to France to work on farms. When I was small and my mother was pregnant with my sister, she went back to Yugoslavia to be with her family. My father, however, did not accompany her. The Second World War had started, and he went to Germany to work in the industrialized factories. He sent money home to my mother, but he did not come back until after the war. My mother wasn't even sure he would come back. I never asked him what happened there. Perhaps it was better I did not know, and he never spoke about it.

I grew up on the farm and didn't leave until I was twenty-two years old. I had heard from family and friends who had emigrated to Canada what a good country it was. I wanted very badly to go to Canada. The letters kept coming, and I decided to leave Yugoslavia and get to Canada one way or another. I was about nineteen then, and I made up my mind I was not going to say anything to my mother. I was afraid she would cry too much about my leaving. But my father understood. He gave me the money I needed to pay a man who smuggled people across the border to Austria. I had heard about this man from others and I decided to try this route. There was no way I could get out through regular channels.

I had some other friends who were planning to leave as well, and we set out at night when no border guards were around to stop us. But the guide got lost, and we wandered around for hours in the fields. Finally he gave up, returned our money, and we went home.

But I couldn't give up. I waited three months and tried again. This time there were five people in the group. Again it was late at night and very dark. Somehow, we got lost again and stopped at a house to ask for directions. To our dismay, the police were waiting inside the house and caught us. They put us all in jail for two days and then sent us home.

I wouldn't let that stop me. I said, "No matter what, I am going to Canada." We had such a poor life that I knew Canada had to be better. We had heard so much about this country and how good it was. I wanted to make money so badly so I could send some home to help my family in Yugoslavia.

When I was about twenty years old, I met the man who became my husband. He lived on a farm not far from my parents' place. Things were so bad for them, too, and he had to go work in the city in order to support his family on the farm. Yugoslavia was a terribly poor country. We had been going out for several years but couldn't get married because we had no place to live. In Communist countries, you have to wait a long time for an apartment. We knew we couldn't stay with my parents or his. There was no room and not enough food for everyone.

And so, my fiance and I made a plan. For months we worked on it to make sure we would get across that border. Many people had tried to cross at the place where I had been caught the last time. But I knew some had made it over. They were luckier than the others. We went to see the guide, and again he took money from us for the crossing.

A date was chosen, and we were told to meet him at a place not far from the border. It was about twelve or one o'clock at night. With us were a couple with three small children. My fiance carried one, I carried the one-year-old baby, and the other man held his third young child. We had to keep our hands on the children's mouths so they would not talk or cry. Any noise would alert the border guard and we would have been stopped and probably arrested.

We pushed our way through a wheat field. The wheat was as high as our stomachs. Because it was night and a heavy dew had fallen, the wheat was soaking wet. All our clothes were soaked right up to the waist. There was no moon and it was very dark. It may have been good for us because no one could see us running, but on the other hand, it was very hard for us to see where we were going. It was easy to trip and fall, especially carrying small children. We were all so afraid.

We crossed a small stream. It was ice cold and there was no bridge. The air was cold and we were dripping wet and worried we would get sick. As soon as we crossed the border, the guide left. The night was so dark, and he was so quiet, we didn't even know when he disappeared into the night.

Up ahead was a house and we decided to knock at the door and ask for help. A man opened the door and told us where to go. He said farther on was a village where there was a police station. He must have been used to people like us asking for help. We stayed at his house for a little while just to rest and then continued on. It was already early in the morning and as we walked down the street, the police saw us and stopped us. They took us with them and kept us in the police station for a day. Then they took us to a lager, a camp in Leibnitz. The camp had been set up for people like us who escaped across the Austrian border. There were many Yugoslavians there. We were kept there for three days.

The place was like a jail. The police put me into a room with three other women. They put my fiance in the next room. One guard gave me food, and I asked him to take it to my fiance next door. He needed more food than I did. For two days and nights I was with the other women and we talked, but the last night I was all alone. The police took the women to some other place. I cried all night. I banged on the wall with my fist so my fiance would know I was still there. He banged back to reassure me. I cried so much and we kept banging on the wall to make each other feel better. Neither of us slept. If he had someone in his room, he didn't sleep either.

Next day, the police took us to a big lager called Klagenfurt. We spent a week there, but it wasn't like a jail. In the daytime we stayed together, but at night, the men went to one barrack and the women to another.

Then we were transferred to a big camp, named Traiskirchen, and stayed about five months. I had nothing to wear. I had left Yugoslavia with only the clothes on my back and two pairs of shoes. During the summer the shoes wore out. I had to work for a week to earn enough money to buy a pair of shoes and a dress, but I was so happy to have that.

Until we got married, we lived separate at night. We had arrived in May and we married on September 25, 1960. While we were at this camp, we went to Vienna for a day to see the Canadian Immigration people at the consulate. We made papers and applied to go to Canada. The man said we would have to wait.

We went back to camp and got jobs outside. We would return at night just to sleep, and we paid room and board from what we earned. There were quite a few people there who didn't look for jobs and didn't work. They got everything free, and this made many people angry.

My husband found work in a factory. I asked a friend if she knew of anyone who needed help, and she told me there was some work available on a farm. So I went there and a man hired me to work in the fields. He would turn up every morning at the camp with a truck and take a load of people to work on the farm. At night he would bring us all back to the camp to sleep.

It was very hard work. In the summer and fall, we looked after the plants and harvested the crop. But by the end of November many of us were moved to another camp called Asten. I managed to find work on another farm where I pulled up shrubs and small trees and cleared stones from the land. The people who owned the farm were very rich, and one of the women who worked with me said the owner was a princess. She was a very nice lady. She would come out to watch us work sometimes.

By now, I was pregnant and I had a big stomach. The lady noticed and felt very sorry for me. She said this kind of work was too hard for me, but I didn't complain. I needed money to get to Canada.

Not long after, I had to stop working. It was too hard to bend down. It must have been January when I finally quit. Luckily, my husband still had his job.

We were still waiting to hear from Canadian Immigration. We were told it would take even longer because I got married in September and my name had changed. Now we had to go and make new papers with a new name. But finally in April, we were informed that everything was all finished and we were ready to leave for Canada. I was already eight months pregnant and I wanted my baby to be born in Canada. We didn't want to wait any more.

The people at Immigration told us that Canada would pay our way over, but we would have to pay the money back when we found jobs. So we left the camp, took the train to Radgenburg and crossed Germany to Bremen. There we boarded a ship for Canada.

The voyage over was terrible. I was so sick. I threw up constantly and I was afraid I would lose the baby. My husband was so worried he called the nurse, and she came and gave me some medicine to keep food down. I was so happy when we finally reached Montreal.

My sister-in-law took a taxi to the harbour to meet us. I had not written her I was pregnant, and she was so surprised to see me like that.

My son was born on June 16, 1961, and he was a Canadian. I was so happy. I was afraid he would be born in Austria or on the ship and he wouldn't be considered Canadian. Because we had not been in the country for three months, I had to pay the doctor and hospital. For us that was very much money. It meant I had to find work right away to pay the bills and also to pay for the train and ship to Canada.

My husband found work after one month in a garage. He didn't speak English or French, but he was lucky to work with someone at the garage who came from Yugoslavia, and this man helped him with the language. He would explain what the boss wanted.

I stayed home only one month with the baby and then I found work, cleaning offices in a big building from six o'clock to eleven at night. My husband worked days and he would come home and look after the baby when I left the house. We worked very hard. Nobody gave us anything, and we paid back every cent we owed.

Then my husband left the garage and found a job in a stocking factory on St. Lawrence Boulevard. There were lots of immigrants like us there, and they didn't speak English or French either. I kept cleaning offices.

Finally, in 1964, I looked for another job and found one in a factory not far from where my husband had worked before, packing stockings. It was the same kind of work. The hours were very long, sometimes ten and eleven a day. I would start at seven in the morning and although quitting time was at five p.m., I usually worked overtime until after six . . . but no overtime pay. Most of the time I was standing. The most I ever took home was $40 a week. I had started at $1.00 an hour and after two years was earning $1.25 an hour. It didn't pay very much, but I knew there were other immigrants who wanted the job. If I had quit, we would not have been able to manage on my husband's salary.

In November, 1966 I had another baby and this time I stayed home for one year to look after him. My husband got a job with Canadian Copper and has been there for the last fourteen years. I worked and we saved our money. We bought a small house and then a car. My children went to school. I wanted them to learn English and French. For me it was too late to learn, but at least my boys would have Canadian languages.

Even if I worked so hard, I'm not sorry I came to Canada. They stopped me twice and twice I was in jail and lived in camps for one year to get to Canada. If I hadn't crossed the border the last time, I would have tried until I made it. I wanted a better life here and I never want to leave this country.

Canada is a beautiful place, and the people are very good. If you work hard, you make something of yourself. You have a chance to get somewhere, not like in Yugoslavia.

I have a family, a house, and a car. I have a good life here. What else could I want? That's all!

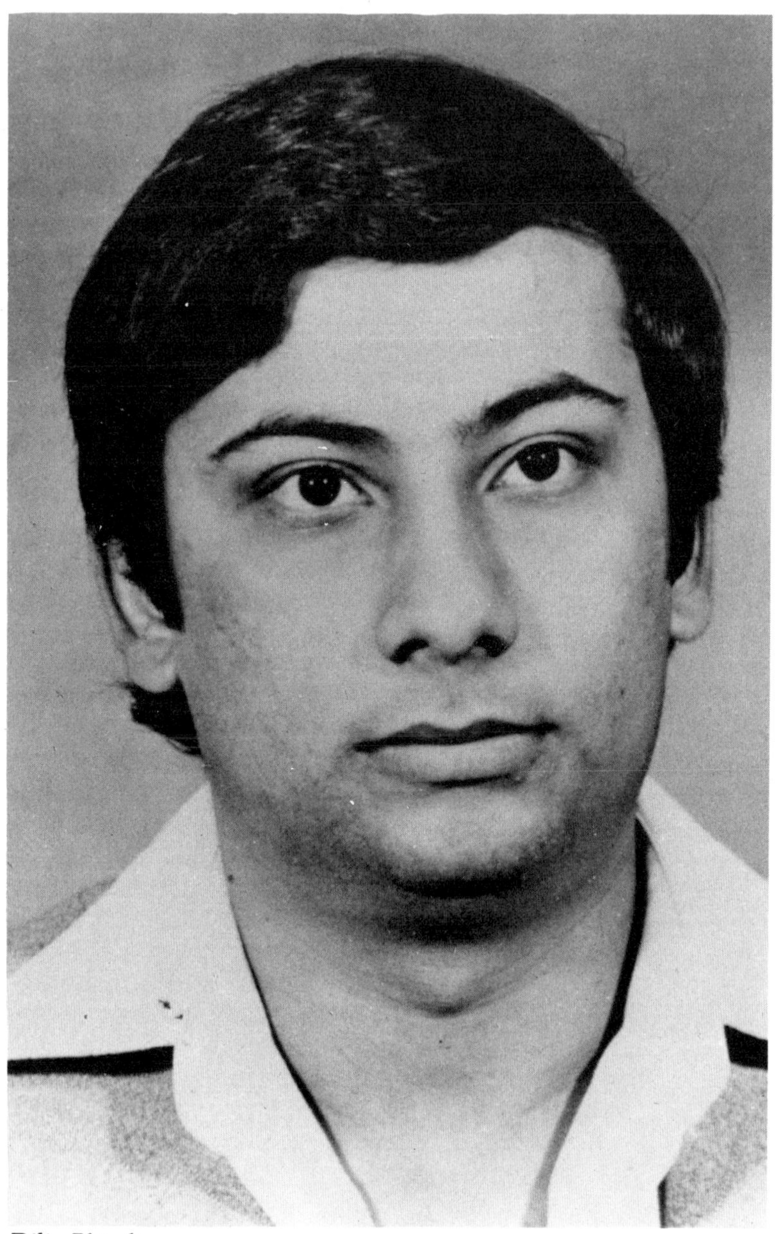

Dilip Bhindi

EXPULSION

From an interview with Dilip Bhindi

If you were to run into any Ugandans today, you would see a cheerful smile on their faces despite all the difficulties they have had to face. They came to this country without a penny in their pockets, and Canada was good to them. I know, for I was one of these people.

I was born in an Indian village near Rajkot in Gujarti State in 1952. My parents were wealthy. My great-grandfather had been a goldsmith by profession, and this trade was handed down from generation to generation. In the 1800s gold wasn't measured in ounces or grams; it was weighed in pounds. The family was considered to be one of the biggest jewelers in the suburbs, and there was much honour attached to anyone in this profession.

When I was one year old, my father left for Uganda to start a family colony. My mother and I were left in the care of my grandparents. When he had established himself in Uganda, he would send for the rest of us.

Uganda had had a history of Indian immigration from the 1900s on when the British began building railways in the country. They brought in cheap Indian labour to lay the track and build the escarpments. They were joined later by many professionals, business people like my father, and soldiers.

My father had been sponsored by a firm, and his employers were so pleased with him that he remained there until the company went bankrupt in 1960. He had no trouble finding work elsewhere.

In 1961 my grandfather died leaving the family without the traditional male head. And so my father came back to India to settle matters and make arrangements for us. He had a business in Rajkot that someone else was running, and when my father returned, he took it over for the year he was there. Finally he decided to sell it because he thought Africa was a better place for business. Because he had been in Uganda since 1953, he had a permit to stay there and so he returned, obtained permits for my mother, sister and myself and sponsored us. My grandmother chose to remain in India.

It was about eight months before we arrived. I was ten years old and didn't speak a word of English. I had to learn it or have problems in school. My father arranged private tutors day and night, and in about eight or nine months my sister and I had learned the language. I began school in 1963 and a few months later was moved up a grade.

Meanwhile, my father was doing very well in business. Although he was working for someone else, he was considered the best jeweler in town and a very good watchmaker. The economy was booming and after Independence, under Dr. Milton Obote, President of Uganda, there was complete freedom.

I finished high school in 1970, and about this time my sister married a boy who had come to Uganda on a visit from England. He returned, sponsored her, and off she went to Leicester. My father went into business for himself and opened a shop next to the man he had been working for.

Suddenly an event occurred that had a profound effect on everyone, not just my family, but all Asian Ugandans. Dr. Milton Obote went to Singapore to attend a conference. While he was gone a relatively unknown officer in his army by the name of Idi Amin masterminded a military coup and took over the country. The first thing he did was close the airport and set up road blocks at all border entries so Obote couldn't get back.

Amin's justification for this coup was that he was acting for the good of the people. He said he would elect a president shortly because he was only a military commander. However, a few months later, he proclaimed himself president and took over. None of us had any idea what he had in mind.

For the first few months, everything appeared to be going smoothly. Exports and imports were moving freely in and out of the country. People were doing well, and everyone thought the new leader was great. Some said he was better than Obote who was pro-British and a smooth politician. My father was encouraged by this lull of apparent security and had money sent from England and India to enlarge his business.

I had an Indian passport and I wanted to go to school in England, but because I needed a visa, I couldn't leave the country. My father said: "All you're going to do is end up working for someone else. Why don't you take care of my shop?"

So I gave up my dream of a university education and stayed while he took a contract to work for a company in Kampala, about two hours away by car from Ginja where we lived.

While my father worked out of town, I ran the shop with two other men working under me. Business was marvellous, and things were so good we had visions of becoming very rich.

It was 1972 and suddenly President Idi Amin made a statement that he had had a dream that the Indian people were taking over the economy, were cheating the Ugandans and not allowing them to rise in the business world. He issued a proclamation that all people who were not citizens must leave the country in ninety days.

It didn't help telling this madman that a family could be a mixture of many nationalities. The mother could be an Indian citizen, the eldest son born in Uganda was a Ugandan citizen and the father could have had a British passport from the British Protectorate period before 1948. Even if the family had three different places to go, and the son was old enough to take over the family business in Uganda, it still would not have changed anything. It meant breaking up entire families in an effort to find one Ugandan citizen permitted to remain. In our particular case, we all had Indian passports and wouldn't even be allowed to go to England.

Amin became enraged when people protested and tried to explain what he was demanding was unreasonable and impossible. For the first three weeks we didn't believe this was actually happening to us. We said: "He's crazy! He won't last, and without the Indians, the business and economy will go down the drain."

Finally we were forced to realize there was no turning him back. He really meant it and wouldn't change his mind. And so we began to sell our things, most of them at a huge loss, and to make plans to put the money into the bank and find some place to immigrate. People began leaving the country by the thousands. We discovered later that about 30,000 went to Britain and the Canadian government invited 6,000 to settle in Canada.

We discovered that even the simple process of leaving was dangerous. We had to leave our property behind; we were stripped of all our possessions, and soldiers were waiting at all border points and at the airport, harassing people continuously. The military police were pushing, beating, tormenting these poor souls and taking their money, jewelry and anything they had of value. In the city, the soldiers confiscated property and anyone who tried to stop them could be beaten, shot or he simply disappeared.

My father and I, with five other people, had taken a taxi to Kampala from Ginja to see the Canadian embassy officials. At a checkpoint, halfway between the two towns, soldiers stopped the car. They all pointed guns at us. For no reason whatsoever, the guard reached in and hit the man in the front seat across the face. Then he asked my father how much money he had. My father took out 200 or 300 shillings, and the soldier asked, "Why are you carrying so much money?" He struck my father in the face and grabbed the money.

Next was my turn.

"What do you have?"

"Nothing."

"Why don't you have money? You know we need money." And he smashed me in the face.

We were lucky to get away with only that. This was happening everywhere in Uganda and everyone was terrified. As soon as the news reached the outside world, British and Canadian embassies were instructed to open immigration to Asian Ugandans. People by the thousands lined up at the embassies to get immigration papers. They would sleep overnight in the lines on the sidewalk just to get their turn the next day.

Most of our small items had been packed and addressed for shipment to India, but as soon as we heard Canada was accepting Ugandans, I said to my father: "Look, we'd better go to Canada, and if we are not happy there, we can always go to India from Canada."

So we changed our tickets and made an appointment at the Canadian Embassy to see an official, Jacques Drapeau. I never forgot his name. That's how important it was to us. I told him I wanted to go to Canada, but I could see people waiting in line with their credentials. There were so many lawyers, doctors and chartered accountants, and we were of the very few who didn't have any of those professions. We were worried and when we were asked what qualifications we had, we were forced to say, "We are not professionals. We are jewelers and watchmakers."

Mr. Drapeau asked me if I knew what Canada was like. I said no, but I would take it whatever it was.

He answered, "That's not the way it works. You have to apply."

"So make an application."

He said he would process it and give me an interview. He gave us two numbers, 1224 for me and 1225 for my father. Numbers given to each applicant were published each day in the newspaper, and I would examine the list carefully to make sure we didn't miss our turn. Finally they appeared in the paper and I went to Kampala for the interview.

"Sorry," said the man, "you cannot go because you lack a few points. You get so many for each qualification. Even though you are good businessmen, there are no openings for your line of business."

The other man with him asked what we did, and Drapeau answered, "Watchmakers."

"Just a minute," he said. He went to a notice board and came back with a sheet of paper. "I have a telex asking for ten watchmakers immediately."

It seemed that a Montreal company had sent the telex after hearing the news about Amin throwing out Asian Ugandans. This company must have figured there was bound to be watchmakers among us.

"Okay," said Drapeau, and passed us. The officials wanted to send us in two or three days, but we asked for five to ten to get all our things together and change the addresses on the boxes we had packed for India. He gave us permission.

Inside of ten days we had cleared whatever we had in the shop. We sold what we could and left everything else, the furniture, the shop and the property. We lost it all. We had to lock up and hand our keys over to the council which took over. We were allowed only one bag per person. We packed what we could and left for the airport.

To our delight, we discovered that the Canadian government had arranged free passage for us. The United Nations security police had set up a cordon so we would not be robbed or harmed at the airport, but before we even got there, the Ugandan soldiers had set up a checkpoint on all the roads leading to the airport and were opening luggage, looting it, searching us and taking whatever they wanted. They did this to all of us — every Ugandan Asian fleeing the country. They held us up for such a long time going through our belongings that we barely made the plane. Until the plane actually took off, we were terrified they might try to stop us.

We didn't know what Canada was like and didn't even get a glimpse of it because we landed at night. I don't even know if it was at Dorval Airport or an army base. The plane was a government-chartered flight and full of Ugandan Indians. The service was excellent. The Canadian government even thought of providing Indian food for us because many of us are vegetarians and don't eat meat.

For most of us this whole thing was a traumatic experience. It was as if we were flying into the unknown. We didn't know what we were going to do when we arrived, where we would live and what to expect. We were completely in Canada's hands.

Once we arrived we were amazed to find that the Canadian people and their government were so kind. We didn't have any difficulty at all. From the plane we were taken to Longue-Pointe army barracks. A man said, "Bienvenue," to all of us.

"Relax," he said. "Relax tonight and we will talk about everything in the morning."

It was already 2:30 a.m. and we were all sleepy. Yet we felt secure for we had our families with us, we were fed and all the officers and people were good to us. We just couldn't believe it was possible.

But the problem was they didn't know what to do with us. It was October and winter was coming. We needed shelter, houses to live in, clothing for the winter and guidance through the adjustment period.

We were told the government had decided to put us up in hotels, and my family was taken to the Queen's hotel where we stayed with other groups for about two months. Everyone was given lodging, board and ten dollars a week for each person.

Once we were boarded at the hotel, the three of us, my father, uncle and myself would go out looking for jobs every day. We couldn't wait. Our clothes and coats had been supplied by the Canadian government. None of us had any warm clothing because we came from a hot climate. By now it was November and it was getting cold. We weren't used to it and were freezing. Walking along the street we would pause, go into a shop to warm up for a few minutes and then leave. We would keep walking until we were very cold again and do the same thing.

On Saturdays, an officer, who was in charge of the group, would take a bunch of people into town to look around and show them the sights. On one of these trips he pointed out Henry Birks Jewelers as the largest silversmiths and jewelry firm in Canada. He said if we could get jobs there we would be very lucky. As soon as I heard that, I told my uncle and father to leave the group, go into Birks to look around, and we would get back to the hotel on our own.

My father and uncle didn't speak much English and depended on me to communicate and translate. In we went and a saleslady, who thought we were customers, came over to talk to us. I guess she could tell by our clothes we were foreigners and asked where we were from. I explained we weren't there to buy anything but were looking for work.

She said the manager was just leaving for lunch, but would we like to talk to him? She called upstairs and told him who we were. He said to send us up, and she took us there herself.

We were treated like kings. Everything was so nice we felt wonderful. What a place! What people! The manager offered us a cup of tea and asked what he could do for us. When we told him where we were from and took out our references, he seemed impressed.

I told him we could fix any watch he gave us, and he asked us to show him right away. We didn't have any tools so he gave us some. Both my father and I repaired a watch, and I guess we must have done a good job. The manager offered to hire one of us. We hesitated, and he said he would take two. But my father said we were a family and had to stay together.

The manager offered us $85 each, but my father told me to ask for more. When I said we were worth $120 each, he said no — all he could give was $100 and no more, but he would take the three of us.

We were to start on Monday, but we had no tools. The company did not provide them. And so on Monday during my lunch hour, I went to a tool company, looked at a catalogue and made a list. The items came to $545 and I didn't have any money. I called the salesman aside and explained I was penniless, but needed the tools. He must have thought I was crazy.

Just at that moment the owner of the store, a lady, passed by, and the salesman called her over to tell her I wanted to buy without money. I explained our situation, where I was from and how we got to Canada. I told her we had just started at Birks and to call them. The salesman did just that, and the report must have been good because the lady said: "Give him what he wants on credit."

And that's how we started in Canada. We paid off a certain amount every week on the tools and we stayed at Birks until 1979. I went to work as a watchmaker for a friend, then switched to part-time work so I could go to school to study computer programming at Dawson. It was hard for me to get in because I didn't have any papers to prove I had finished high school in Uganda. But the administrators were very good about it.

In 1975 I went to England to visit my married sister, and I got married while I was there. My sister had arranged the meeting. Judy was originally from Nairobi, Kenya, and my sister knew my future wife had a 100 per cent good character.

I returned to Canada after three weeks in England and didn't have any trouble getting Judy into the country. I had bought her a ticket in England, and when we arrived here, I went to Immigration and said: "I want to present my wife. I just got married, and she is going to stay here in Canada.,"

"She can't," said the immigration officer.

I explained where I was from.

"Oh, you must be one of the Ugandans. But you know, you can't do this. It is not the way."

I asked if he could make an exception, and he was very nice. He said he would get me a ministerial permit and in one year Judy would be a landed immigrant.

For the first two or three weeks, Judy ran around acting like a tourist. Then she got bored doing nothing and said she wanted to work. I didn't think she would find a job, but she insisted on trying. She went to the bank across the street where we lived and asked for a job. The manager asked her if she had any experience, and when she told them she had worked for Lloyd's of London, the manager had a telex sent to verify her statement. As soon as he received confirmation, he asked her to begin work immediately. But she had to go to Immigration to get permission to work. She went on Monday and Tuesday morning she was at work. And she has been there since August, 1975. Today she is a senior officer in charge of a section and has the keys to the bank.

In the ten years I have been here, from the $10 the Canadian government gave us, we have worked together and built up capital, bought a house, furniture, cars, and we have traveled to England, Switzerland, Holland and Florida. I have learned to handle electronic watches, learned the diamond trade and how to evaluate jewelry. I studied French and took courses at the University of Waterloo in management science, human relations, psychology and personality.

You could say I have had an advantage because I speak English and learned some French. But take a man like my father who is older and doesn't speak either of the two languages. How do you explain his success? He says he is a businessman, and the language of business is business. It doesn't matter what languages you speak. If a man is good at his trade, he will always be a success.

He worked very hard the early years he was in Canada, and in 1978 he moved to Ottawa with the company he worked for. For two years he worked in their watch repair department in the Billingsbridge Shopping Centre. In 1980 he noticed someone putting up a bankruptcy notice in a store window and immediately went in to rent the place. He signed the deal the same evening and had a friend in England wire him the money the next day to pay for the initial investment.

My father works fast when he wants something. There is a certain type of furniture he wanted that is made in Quebec City. We went up there, and the owner said it would take six months to build. My father offered him $500 more if he could take his samples.

"For that kind of money, you can take it now," said the man.

Then my father approached watch companies and got merchandise from them. He even went to the company he worked for, told them his plans, and they were very nice about it. They let him leave and didn't say anything about his opening in the same shopping centre.

Today there are three shops like his in the centre, and all the watchmakers come from the same Indian town. The centre sometimes is known as the Indian Jewelry Shops because we have a monopoly of this business in the centre. In the few years he has been in business — and I have gone down to help him a couple of days a week — he has done very well. We expect to do even better and will make up for the business we left in India and the one we lost in Uganda. My father's motto is, "Good service, good prices and a smile."

I often look back over the last ten years and know we have been very lucky. Canada has been very good to us. There wasn't a thing the government didn't help us with. We had a few difficulties finding an apartment and the government helped. They paid the first month's rent and even guaranteed the next month's rent if we could not pay. We were even supplied with food the first day in our own apartment. I can't say we had any real hardship — we just didn't have any money — but our hard work improved things tremendously.

The government arranged for an adviser to counsel us, and we were given a phone number we could call day or night if we were in any trouble. I remember we had a problem with our personal belongings which we had sent on ahead to Canada. Because we didn't know where we would live, we sent everything in bond, care of Montreal customs. We asked the counsellor if we had done the right thing. He checked into it and traced the boxes. Two days later they were at our door at no extra charge.

I was very impressed by what the government did and even more by what ordinary Canadians did for us. I can truthfully say I never came across any cases of prejudice since we arrived. Among the people I worked with was a Japanese, a Swiss, a Hungarian, a German, a French Canadian, two Englishmen, and we all got along. I was always treated like somebody, and the manager was so kind he even gave us a radio when he learned we didn't have one or even a TV set.

When we bought our house and had just moved in, the minister of Lachine church, Tom Miles, and a family by the name of Meadows, came to visit and welcome us to the parish. They offered to help and took us to church where the minister made a speech before the congregation. He held us up as an example of family life and hard work. He praised our efforts, and everyone stood up and clapped. They made us feel so welcome.

Mr. and Mrs. Meadows came to our house, looked around, and a few days later a truck arrived with a chesterfield, a TV set and some other things to start housekeeping with. They helped us fill out papers, attend to legal problems and showed us how to get the children admitted into schoool.

Slowly we began to fulfill our ambitions. Because I had to work as a go-between for my father and help him translate, I could never realize my dream for university, but the hope never died. With my wife working, I decided to take courses in computers and, along with cameras, will introduce them into the shop. Hard work has brought me this far. Working from 8:30 a.m. to 11:30 p.m. never bothered me as long as it meant getting ahead.

Today the majority of the Asian Ugandans who came to Canada as refugees are holding good jobs, have families, homes, cars and in another ten years will be even better off. Their main ambition is business, which they have done in India and Uganda for generations. I know we were not liked because we were very good at our work. Resentment builds up when you become successful. But I know that the plane load of people we came over with have all done well. We were such a closely knit group that to this day we have kept in touch. I know them all, where they are, what they are doing and what their children are accomplishing. They all seem to live in areas near one another. One from our group recently graduated with a Master's in Business Administration. Everyone was very proud of him.

We have made a success of ourselves here. I know it is difficult to do this in other places in the world. Canada must have seen us as a good investment, and because we are primarily businessmen, we will contribute a lot to the economy of Canada in the future.

Multiculturalism really works in Montreal and I have always been well treated. In addition to English and French, I speak Hindi, Gujharti and two Swahili dialects. I am a Canadian citizen and consider myself very lucky to be here.

So far everything has been good, and I have no complaints. But who knows what could happen tomorrow?

Look what happened in Uganda because of discrimination!

Budapest, 1956, Hungarian Revolution

GOODBYE TO MY HOMELAND

From an interview with Ernest Ban

Do you know what hunger is? Have you ever lived through a war? If you haven't, you can't understand. It's something you want to forget, but you never can, no matter how hard you try.

I was born in Budapest in the early 1930s, but my memories are centered around the war years. The most traumatic episode I remember happened at 10:00 a.m. on April 13, 1943, when the Allied bombers attacked our city.

We lived in low-rental attached units very close to a railway, chemical factories and oil refineries. From above, our homes must have looked like factories to the pilots. The sirens went off, and the planes dropped their bombs on us. I was home with my sister, and my parents were at work. I remember my only pair of shoes were at the shoemaker and I ran out in bare feet.

Trenches had been dug in the ground to be used as air raid shelters, and we ran for them, but in the confusion I lost my sister. I didn't know where she was. When the bombs hit, the ground shook as if there was an earthquake. One hit our shelter right in the middle. The whole thing collapsed. Luckily for me, I was at the other end of this sixteen-foot-long trench, and with me in the few feet of space were about twelve or thirteen people. You should have seen these men and women crying, kneeling on the ground and praying. I didn't understand it at all. I was only ten or eleven and I was thinking: "Aren't they ashamed, acting like babies!" The seriousness of it hadn't hit me.

It was a good few hours before people on the surface dug us out. I wanted to see my sister right away. Miraculously she was unhurt, down at the very end on the other side. We climbed up to horror.

The air was thick with yellow and black smoke. We were coughing and gasping. Hardly any houses remained standing. Many people had run to the woods nearby to hide among the trees when the sirens went off. The Allies were using a certain type of bomb that didn't explode on impact. It was set to explode at a certain altitude so far from the ground, and the shock waves flattened everything around it, not to mention what the shrapnel did to anything in the way. Those poor people in the woods were blown to bits. There were pieces of human bodies, limbs hanging from the trees left standing. There were so many killed. It was awful.

I moved around like a sleepwalker. No one even looked at me. I noticed that most of the shelters had either been hit by bombs or had collapsed from the vibrations of direct hits on the houses. We had been lucky. Our shelter had been made of wood and could withstand the shaking, but those that had been built of bricks and cement and were too rigid had fallen in. The streets were covered with corpses laid side by side. People were spreading newspapers, blankets, anything they could find over the bodies. As long as I live I will always see this scene.

My parents came running home from the factory. My mother was worried about us and she was running toward our flat with a friend, a co-worker, about 100 feet behind her. My mother ran across a field and what looked like freshly raked earth. Her friend was just a minute or so behind her and bang . . . the earth blew up. As her friend hit the spot, a bomb exploded and she was blown to bits. My mother was very lucky. It could have happened to her.

After these incidents, my parents were terrified we would be killed, and we moved out of the city to the country, about thirty kilometres from Budapest, where we had some distant relatives. We rented a small house. It was really pitiful for city folk to try to survive without any knowledge of farming and no jobs.

During the summer, my mother and father would go out picking beans, fruit, anything that grew on nearby farms. We kids would steal food. There were lots of vineyards and grapes, and we would pick at least thirty kilos which my parents would sell in the capital. We stole firewood and carried it home. We cut down trees to get the wood. We were like a pair of scavengers, but we had no choice or we wouldn't have survived. We would salvage the smallest thing we found, even if it was frozen. A half-rotten cabbage, a carrot, were treasures.

Do you know what my parents did that winter? They became beggars because we couldn't get any food. But they didn't beg in the same village. They were ashamed. They would walk four or five kilometres and beg in other places. They'd come home with a piece of dry or moldy bread, a few rotten apples or a piece of spoiled bacon. We had a watchdog called Pajtas that a neighbour wanted. We sold the dog for a sack of corn. We lived on corn and water for a month, and that's all that kept us alive. We stayed in that country place for a year and then moved back to Budapest.

There were many people out of work, including my father, and he got a bleeding ulcer. He was in the hospital for six months and had two operations. There was food in the hospital and when my mother walked there and back every day because she couldn't afford a streetcar, she would come back with a bag of cheese peel. You know the wax that is put around cheese to preserve it? My father would go around the wards after meals and collect this peel. There was at least an eighth of an inch of cheese on it. We ate this stuff, wax and all. It lasted for weeks.

The Russians occupied the country in 1945, but it was a while before conditions improved. I remember breaking into an abandoned house and searching for food, pots and pans, anything I could get my hands on to sell so I could buy something to eat.

A crazy, drunken soldier spotted me and began chasing me all over the place, firing his revolver at me. I escaped through a back door into the garden, running like crazy. I was about twelve at the time.

Finally, my mother got a job at a small factory where they made paper bags and envelopes, and one day she came home with a bottle of honey she had found sitting in a window at the factory. I think we had some bread. The honey must have been sitting there for a while because it was thick and gooey and hard to spread. We were so hungry we didn't care. The next day she came home from work and said: "Kids, I hope you didn't eat that stuff. It was glue!"

The foreman had been looking for it to use on his envelopes. We didn't eat the whole thing, but it was lucky we didn't get sick. We were so poor, and there wasn't any food in the house, except one big onion. We hadn't eaten in two days. My sister and I took this huge onion and ate it raw. We got so sick, we felt like dying. But it wasn't only us who were suffering. It was a general condition. I missed a year of school with everything that was going on.

But once the Russians settled in, things began to improve. The army quartered two officers, lieutenants, in our house. My mother got a job in the kitchens of the officers' club at headquarters right across the road from our house. These two officers were nice guys and they would bring food home for us from the club. My mother was also allowed to bring home bread, meat, everything that was left over. At least we weren't starving any more.

The officers who stayed with us were generally across the street playing cards or drinking at the club. The colonel and chief of police were stationed there as well.

One night, when the soldiers were over there and we were getting ready for bed, someone knocked on the door. My mother thought the men might have forgotten their keys, and she went down in her nightgown and robe to open the door.

Standing there were two drunken Russian soldiers. They pushed their way in and wanted to rape my mother right in front of us kids. One of the soldiers had a grenade in his hand and said if she didn't cooperate, he would blow us up.

My mother said, "Wait, let me close the door first." And she went through that door like wow, running down the street, screaming her head off, "Patrol! Patrol!" There were guards stationed right in front of headquarters across the street and a major — I'm sure he was a high-ranking officer — ran out.

My mother yelled what was happening and while she was doing this, the two drunks staggered out of our house and began running down the street toward the highway. Our house wasn't too far from the well-lit highway. The major yelled orders to the guards to shoot the drunken soldiers. Right in front of us, as we watched, the bullets cut them down.

Don't forget the first wave of soldiers that occupied the country were the cream of the crop, but then came the Mongols, the worst barbarians you ever saw. They raped anything, even eight- and nine-year-old children. They were monsters. I saw one of these drunken Mongols staggering down the street dragging a guitar behind him on the sidewalk, peeing as he moved along, and he exposed himself right in front of everyone.

The two soldiers who stayed with us were gentlemen, and hanging around with them and the soldiers across the road, I learned to speak Russian. Finally they were posted to Berlin, but one of them stopped at our house on his way back to Russia about a year later to tell us that his friend had been killed in Berlin. We felt badly, but imagine this one coming by to look us up and say good-bye before he went home!

When I got back to school, I did badly. Before the war I had been first in my class but now I failed twelve subjects. Before I had been teacher's pet, and she had taken me home to help her correct other kids' papers. Now I was so unused to school that I got into bad company. We discovered girls and started fooling around. I didn't even go to church. I'd get a friend to stamp my ticket to show I had been there, so even my parents didn't know what I was up to.

My father was a postman, and he wanted me to follow the same position. I didn't want it, and my mother said no: "No way; the boy has brains. He's going to school."

At the time the government was looking for bright boys and girls to push them toward education in the hope that these students would be the new members of the Communist elite. So they gave accelerated courses to do four years in one in order to get into university. This was to make up for the years of schooling most of us had missed because of the war. Would you believe I finished with 99 percent? By 1950 I was in university. In 1956 I graduated as a textile engineer in mechanics, and got a job with a textile firm.

Immediately after graduation you had to serve three months in the army. It was compulsory service, and every year you had to spend one month of training as a reserve. When the uprising broke out in 1956, I was in the army. We were released and with a bunch of other students, hitchhiked our way back to Budapest. We ran right into the shooting.

Since the university students had started this whole thing, naturally all students were suspect. I wasn't even there when it happened and I could prove I was in the army, but all the same, we were stopped, questioned and some of my friends were picked up and disappeared — you know, a one-way trip to Siberia. I never saw them again. So I was afraid to stay.

It was then I remembered something the father of a girlfriend had once said to me. I had known her years before and wanted to marry her, but she went out with someone else. Her father had told me that if I ever wanted to leave, he'd help me. He was living right beside the Austrian-Hungarian border.

I looked him up and asked him if he remembered what he had said, and he told me he'd help me only if I married his daughter — either/or. So two weeks later we went to the City Hall in Budapest and got married.

One of my friends came to pick me up with a motorcycle to take me to his place. I didn't notice that he was driving without a headight, and we were stopped by the police and taken to the station where we were kept overnight. This was my wedding night, and I shared a cell with a murderer who was talking casually about his girlfriend and her mother and the brutal way he killed the old woman because he didn't like her. I don't have to tell you how much sleep I had.

In the morning the captain came in and began questioning me. I had to convince him that I was a solid citizen, that the government had paid for my education in full and that I was an active member of the Communist Party.

He appeared pleased to hear this, let me out and told me not to ride on bikes without headlights. So I went home, and told my new wife we were going. I was too afraid after this incident to want to hang around. With only the clothes on our backs, we headed for the railway station to get the train to her father's place. I wanted to take my diploma with me, but I figured that if I was caught and searched, I'd be in big trouble.

There we were at the station having a beer and waiting for the train. With us was a friend of my wife's and her father. I looked up and three big guys in leather coats were coming toward our table. My heart sank. I knew they were the secret police. They began asking questions and wanted to see our IDs.

"Where are you going and what are you doing?" And on and on, one question after the other, they asked. You can imagine how frightened we were, but I said we had just got married, and my wife's parents wanted a church wedding and that we were going to visit them and get it done there. Fortunately, I had been there before, and my papers were stamped to prove it.

The policeman said: "Well, I see you've been there several times before. This is very nice. This is the kind of thing we like, that you believe in the future of Hungary and even in troubled times like these you get married and you are sure the future will be rosy . . ."

And they shook hands with us and imagine, they wished us good luck. Little did they know we were escaping over the border. We were scared stiff that we might give ourselves away, and they'd stop and arrest us. So we traveled to my father-in-law's place, and the old man slaughtered a pig. We had a feast and stayed there for three days. Then he guided us through the woods right to the border. Arm in arm I walked across with my wife and a few metres on the Austrian side, I turned around, raised my arm and said good-bye to my homeland, Hungary. I knew I might never see my country again.

For three months we remained in Austria. They treated us well, the Austrians. I had only the suit on my back, and we were given clothes and fed wonderful meals. People came from different countries recruiting immigrants — people from the United States, England and Canada. They distributed application forms. My first choice was the United States, but I filled out forms for the U.S.A. and Canada and decided I would take the one that came through first. I didn't think I would have any trouble, but maybe I was a little overly confident because I was a college graduate. We had heard rumours about Canada, both good and bad. I heard about the Indians and had read some history books so I thought Canada was half-civilized. Reading those stories about the Mohawks, I guess I got the wrong impression about Canada being primitive and a backward country.

We had also heard stories about people getting sixty to sixty-five cents an hour washing dishes, and that some who were very lucky got a dollar an hour. I thought a dollar an hour for a university graduate was terrible. It couldn't be possible, but some of the people we became friendly with had received letters from relatives in Canada, advising them not to come because things were so bad. I thought, "My God, if relatives write letters like that, there must be something to it."

Finally our number came up . . . for Canada, and I said, "Okay, we are going to Canada, destination Montreal." And with that decision made there was no turning back. We arrived April 13, 1957 and were taken to St. Paul d'Hermite. It was similar to Eisenstadt in Burgoland, Austria. The buildings were different in structure, but served the same purpose — refugee centres.

My first impression of Montreal as we drove from Dorval Airport was how dirty the streets were, newspapers flying around in the wind on the streets. I couldn't believe it was such a mess. Of course, it is much cleaner now. And I was amazed at the number of cars. I never saw anything like that in Hungary.

We stayed at the refugee centre for over a month. One day one of the directors called me into his office and asked: "Mr. Ban, are you an engineer?"

"Yes, I am."

"Okay, there's a man who would like to see you. He wants to hire an engineer."

So I was sent to another office and there was an old farmer sitting there in dirty boots and jeans with the translator. We started to talk. First he asked me if I spoke English. I said, "No." He wanted someone to repair his farm machinery. I told him I wasn't a mechanic. I was an engineer, and the deal was off.

After a few weeks, I was getting frustrated. I couldn't stay there forever. I wanted to work. I had to have a job. I never liked handouts from anybody. I am an independent person.

So we left and came to Montreal and we were put up in a jail on St. Antoine Street. It was a jail then, but one part was reserved for aliens. It didn't have bars where we were, but people who were in the country illegally were kept there temporarily and deported. We weren't caged in, but we were eight to ten in a room, men and women, husbands and wives. There was very little privacy. The good thing was that the cook was Hungarian, a real nice guy. I was able to talk to him.

When we landed we had been given five dollars and were told that if you show your money you could get killed. We were frightened and then being in that jail, listening to the fire sirens, the police and ambulance sirens scared us even more. We kept hearing stories about rapes, muggings and killings, and I was wondering if we did the right thing in coming here. The future didn't look very bright.

A girlfriend of my wife's got in touch with a Hungarian priest who had found a job for my friend. He was married to my wife's girlfriend. And what kind of a job did he get? He worked in the cemetery digging graves. I thought he was lucky and asked if I could get a job there, too. Next day I was told I had one. So the two of us would go every day together and dig graves in the cemetery. Imagine, me, an engineer, on my first job in Canada!

I was working only two days when one of the supervisors at the jail found out I had a job and threw us out. They figured I was going to get a salary on Friday, as little as it was, but they didn't consider that we had nothing to live on, nothing for food, and that we would have to pay for a room or place to stay.

I don't know if it is done differently now, but they made it very hard for the new immigrant then. They should have given us a few weeks on a job to get ourselves together before kicking us out. I had been getting a lunch from them, two sandwiches, but since they figured we were getting paid, we wouldn't be allowed to stay there for nothing. I hadn't even received my first pay cheque.

The last thing they did for me was to find me a room. They contacted a landlord and what they did was pay the first week's rent which was ten dollars. The landlord even picked us up and took us to his house. I kept working in the cemetery. However, the gravedigging lasted only a week, and I was promoted to mowing the lawn along with my friend. There we were pushing machines around with one hand and with the other I held a dictionary, trying to learn English. Another friend of mine was hired as well, and we worked together for months.

One evening I went home, dead tired, and there was a French couple visiting the landlord. We began talking and believe me, it wasn't easy with the language problem we had. The man asked me what I was doing and how much I was getting. All I received was eighty-five cents an hour and he told me he knew someone in construction who would pay me a dollar an hour. A dollar seemed like a fortune to me. It was then I remembered the rumours I had heard in Austria and disbelieved. I found out the hard way how true they were.

He made a phone call and then took me down to a restaurant on Ontario and St. Denis Streets where a man was waiting for us. He hired me on the spot. It was a hell of a job. I worked at covering wood-frame houses with bricks or stone. What I did was mix the cement, carry it up a ladder, one or two storeys high, come down, carry the bricks up, run down, mix the cement, back up, down, up that ladder . . . by the time noon came around, I was so tired, I couldn't even eat my sandwiches. I couldn't swallow from exhaustion. This lasted a couple of months, and then the bosses went off to Belgium and one of their relatives offered me a job making imitation stone. In a couple of months I was such an expert, putting this stuff on a house and spraying it, that I was doing it all myself while my employer sat in the truck drinking beer. We had so much work at one point that he hired half a dozen guys and I became the foreman. He liked me and wanted me to stay with him.

"We're going to make it big," he said, but no way was I going to spend my life doing this kind of work. I was an engineer. So I found another job in the stock room of an electronics plant. They imported the parts and then the radios, record players, etc., were put together at the factory.

My mother sent my diploma from Hungary. After five years I applied to become a member of the Order of Engineers. The Hungarian University for Engineers is world-famous. So finally I was getting back to my profession. I got another job working for a company that built custom-made machinery for business forms. First I was assistant-head engineer, then I went to another firm as chief engineer, and now I am with a very large, multi-national company. I finally made it, but somehow I don't feel that I did enough, that maybe I didn't have enough ambition. I just drifted with the current. I always wanted to go into the fast-food line and I am still thinking about it. Maybe I will do it one day.

I went back to Hungary in 1975 and found everything there so strange. I could find my way around Montreal so much better than I could in Budapest. The people I had known there before were no longer my friends. The feeling was different, and I knew there was nothing for me there. The customs seemed to be different, and I felt totally lost — like a stranger. It was then I realized that Canada was more my country than Hungary. When I left, I realized that I had changed and my goodbye to my homeland was final.

I love Canada; it's a great and beautiful country!

Max R. de Bruyn

A SEARCH FOR IDENTITY

by Max R. de Bruyn

MOTHER'S STORY

The morning of November 11, 1944 in Rotterdam was bright and cold. As I rolled up the blackout shades of our corner bedroom, I found myself looking directly into the barrel of a machine gun mounted on the sidewalk below the window. Bernard, his face chalk-white, came into the room. He shook his head for he knew there was no time for him to hide anywhere. The house was surrounded.

We heard a loud banging at the front door, and two S.S. officers entered. I did not feel panic-stricken — just cold and dead. The officers were doing their duty. They had caught a dangerous enemy, but they were courteous about it. They told Bernard to say good-bye to me and the children and turned their backs while he did so.

The rest of the day was a nightmare. Soldiers came and searched the house for hidden radios and other evidence while most of the neighbourhood men in the same situation were taken away in what we called a "Razzia". During the afternoon other German soldiers came and ransacked closets and cupboards. I asked them where they were taking the men.

"They are all to be taken to the Bus barn," said one of the soldiers.

"Could I possibly see my husband there?"

He looked at me. "Yes, if you are brave enough."

My sister Jo came, and we packed warm clothes and food for Bernard and then prepared ourselves for the hour's walk to the Bus barn. The children were warmly dressed, Max in the carriage, with Paul sitting at his feet. The parcel for their father was tucked between them.

We discovered we weren't the only brave ones when we arrived. There was such a crowd of women that the Germans turned fire hoses on us to spray us away. Soaking wet and bitterly cold, we somehow managed to get into the barn and see the streetcars lined up and filled with men, all driven from their homes by an occupying force whose last desperate attempt was to break the spirit of a proud people.

Jo and I took turns yelling Bernard's name as we walked along the lines of streetcars. Jo found him. Although guards with guns were everywhere, we managed to get the parcel to him, and I was allowed to say good-bye once more. He gave me his wedding ring to wear and made me promise to protect the children. Our good-byes were even sadder for we knew we probably would not see each other again. We left without looking back and returned to a very cold and empty house.

Things went downhill rapidly. I moved in with my parents, joined the soup lines and waited and waited that long, horrible winter of 1944.

Shortly before Christmas a girl on a bicycle called on us. She was a courier, one of the unsung war heroines, carrying verbal messages from our underground Dutch forces to other groups to maintain contact between them. She handed over a parcel with bacon, flour and rapeseed oil, a contribution from my uncle Geuko to his hungry relatives. The courier's message was that this would be the last parcel because the Nazis were holding the Yssel* river and its bridges. No one could get across. But if someone had the courage to try, he would be welcome in his home.

At this point a decision had to be made. The city was in ruins from the bombing, there was very little food to be had and with no husband to help me obtain the essentials, I decided to go rather than wait and starve.

On January 5, 1945, I left Rotterdam on foot, pushing a baby carriage containing my youngest son and a few meagre belongings while my oldest son walked beside me, holding on to the carriage. In my womb an unborn fetus gave a greater urgency to my flight. I left behind me the devastation caused by the combined bombing of Allies and Germans while inside I felt the emotional devastation of not knowing where my husband had been taken in retaliation for his underground activities.

There were many other refugees on the road, ill-dressed for the cold weather. I had to beg for hot water to prepare the children's powdered food. I had barely reached my uncle's farm when he, too, joined the ranks of internees along with many others as the Nazi soldiers continued to pick up all able-bodied men.

My final refuge found me in the village of Midwolda* where I was liberated by a Polish division on April 15, 1945. My limited knowledge of English was enough to get me a job as an interpreter to the Polish commander whose minute English vocabulary was infinitely better than his knowledge of Dutch. For this I received the squadron's sewing machine, a bar of bath soap and a bar of chocolate. I had not tasted the latter for years.

*Ijssel in eastern Holland.

*About 30 km. east of Groningen.

After the ceasefire on May 6, 1945, I stood waiting by the highway leading through the village, asking all emaciated skeletons coming from various liberated concentration camps if they knew my husband and had seen him. I knew he had been taken to Germany for he managed to drop a message on a scrap of paper from the train taking him there. It had been found by a member of the underground and delivered to me by courier.

Meanwhile my husband had reached the border from Nordhausen camp near Leipzig where he had been interned. He avoided compulsory quarantine for returnees, when a fellow churchman working at the border station found him and took him home. Bernard's first night in his home country found him dressed in his host's carefully preserved wedding suit, attending a birthday party. Bernard's clothing was in tatters. At the party he was told there were no Rotterdam survivors. They had either been killed by the bombardment or had died of starvation.

But Bernard was certain that I had fled before that and had probably gone to my family in the north. Somewhere he obtained a bicycle and set out to find me.

I had given up my vigil on the road, not only because I feared the worst but because my advanced pregnancy made it difficult for me to stand for any length of time. Without my knowledge my youngest cousin Edzo, fifteen, had taken over my post.

On one of the very last days of May, Edzo came running home. We heard the clattering sound of his patched wooden shoes. Because of our dietary deficiencies, we all had diarrhea. Edzo had it worse than all of us, and we thought he was merely running for the outhouse again.

His eyes were sparkling, his face beet-red as he shouted: "Bernard is coming!" I was thunderstruck, unable to move and sure enough there came a bicycle rider on a bike with no tires peddling up our sandy country lane. I did not recognize this man whom I had known for nine years. He probably weighed no more than 100 pounds. His face a deep bronze, he sported a moustache and was wearing a pair of American army fatigue pants and a German uniform jacket over a bare torso. Those were his only clothes.

The reunion was short-lived. A few days later on June 8, 1945, I went into labour. Bernard found a cart and horse and set out for the nearest hospital. The horse had to be coaxed all the way and by the time we arrived, I was ready to deliver. The hospital was short-staffed and had no doctor, so Bernard delivered his daughter Didy himself. He had been unaware that I was pregnant when he left.

Ten days after Didy's birth, we rode back to Rotterdam on top of a load of potatoes. It took 24 hours to return — 24 hours without food or water. My milk had run dry so that when we arrived at the home we left eight months earlier, the first thing we did was send for the doctor who helped us revive a tiny baby who was so weak she had to be fed with an eyedropper.

MY STORY

These were my parents. I was two years old.

Shortly after this period, my parents began to attend some evening meetings which were not church-related. I couldn't help overhearing some of the conversation. I heard that someone had approached my father, who had appeared troubled, and had told him he looked like a typical prospect for emigration.

As time went on, literature appeared in our home about a strange place called Canada. There were beautiful pictures of mountains, lakes and large open spaces without canals, church steeples and windmills. The grandest sight of all for a kid mesmerized by cowboys was a picture of a Mountie on horseback with Lake Louise as a backdrop.

Something else happened to make emigration even more inviting. My father had put down a sum of money on a store, and when the owners heard about emigration plans to Canada, they demanded immediate payment. Banking arrangements could not be made, and somehow the store reverted to its original owners with my father forfeiting his down payment.

I was in second grade and suddenly the word "immigration" became a catalyst and reason for everything that could go wrong in my short life. Emigration was the reason I no longer lived in a nice home in a fashionable district, and it was the reason my father was pushing a heavy milk cart on a daily route instead of standing behind the counter in his own store.

This bleak picture of reality was embellished by constant tales of better things in a faraway land waiting for people like my father — a land waiting to give him a job, a home and a bright future.

One night at the kitchen table I overheard my Dad say that the man at Immigration told him the only thing he needed to take to Canada was a good pair of coveralls and workboots because they couldn't be bought there. "Why should he take things to Canada that he didn't need in his own country?" I thought. "Why should we leave behind all the things we enjoyed?" Dad had warned us that we might not have carpeted floors in Canada. He said the average home had packed earthern floors which were cleaned and swept with a broom made of twigs. And here we were using a vacuum cleaner on our floors.

That summer I went to my maternal grandparents' house for school vacation, but my stay was short. The realization of leaving came the day my grandmother asked me to help with a large package with which she was struggling. When I asked what it was, she gathered me in her arms and with tears rolling down her wrinkled cheeks said it was a traveling crib for my baby brother to use on our voyage to Canada. We would be leaving in a few days by boat. There was no feeling of saying good-bye to everything that was familiar. Instead, there was a sense of excitement for the great adventure ahead.

My grandmother dressed me that sunny day in June, and as I walked ahead of them, I realized my grandparents were sharing a feeling of loss. I do not remember giving my grandparents a good-bye kiss. If I had known that emigration was going to take me away from my beloved grandparents forever, perhaps I would not have been so blind to all the emotion that was taking place around me. I couldn't understand those silly women crying at the dock and my Dad unable to talk to us and answer the barrage of questions because he had developed problems with his voice and couldn't speak.

How much strength was required to walk up the gangplank that day into the unknown and stand at a rail watching familiar landmarks glide by as the ship's PA system played a version of "Auf Wiedersehen" over and over again!

The ship contained people from every region of Holland and every walk of life. Most, however, were from rural areas and thus were mesmerized by the intricacies of formal dining table layouts, strange fare and other attitudes like religion and the functions of indoor plumbing.

The problem of strange meals didn't last too long because once the ship reached open water, seasickness became an epidemic, and the dining room was virtually deserted except for a few with hardy stomachs. My father was bunking with six other men in the lowest deck of cabins, and the stench was terrible.

All things considered, the seven-day voyage from Rotterdam to Halifax was like a vacation except when my brother had his front teeth knocked out after he lost his footing on the pitching deck and smashed into the guardrail. A foot to the right and he would have been overboard.

When land was sighted and we crowded to the rail to see Halifax in the distance, I recall a sense of impending dread descending, not only over me but the entire ship's company.

This was why we had all come. This was the first sign of the Promised Land. The last trace of Holland would be removed like an umbilical cord cut to separate mother and child. When we walked down that gangplank, the connection with the motherland would be severed.

We spent the last evening on board the ship tied at the dock. The new day and a new dawn beckoned us to proceed — to begin a new life in a new land with the same God to be our inspiration and our mental support. It was June 28, 1952.

We walked down the gangplank to a large dock-side warehouse and into a processing procedure that resembled a Friday auction at the stockyards. Herded and harrangued like cattle, we left the warehouse and had our first look at the train which would take us to our destination. The pullman we were assigned to had probably been used as a troop carrier by Canadians during the war. The seats were wooden uprights, the berth a platform that pulled away from the ceiling and contained a blanket of coal soot.

The Dutch are obsessed with cleaniness, and horror was clearly marked on the faces of the mothers when they saw their surroundings after the sterile cleanliness of the ship. The scrubbed pink-faced children wearing their Sunday best for the first day in the new land were soon reduced to a rag-tag mob of chimney sweeps.

Perhaps it was a breakdown in communications or the language barrier, but we heard that the only food available on the trains would be sold by a vendor roaming the aisles. The limited variety of soggy sandwiches and packaged candy was not the kind of sustinence we needed for days of travel. Therefore, my father with his limited command of English set out into the streets of Halifax to look for groceries.

I do not remember the shop's name, but word of mouth must have provided the owner with the biggest bonanza of shoppers he'd ever had. The store was crammed with Dutchmen using the international language of gestures and facial contortions common to all who are unable to communicate. We came out of there with a few bags of food purchased with the strange new currency of our new land. Our money supply was extremely limited and intended for dire emergencies. But this undoubtedly was one. We returned to the train with a supply of bread, butter, jam and peanut butter, but the joy was diminished when we first tasted the mushy white stuff that passed for bread and the alien taste of strongly salted butter. And when we realized there were others on the train who didn't have Canadian currency, sharing what we had became a Christian duty.

The trainload of people who left Halifax that day were a far cry from those who had disembarked full of hope and expectations. The railway car was a picture of filth and despair. Sickness, hunger, wailing infants and disgruntled aged were totally ignored by we enlightened young. Embracing lovers and quarreling partners were equally disdained. For us this was a great adventure. We were not going to let adults and crying babies ruin it for us.

Two days later this monotonous journey finally ended on a railway station platform in Chatham, Ontario. There was a clear sky, and bright sunshine streamed down on our forlorn little group as we waited for the reception committee which didn't arrive for a long, long time. Finally two young men showed up and loaded us into two cars with our baggage. After a long drive, we arrived at a nice home on a tree-lined street, which I thought was to be our new home. Instead the house belonged to the minister of the Dutch Reformed Church, and the reason for the long drive, which should have taken only ten minutes, was that the young men didn't know what to do with us. So they just kept driving around until my father insisted we be dropped off somewhere. Thus we cooled our heels at the minister's house sitting on our suitcases until we were loaded back into the cars for another journey. We were taken to the countryside of Kent County, and when we turned into the lane of a farm, it certainly wasn't what we had expected. I can understand the shock my parents must have felt to have come this far and paid such a terrible price for this.

The laneway was deeply rutted and the land totally overgrown. Probably it had not been maintained for a long time. The house itself was in desperate need of repair. There were leaning doors, hanging eavestroughs and grey clapboard siding. Except for the telltale path leading to the outhouse a few feet from the water pump, the place looked totally uninhabited.

We learned to our distress that we had to share accommodations with another family of immigrants who had arrived from the Netherlands only seven weeks before. They were not at home and were totally unaware they were having houseguests who were already standing at their locked door.

My mother set up a bit of lunch on a sheet on the grass, making the most out of what was obviously a terrible situation. My brother and I went exploring and as my father suggested to the sheepish-faced young men that we go back to Chatham, the family living in the house drove up and found their front yard occupied.

Our hosts were humble people, but they did what they could to make the best of the situation. There was very little furniture in the house. We were shown to a barren back kitchen. My mother put us to work immediately to get our minds off the day's disappointments. We had left a comfortable home, a loving family and a familiar country to come to a desolate farm in a foreign land and share a dilapidated farmhouse with another immigrant family whose ideas and lifestyle were totally foreign to us. We were not to have a home of our own, and my father had no job. For this we had paid $5,000 as crossing fare and entry fee. The dream had vanished, the voyage was over and the adventure had ended. Reality was a grim taskmaster.

Mother sent us out to find straw for the mattress covers she had brought with her in case we encountered unhygenic mattresses. At least we would have a soft place to sleep, softer than the hard wooden benches we had slept on the past few nights in the train.

There was no indoor plumbing, and we had a new experience with the pump. Our hostess showed us how to prime it and how to tie a small linen bag around the spout as a filter to catch the flakes of rust. We had to bathe in a large pan filled with cold water, casting aside all thoughts of privacy in the need to be clean after the two days of travel and oppressive heat.

As a fitting conclusion to one hell of a day, a violent thunderstorm capped the humid summer evening — a storm that scared the living daylights out of us. The violence of the elements probably helped my father express his anger for the shattering of his dream. I can only guess what words my parents exchanged that night. Years later my mother told me.

They spoke of that last farewell, waving to her family who were standing on top of their car at the end of the road as the ship made its way past the hook of land to the sea. Her mother was wearing a light green coat and waving a large, red headscarf.

"Whenever I hear that tune 'Auf Wiedersehen' I still see her there because it was the last time I saw her in this life. It still hurts," she said.

"As soon as the coast of Holland was behind us, your Dad and I walked hand in hand to the bow of the ship and decided we would not look back. We were going to a new country and even if we did not know what lay ahead, it was going to be our future. If we were new immigrants, we would be the best immigrants that Canada had ever laid eyes on."

The shared accommodation was part of an agreement our hosts had with a farmer for whom they were sharecropping. My father felt guilty about sharing their house and meagre food supply and volunteered to work with them. But after two days, they asked him not to go again or they would be finished too soon. They were paid by the field. I went the second day, but I botched my first attempt at thinning sugar beets.

The following day Dad went looking for a house for us without the aid of newspapers, transportation and no idea where to hunt. His implicit faith in the Almighty must have been rewarded because he returned a proud man to tell us he had found a nice place. We closed our suitcases which we had been living out of, and were ready to move the next morning to a humble frame house. For us it was a palace because it was our own.

Our house was on a farm near the hamlet of Florence. The owners, Mr. and Mrs. Stacey, lived in a new house on the other side of the vegetable garden. It was their assistance and sympathy that allowed us to overcome the setbacks and prepare ourselves for our new life in Canada. I say this because up to this point there had been no assistance from the very people we thought would give us direction and a foothold.

To explain our profound disappointment one must understand the system of immigration at that time which required a new immigrant to have a sponsor who would ensure a job and house on arrival. This had been arranged, and we had been on our way to Leamington, Ontario, where a house and job were waiting for my father. As a draftsman he would be working in an automobile manufacturing plant. But when we were in the middle of the Atlantic ocean, my father received a cable from a former minister he had known in Rotterdam. It advised him that for the sake of the church it was my father's duty to go to Chatham where a new congregation was being set up.

Anyone outside the Dutch Protestant community would not understand this. The Dutch take their religion so seriously that they believe their church is the only ticket to salvation. Great rivalries existed in the Netherlands between the Protestant denominations, and whatever the "Dominee" said was accepted as Gospel. This rivalry and pastoral influence was transplanted to the new world, creating a competition to stock the flocks of the Reformed Church, Christian Reformed Church, Free Christian Reformed Church and the Canadian Reformed Church. That was how my father answered the call to the Free Christian Reformed Church of Chatham.

I have never been able to understand the differences and obviously neither could this particular minister for he changed his name and denomination back and forth before he was called upon to explain the difference to his ultimate Master.

My father followed blindly as he had been taught from infancy, and that was how the minister came to send his son to drive us around Chatham while our fate was being decided by the minister and his family. The new congregation appreciated the addition of new members to the flock so much that not one offered any assistance whatsoever in helping us find a place to live. The first time we saw the minister was when he came to pick us up for church on Sunday and honked his horn at the end of the lane — the shepherd calling his flock. I have tried hard not to hate him, but reliving this memory does not help that resolve.

The ride home afterward was usually the result of an argument between members as to who would be saddled with the job of returning us to the farm.

Our neighbour across the road was a member of this congregation and he gave my Dad a job working in his fields weeding acres of beans and tomatoes with an ordinary hoe. I remember my father coming home in agony after all day in the sun with burns so bad right through his workshirt that he should have been hospitalized.

As soon as Dad heard an airbase was being built in Centralia and labourers were required, he applied. But he would have to board away during the week and come home weekends. Home was a place without furniture. Our crate had gone to Leamington first, and the railway people had lost track of Bernard de Bruyn and his family.

With Dad gone, our food supply dwindled to boiled barley and the blueberries we picked. When Mrs. Stacey, our landlady, walked over and saw what we were eating, she offered us the peaches which had fallen from her tree. Shortly after, Mr. Stacey came by and said he had bought a cow and would teach my brother to milk. In payment we could have all the milk and cream from the morning's milking. Now Mr. Stacey needed another cow like he needed another leg, but how could he allow a proud family on his property to live on nothing but thin barley? So now we had come to a land of milk and honey, and my mother joked when writing home to Holland how rough things were, but that even when we were broke we could have peaches and cream.

My brother and I became good friends with our Canadian neighbours who took us under their wing and tried to teach us English. But I spent more time weeding in a neighbour's garden, and she would treat me to a new-found delight — freshly baked apple pie and a glass of ice-cold freshie from the fridge. It was three years before we had a refrigerator. I didn't worry too much about learning English because my stomach came first. Mrs. Stacey just smiled a lot and I smiled back. Her cooking and I got along famously.

The crate with our belongings was eventually found in a freight car at a siding in Thamesville. Mom had to coax our neighbour across the road to take his tractor and flatbed wagon to pick up the crate and bring it home. There was no delivery service like today. Along with the crate came a government inspector for the seal had to be broken in his presence. He examined every item that was removed and kept repeating the same word with each thing. Although mom knew enough English to understand, she couldn't make out what he was trying to say. Finally the inspector got angry and said: "Damned immigrants! I try to speak their bloody language, and they still don't understand."

Our neighbour straightened it out. The inspector kept asking "Flesh?" when he meant to say "Fleish" which is meat in German. But meat is "Vlees" in Dutch, and he thought we should have answered "no" to all his questions. He wanted to know if we had any meat in the crate.

As if that wasn't enough, we saw what care had been taken of our belongings. Piece after piece came out of that crate with some form of damage or another. My mother had lived for the day that crate would be delivered so she could make this strange house in a strange land into a home surrounded with familiar things. As it was, there were precious few for my parents had sold most of their belongings to pay the costs of emigration.

Dad didn't stay at Centralia very long because he couldn't make enough money. Shortly after he was lured by the promise of fabulous wealth in the tobacco harvest — double salary and prosperity. But the reality of dealing with life on a tobacco farm during the harvest with all the transient labourers and their alien behaviour soon proved why good money was being paid for this back-breaking work.

From picking tobacco we went to picking tomatoes. We all worked and enjoyed it and could eat all we wanted. Unfortunately, the job didn't last long. There was a freak hailstorm over the weekend, which flattened the crop and when we arrived on Monday to try and salvage something under a broiling sun, the nauseating smell of rotting tomatoes hung in the air. Since that day I have not been able to eat tomatoes.

Letters from home came regularly, but it reached the point where I hated to see the postman putting mail in our box. Mom would disappear and come back with red eyes. We were all homesick, and it wasn't until my grandfather wrote a few words to me that I realized how much we missed the family. There were times I asked myself why my parents didn't crawl back on their hands and knees and go home. What monumental pride kept them from admitting they had made a mistake in coming to Canada?

Why didn't they go back to family and friends, back to a home with toilets and proper bathrooms, public transportation and stores with all the things they loved to buy? Why didn't they go back so they could dress in the latest fashion to walk to church on Sunday instead of being hassled by Christian brothers and sisters over a ride? They could have returned to a home where they tucked children into beds covered with proper bedclothes instead of a straw bag. Why couldn't my father go back to a land where he had always been able to provide a comfortable existence and a warm hearth for his family?

As a married man and after so many years, I still ask those questions because I know what kind of agony I would go through to leave a secure profession and income for the unknown. While I can appreciate my father's implicit faith in the Almighty, did he stay for the church in Chatham? They didn't care. He was just a statistic. After going through the unspeakable deprivations of a Nazi labour camp, why did he voluntarily put himself through virtual slave labour when all he had to do was pack up and go back?

We began school that September and with a bravado we did not feel, went off waving good-bye to Mom standing at the mailbox. There were four grades in my classroom, and the teacher was an old woman who didn't like to move her considerable bulk any more than she had to. The kids had to come to her desk for assignments and lessons. I didn't know this and stayed in my seat except when I saw all the kids leaving the room. Then I followed them.

But a funny thing happened that puzzled me. Some of the children would wave their hands in a very agitated manner and yell a funny word. After considerable waving, jumping and squirming, the teacher would acknowledge them and they would leave the classroom.

When we arrived home that day, mom asked us about our experiences, and my sister Didy and I decided we should tell her about this peculiar behaviour because we might be missing something. So we imitated what we had seen and yelled that funny word. It sounded like "Mayliedrom". That night we had a family council with my older brother and again had to seek the advice of a neighbour who came up with the answer after I went through all the motions.

You can imagine how many times that story was told, retold and laughed at by everyone who heard it, but how I envied those kids because there were times I had to go to the bathroom and didn't know how to ask.

I must admit I was disappointed that the teacher and rest of the class did not offer some assistance in translating. There were other Dutch kids who could have explained the routine. It wasn't until very much later that I understood why they hadn't. The children reflected the parents' attitudes and that was to give us space to acclimatize ourselves to this foreign environment and system. All I had to do was ask, and they would have answered.

Just as I was getting used to this new system of multi-grades in one room, we found we were moving. Dad started talking about a new job somewhere else, and one day an old friend who had been a colleague on the Rotterdam Police Force turned up with a truck. The loading began and toward evening when a cold wind was blowing the dry golden leaves of the soft maple on the lawn, I climbed into the pickup truck amongst our furniture and watched the house disappear through the cracks of the homemade racks. I said my good-byes to the house I had grown to love as a home and good-bye to that big old tree sitting in the middle of the large front lawn. For some reason I didn't want to leave it.

The trip from Florence to Lynden, Ontario was not very pleasant. Halfway through the city of London it began to snow. By the time we arrived I was cold and stiff. We stayed in Lynden for a few days until Dad arrived with the rest of the household effects and then went to our new residence on a farm near Copetown. Most of our first winter in Canada was spent on that farm. It was to be a difficult one. School was not pleasant because of the language problem and the strange customs and traditions of the Christmas season. We had always celebrated the coming of St. Nicholas on December 5 with Dutch religious carols. Now we were learning new songs like "Jingle Bells" and "White Christmas" and thought it sacrilegious to mix these with "Silent Night" and "Away in a Manger".

Our Christmas tree was a scrub pine we decorated with popcorn and coloured paper. We even made window decorations and a door wreath. Our landlady gave little Benny a toy, and we shared his joy for it was to be the only toy this first Christmas of 1952 in the new land.

During our stay in Copetown, Dad bought our first car, a '28 or '29 Plymouth. He bought it from a Dutchman, and it didn't run too long after the purchase. There was no guarantee. It was just another form of assistance extended by one of our former countrymen.

The winter layoff forced dad to get another job with a businessman in Sheffield. The man had bought a farm in Puslinch Township and needed a man to work and live there. He came to pick us up and deliver us with our belongings. The house turned out to be a dilapidated log cabin with a few clapboard additions. Words fail me in describing it, but I do know that we had hit bottom. The old car died trying to climb the hill to the house and stayed there. So did we.

It has been said no man is an island, but let me assure you that this family was an island, virtually isolated for the time we stayed on that farm. The owner of the place also had a grocery store in Sheffield so my mother would order what she needed, not wanted, and then he would bring out what he thought she needed and deduct the price from Dad's wages.

That summer our first real Canadian was born. My little brother Ed was born in a hospital, the first to have that distinction. Dad had to walk and hitchhike to Galt to visit mother and his new son. The old car still sat where it had died. I discovered later what an effect all these problems were having on my father. On one of those trips from the maternity ward, he was so terribly tired that he went to a parked car in front of a house. Had he been able to start it, he would have stolen it. That was how desperate he was. He had to go home to a young family left alone in the sticks without adult supervision, and he had doubts as to whether he was well enough physically to make it back. I remember that night. My brother Paul and I waited anxiously while the hours dragged by and finally I crawled into my parents' bed, knowing his return would awaken me. I opened my eyes to see him on his knees at the side of the bed, and he stayed that way for a long time. Knowing him the way I did, he probably was asking forgiveness for even contemplating the theft of that car.

We moved again in August to the village of Lynden, and that house was our first step to a normal existence. It was on a street with sidewalks and it had a fence, a proper kitchen and central gravity furnace. But there was no sink or running water, and the pump was usually dry. The furnace had a voracious appetite, but at least we had a proper home. Dad was working on a construction site, and mom had some neighbours to talk to.

It seemed we had survived that period of probation other immigrants had described. Dad worked at various jobs — delivering coal in the city of Hamilton without a driver's licence, as a labourer, and at a service station maintenance company. There was a period of unemployment when he quit his job to go to another on the advice of a Dutch colleague. It turned out his friend had the wrong information because he didn't know enough English.

Finally Dad got word about a job near Peterborough, and my parents went to check it out. They came back with a glowing account of the work, wages and a house waiting for us. Mom would be able to work as well and assured us of a good income. Off we went again arriving late at night at a farm in the hamlet of Ida. We were met by the owner and his family who had prepared a table loaded with food for the weary travelers.

At last I was in a real Canadian kitchen with polished linoleum tiles, sparkling white appliances, two chrome water faucets and a stainless steel sink. Sitting down at the table was an unnerving experience because it seemed as if we were on display. I was conscious of our appearance because of our clothes when our hosts were standing there in the finest traditions of Canadian affluence. Didy didn't react well and wouldn't eat. It seemed as if she was making a spectacle of herself by not liking these alien dishes and sandwiches. Noticing her discomfort, Mrs. McIndoo Sr. asked Didy if she would like something that wasn't on the table. Didy asked for a peanut butter sandwich. It was her way of coping with a fishbowl situation.

In this environment of hospitality and friendship, I began to recover from the last eighteen months of hardship, grief, loneliness, homesickness and ridicule. I developed a fierce pride and determination to work toward a real identity and to come back some day and repay these good people for their love and kindess. It was apparent from that time on that we had truly arrived in Canada and were ready to be like these Canadians sharing their table and home with us. The next step was integration.

Life was difficult, but my parents found their salvation in work, an ethic common to most immigrants. For me work would be the means of developing an identity as far removed from the Dutch immigrant as possible. What I didn't know was that this quest would only cause me to deny my heritage and push me toward anonymity.

In our home, the language was Dutch along with all its traditions. Therefore, we would not be allowed to watch TV on Sunday. We would always be different because we didn't go to the United Church on the corner like the others. Instead we drove to Peterborough twice every Sunday to attend services in the Y.M.C.A. gymnasium given by and for Dutch people. It wasn't so much a matter of affording a TV. The danger was in bringing the devil into our home by way of the screen. We heard this from the pulpit, and it wasn't difficult to understand the dangers of TV when we were forbidden on religious grounds to go to the movies as well.

It was hard for a youngster to understand because all I wanted was the Canadian way of life and that didn't seem immoral. As a family we had good contacts with the neighbours, and all appeared to be well, but the separation came on Sunday when we went to a different church. I couldn't understand why this double trip every Sunday was so necessary. It made my Canadianization so much harder for when I said my prayers to God, they were in Dutch. I had grown up speaking to God in that language, and it didn't seem right to speak to Him in any other tongue. I was living in two worlds, even in religion.

In due time I began to realize that for these immigrants their God provided a social function for meeting their fellow countrymen. He was there not so much to maintain their heritage, but to allow them to share their experiences in this strange and sometimes savage land.

Outside our home I was striving for acceptance as an equal. I thought to do this I would have to stand out and do everything a little better than the others. In that respect I was successful. At home everything was dominated by church activities, and everything in it smacked of another culture, another time. I wanted no part of it, and Paul and I would find ourselves defending this country, its customs and its people from parents who were only trying to maintain a portion of their heritage within the four walls of their modest little home. It wasn't what they had been accustomed to before emigation, and it wasn't their own home, but it was in this place that the real integration of cultures began.

Slowly the traditional recipes of the community superceded the old Dutch recipes. More English was spoken at home, and after my parents bought an old upright tread-pedal organ which mother would play on Saturday afternoons, we would sing not only hymns of Holland but those translated into English and United Church hymns. She was a busy woman with a large family to which additions came regularly. She worked during the day sorting eggs and did the housework without the modern conveniences. It was fascinating watching those work-roughened hands make such beautiful music on the organ's keyboard.

The months became years full of normal life events. A brother and sister were born while another baby didn't make it out of the hospital. The community got together and plowed snow from miles of road by hand so mom could come home from the hospital when the municipal plow couldn't get through the drifts. There were deaths, sad deaths, because they were announced by way of telegram from Holland, and there wasn't enough money for airfare to attend funerals. Our grandparents went to their graves without ever seeing their children again.

Work on the farm was constant, but it helped us become a part of something — a small identity perhaps but an important one nonetheless. By the time my brother and I were in our early teens, we were doing a man's job along with the other hired hands. We were a part of the farm and farming community.

I have said earlier that I lived in two worlds. Actually I was living in three. One was away from home, the second was at home and the third was an obsessive, imaginative world into which I would withdraw with clockwork regularity. Early in the evening, particularly in winter, I would dive into bed upstairs and in the darkness I would become someone else. This imaginary world began to consume more and more time, and I earned the reputation of being a loner. Only when I developed a fascination for the opposite sex did my imaginary world begin to decline. I went through all the stages of puppy love and it was a problem because the girls I met and played with on Sunday were a different breed from the ones at school.

That last year in elementary school, a new family moved into the area. We heard they were on welfare, which was a foreign term to us. There were a lot of children, and they lacked good manners and were not too clean either. Two of the boys called me a name I had not heard in a long time. They were ill-mannered, ill-groomed and ill-fed, yet they called me a D.P. regularly. I should have realized they were only repeating what they had heard at home, but it didn't matter. It still hurt terribly, and when the term caught on among the others, it became a battle cry which resulted in some violent episodes. The words, "Displaced Person", were like waving a red flag at me. It became an expression applied to all immigrants and it was galling. We certainly didn't go through all those trials and tribulations to be harassed by a few dummies who were mean and spiteful. When I was older, I was able to deal with it better and could agree with a contemporary interpretation which described D.P. as a delayed pioneer.

Graduation came and I was on my way to high school in the city. It was a totally different life. I was in heaven for I was one of "them" during the day.

But I discovered the term D.P. was more common here, and those who used it learned to regret it. I achieved some notoriety, and it became difficult to hide the telltale signs of these scuffles. Some of the teachers would ride me about it, but at home I could always blame my disheveled clothing on playing football at school. It was accepted but not appreciated.

Another problem was the dress code — blue blazer and greys, but my parents couldn't afford it. My brother had to go through it, but by the time I entered, the rules had been eased as long as no one wore blue jeans or cords. Because my wardrobe was limited, I regularly visited the vice-principal's office where detentions were handed out for violating the dress code. It became easier to develop the tag of rebel rather than reveal our financial position or ask my parents for things they couldn't afford.

From the vice-principal's office I was sent to the guidance office where they spent a lot of time trying to talk me into conforming. If they only knew how much I wanted to be like the others and wear V-necked sweaters, spike pants and penny loafers. I wanted to go to the prom in a navy blue suit with a corsage for my date. I would have enjoyed wearing a blue blazer and crest for the school picture, but to admit this would have been an admission of poverty and that we were immigrants working our butts off to survive.

But I was still of dual nationality. The slightest mention of dating a Canadian girl brought admonishment and counselling. There was more of it in catechism classes every Friday night, and the same procedure would continue on Monday night when it was time for the Young People's meeting.

In past summers I had attended a church camp sponsored by our employer and the United Church. I had been a counsellor that last summer and as a result I was invited to attend a seminar held in Peterborough for counsellors.

It was my first convention and first lodging in a Canadian home. When they sang a song, I mouthed the words because I didn't know the lyrics. By the second refrain I had memorized them and sang louder than anyone. I called my sister at home to ask her what piece of cutlery to use after I saw my hostess set the table differently from the way my mother had. When I was informed I would have to say grace because I was a guest, I excused myself, went into the bathroom and translated from Dutch into English the prayer that dad used onto a piece of toilet paper. I hid it in my lap to read while all eyes were closed.

Because of that seminar, I was nominated to be the Peterborough representative for the Ontario Older Boys Parliament held annually at McMaster University in Hamilton. The honour didn't sink in until I arrived and saw the preparations and accommodations. I was to sleep in a college dorm, eat in the dining room and participate in a parliamentary debate with representatives from all over Ontario before a gallery of spectators. My picture and a quote would be printed in a major newspaper, and I was only fourteen years old.

Sunday morning found me reading a Scripture lesson in a huge church packed with people dressed in post-Christmas finery. It felt good to think that the kid from Peterborough, not the kid from Holland, was reading the Scriptures. It was an opportunity I would not have been permitted in my own church unless I was an elder. When bread was broken and the grape juice poured, I couldn't take it because it was not allowed in my church. The minister noticed my hesitation and whispered to me: "You have read to us from His word; now join us at His table."

I felt clean, whole and I could have walked on air. I was representing a Canadian church from a Canadian city participating in a Canadian tradition with Canadians! That night I prayed to my God for the first time in English.

When I arrived home I was informed that our minister had told my parents that I should be using my energies in our own church activities and not participate in the inter-denominational efforts to which I had just committed myself. Since then I have not participated in any major church-related activity other than singing in a choir, and it has been almost 26 years.

The following year was a disaster. I developed personality conflicts with two of my teachers and as the possibility of passing went from slim to remote, I stayed away from classes. Eventually the principal stopped by to say I would be doing everyone a favour by leaving and attending a fine agricultural school. One of my teachers even blamed my behaviour on my ethnic background. It was obvious I was going nowhere; therefore, my parents decided I should learn a trade as soon as I finished grade 10.

My first employer was a Dutch contractor who said he would teach me to be a carpenter, but the only thing he taught me was how to exploit your fellow countrymen for peanuts while he dangled promises before their noses. I quit and went to work for another Dutchman at $1.50 an hour, mixing concrete. But the job didn't last long and I was laid off. Standing in line at the unemployment office was another education. It was 1959, and the lines were long and slow. Resentment was heavy, and it was directed at "all those God-damned D.P.s". They were at the root of all the problems and were taking jobs away from the deserving. I just stood and listened. I wondered what would have happened if they knew I was one of those D.P.s. I looked just like the others in line, but even here I couldn't lose my double identity.

There were a few more odd jobs here and there, and when an old friend came from Woodstock for a week-end visit, I asked if I could go back with him and look for work there. The family debated and finally agreed. And so I left home and was on my own at sixteen years of age.

Just before I left, I had filled in an application to join the Canadian Army. I wasn't in Woodstock long when the army called to say I was due for processing and had to return. I was told to go home and stay until September and then report to Ottawa. For the rest of the summer I worked with a construction company doing all the dirty jobs. The crew were all Indians, and I was the only non-Indian on the gang.

What would my father have thought of me? He had come to Canada so his children might have a better future, and here I was doing the same thing he had been when he first arrived in Canada.

We were usually paid before lunch on Friday, and all of us would disappear into the hotel bar and drink our lunch. If anyone questioned my age, all the guys would stand up and the waiter, intimidated by the rough-looking crew, would hurry away to get my order. My gang may have been a tough-looking bunch, but they became my friends. When I left, the leader shook my hand and told me to do well so I would never have to work like this again.

I had come full circle. I had become one with the real Canadians of this land and I was their friend.

On the September morning I left Peterborough by bus for Ottawa, my feelings were similar to those the day we left the docks of Rotterdam. This time, however, I was aware of my destination and what I would be doing. I was on my way to start a new life far from Dutch influence, farm chores, baby sitting and religious hypocrisy. I was going to become "somebody". I wondered if my parents had felt this way when they left the old country.

Someone met me at the Ottawa bus station, and I was taken to Depot No. 13 to meet the rest of the inductees. We became buddies and acted like men going off to war. But I felt good. No one asked me what country I was from — just what was my hometown.

I wanted to go into the Signal Corps because I was fascinated with radio transmitters. But when the officer reviewed my file, he said with apparent regret that I couldn't get the security classification because I was a foreigner.

I had not expected this. It was a blow.

Canadian citizenship took five years to attain, and then the applicant had to appear before a federal judge. I would have to answer questions on general knowledge about Canada, receive a certificate and take an oath of allegiance. My parents had been through this, and I had assumed I was included in the process as their child. When I told the officer my parents were Canadian citizens, he asked if I wanted to be one as well.

The look on my face must have spoken a thousand words. He asked me to wait while he checked to see what he could do. Later that day we entered a staff car and drove up to Parliament Hill. When we stepped out, a Mountie on duty saluted us, and I was ushered into an office to answer some questions. A tall, grey-haired lady came out of another office, smiled at me, shook my hand and said she was happy to meet me. After she left, the officer informed me I had just met Mrs. E. Fairclough, Minister of Immigration.

Once back at his office, he asked me to place my right hand on a Bible, raise my left and take the Oath of Allegiance. Then he shook my hand, welcoming me into the Canadian Army as a Canadian citizen. I was in a state of total euphoria. In one afternoon I had become a citizen, a member of the armed forces, had met a government minister, was going back to school and learn a fascinating trade. I was on my own in a Canadian institution and a full-fledged member of Canadian society . . . well, almost.

Because processing my citizenship papers cost $5, I was called a $5-recruit by one of my buddies during the second week of training. It was like a slap in the face, but I didn't react in my normal fashion for I had heard enough horror stories about army detention barracks and practices. I had seen some of the boys doing extra pack drill every night for committing minor infractions. But one day that term "$5-Canadian" was used by the wrong person at the wrong time, and he became the recipient of all my pent-up anger. I paid for that action many times over.

One of my buddies made me see what a fool I was to be so sensitive about my ethnic background. He told me to be proud that I had a document stating I was Canadian and I had to prove I was worthy of it. His citizenship was an accident of birth. That conversation, as we sat on the edge of my bunk in the barracks, changed my attitude from then on, and it enabled me to become friendly with a group of guys who came from all walks of life and ethnic backgrounds.

I discovered that my project of Canadianization, of assimilation, was all wrong. I had tried to identify with a single group and have a single identity. Even native Canadians preferred identification by tribe and council. A Canadian was one who had come from elsewhere along the line. Canada was a kaleidoscope of nationalities thrown together with a common purpose — to survive and become "somebody".

By the end of the first year, I was certain my citizenship was complete. My English was good, and my profanity was colourful and explicit. I was totally self-reliant and able to help others stand up for themselves where they had not been able to before. I wore the uniform of my country with pride, sang the national anthem and chided others for not being more nationalistic. I had become a citizen and had paid my dues, but the account was not yet closed.

By this time Dad had finally realized his dream which was the same for most Dutch immigrants. He had saved enough money and with the small inheritance he had received from his mother he bought his own farm.

This particular Christmas was to be the last in Dad's tenure as a hired hand for Mr. McIndoo. There was a certain amount of sadness that this happy association with these good people was to end. That Christmas eve the white clapboard house sat in the winter snow under a clear, cold starlight night. As I walked toward the warm glow of the bright windows, the snow crunched under my feet. I watched the smoke trail rising from the chimney almost vertically in the windless night. A good supply of wood had been stored in the garage for the big kitchen stove and the front room oilheater burned continuously — a luxury for us. There were new kitchen appliances and the pantry was brimming with a variety of treats in anticipation of the holiday. There was even a store of wine and liquor that hadn't been around our house for a long time partly because of lack of funds and partly because of the teetotal nature of the Dutch community.

Rising from a pile of colourfully wrapped presents, the tree stood majestically arrayed in the front room. This holiday was to be a festival of plenty, a religious experience combined with a newly gained affluence and membership in the community. We had much to be thankful for. It was to be a Christmas like the ones I had heard my schoolmates talking about for years. I felt like a nouveau riche.

On Christmas eve, dressed in our finest, we gathered around the tree and unwrapped the presents, enjoying each other's surprise and delights. The emotions of gratitude blurred many an eye that memorable evening. Dad read from St. Luke, and after the little ones went to bed, we stayed up late drinking spirits, eating the delicious traditional tidbits and drinking mother's rich coffee.

That night when I went to bed I thought how we had just celebrated a traditional Canadian-style Christmas in our own way. I was very happy. The two cultures were beginning to merge where it mattered the most.

Right after Boxing Day I was to return to base and had packed my gear into my car the night before. It sat in the garage, my most cherished possession, which I had inherited from my brother Paul. It was a blue 1953 Pontiac complete with "music, heat and four white feet". Dad's car had been taken to Oshawa by my brother that night, and I was assured of an easy start in the cold weather.

Very early in the morning, we were awakened by shouting. Mr. McIndoo, who lived on the other side of the lane, was yelling Dad's name over and over again.

"Ben, Ben, for God's sake, get out of the house! It's on fire!"

I got up to verify this alarm, and sure enough flames were casting an eerie glow against the solidly frozen window panes. I got dressed and miraculously we all made it downstairs past the roaring flames which had already consumed half the kitchen. Not long after we got outside, the second floor caved in. We were standing outside watching the place burn when dad mentioned how cold his feet were. I looked down and realized we were both standing up to the ankles in snow in our bare feet. I ran to the house and tried to break through the front window to salvage the FM radio Paul had given Mom for Christmas, but the heat and flames drove me back. I followed Dad back to the main house and watched the rest of the destruction.

It was the second time in my life I had seen Dad cry. The first was when my little sister had died of diphtheria in Holland. He stood there in anguish watching everything he and mom had worked so hard to attain go up in flames. I felt the loss of the car and everything in it as well as the future loss of mobility. How could I pass next Friday morning's inspection without a proper uniform and what about transportation getting back to base? It sounds terrible now, but age dictates a different set of priorities.

If there was any doubt about our family belonging to a community, it was dispelled by the way everyone combined to put us back on our feet in a short time. The clothes that came were taken out of closets and drawers. Household effects donated were functioning in homes of donors. Earl McCarroll, a neighbour who was dad's size, brought a sweater he had received from his wife that Christmas. It was still in its wrapper. He was not an isolated case. One final example was the insurance agent, a neighbour. Dad remembered the day after the fire he had forgotten to pay his fire insurance premium and was a week overdue. The next day we received the maximum coverage allowed under the policy with a handshake and best wishes.

To all the members of that community, one and all, went our thanks and love.

Another event occured while I was still in the army. I received a letter from Mom informing me that the people who had taken my father in after his liberation from the German concentration camp had emigrated to the United States and were coming to visit. Would I come home if at all possible? I got a week-end pass to meet these people who had played such an important and humane role in our family's past. Didy had corresponded with one of the daughters, and my sister and I played the role of host for the couple's daughter and son. I fell hopelessly in love that weekend. I gave her my squadron ring and we continued this long-distance courtship for a few years before I got tired of hitchhiking 1,400 miles on a week-end pass and decided to marry her. So much for my resolve not to marry a Dutch girl. By marrying one I had tied myself right back into the family's history.

While I was at Camp Petawawa, the entire pattern of my life and my family's changed when I received a call that Dad had been in a serious accident. I arrived to find him in intensive care. He had been cutting dead wood from fences and dragging the pieces across the snow with the tractor into the barnyard. The tractor had rotated backwards in a layered snowbank, pinning him underneath. Impaled by the muffler, he lay in the snow a long time before he was found. He had numerous injuries, frostbite, and his right leg, including the knee, was horribly crushed.

I got three months of extended compassionate leave from the army. The doctors I spoke to said there was no way Dad would ever walk again without the use of a prosthetic device, but he was adamant that he would walk again on his own. Eventually he did. Mother knew how long this period of convalescance would take, so she sold the farm and bought a house in the city. She got a job at the hospital as a nursing assistant. And when Dad had confounded them all and walked again, he got a job as an orderly in the same hospital. Sheer pride kept him mobile, and few people knew that he virtually had no knee, that one of his legs was shorter than the other. However, the constant agony was too much, and an operation forced him to retire a year before his 65th birthday.

It had taken eleven years and a lot of hard times, but these city folk from Rotterdam were finally back in a proper house in Peterborough, doing a job they enjoyed.

Eventually I did a stint overseas, wearing the sky-blue beret of the United Nations. After my return, I was much more appreciative of everything this beautiful country had to offer and had no patience for anyone who wished to discuss this land negatively. After five years I became disillusioned with army life and requested a discharge. My wife and I decided army life was not conducive to a happy marriage.

I applied to Peterborough's Fire and Police Departments and the Ontario Provincial Police. The fire department came through first, and on my 21st birthday, July 13, 1965, I started my new career at headquarters in Peterborough. I never forgot that first day for I was introduced to something I had not come across before.

After roll call I was shown the facilities and on my way past the duty office I heard the platoon chief ask the duty captain what the new man's name was again. The captain said: "Maxie Rosenbloom".

"Maxie Rosenbloom," shrieked the chief. "Well, I'll be . . . go to hell, First we let in the Micks and now they are hiring Kikes as well."

I had been prepared for ethnic bias, and this was my first confrontation with religious bias. It was my introduction to a very Orange department.

That day at coffee break one of the men asked me what I had disliked most about the army. My answer cast serious doubt about the parentage of all Military Police (meatheads). As soon as I finished my criticism, an officer stood up and left the kitchen. After his departure, my questioner informed me this man had been an M.P. during the Second World War. I managed to get through the rest of the day without putting my foot in my mouth again . . . until the afternoon coffee break. It was the same room, same table, same questioner and the same officer sitting within earshot. Trying to play it safe and wanting to vindicate myself, I described a small city in one of the western provinces in a very uncomplimentary fashion. The same officer stood and left immediately. I was informed, rather gleefully, that the place I had described was the officer's hometown.

The kitchen was in an uproar, and when I returned home that night, I had to explain to my wife how I had just blown my career with my big mouth. The following morning I was an hour late for work. We were newlyweds and didn't have an alarm clock. I was promptly informed that I was fired. Only an act of council could reinstate me. I went home with my tail between my legs and told my wife. How could I tell my parents? Thank goodness I didn't have to, for as soon as I got to their house there was a message waiting that the fire department was looking for me. I went back and was told I had been reinstated because no one had explained rules and regulations that first day.

That evening we bought an alarm clock and I was never late for work again.

The next thirteen years were happy, productive and satisfying. As a contributing member of the community, I had shed the cloak of immigrant status, or so I thought. A new challenge arose, and as I left the department for employment with the provincial government, one of my colleagues said his good-bye in the following manner: "Little Dutch boy makes good, eh?"

It didn't matter any more because those who truly counted had sent me congratulations and letters of regret on my leaving. However, that incident did bother me because I had worked so hard to become a Canadian and downplay my ethnic background. I had begun to hide my own identity trying to become someone else, until finally I realized that it was enough of a chore just to be myself.

Today I am the father of three daughters, two of whom are teenagers. Born and raised in Canada, they still look like typical Dutch girls — blonde, blue-eyed and tall. They ask many questions about Holland and sometimes state their displeasure at not having been taught the Dutch language. This happens especially when company arrives from The Netherlands, and they cannot understand the conversation.

On the surface we are a typical Canadian family, yet there is a difference. We are raising children in areas where we had no knowledge. We had no contact with aunts, uncles and cousins. We never saw grandparents. How can I tell my girls that this contact is available here?

There is a cultural split in our home. My estranged wife and I shared a common heritage, but our cultural differences are as different as day is to night. She was raised in Holland until, as a teen-ager, she came to live in the United States. I was raised in Canada by Dutch parents who based their principles on the Holland they had left. I only wanted to become a Canadian.

These differences are more pronounced whenever we have visitors from the old country, and it is then my longing to go back to my roots becomes more desperate. I must visit, but I am afraid to go — afraid to destroy the boyhood images, afraid of disillusionment. I have to go back and walk the streets of memory where I lived as a boy. I want to stand at the graves of my grandparents and say a proper good-bye. I want to meet those aunts and uncles who are only names, not even memories. I will not go as a tourist, nor as a prodigal son, but as a collector — to collect a state of mind and complete my understanding of who I am.

And this story, which started as a labour of love in answer to a request for immigrant stories in a newspaper, finished as a search for identity. I hope this work provides some insight into what it was and still is to be the child of immigrants. I hope I was able to convey my regret for trying to deny my heritage as well as my joy in rediscovering it. Above all, I hope my love and admiration for this country were apparent throughout, and that my readers will appreciate why I do not want to be referred to as a hyphenated Canadian.

I am a Canadian!

Lillian Sulteanu

APPRECIATION

From an interview with Lillian Sulteanu

Ever since I came to Canada from Roumania when I was sixteen years old, I have been trying to convince people how great this country is. No matter how much I try, they still don't realize what they have here. You just cannot instill that feeling of appreciation in people who have never been immigrants and have never suffered traumatic experiences.

For many years I couldn't talk about the things I went through before we came to Canada. I used to sit and cry a lot, but now I realize that there were many others who had it worse, especially those who survived the concentration camps. My experiences were traumatic because I had lived such a sheltered life and wasn't prepared for the reality of life outside my home.

My father was born in a small town about fifty or sixty miles from Bucharest where I was born. My mother and her family had been born and raised in Bucharest, and for the first five years of my life, we traveled back and forth between the two places, keeping up the family ties on both sides.

We were in the small town when the Nazis came to power in 1939. My father knew someone in the Nazi Party who warned him to leave as quickly as possible. We didn't even lock our doors when we fled to my grandparents in Bucharest. There had been only two Jewish families in the town, and because there was prejudice, a Christian friend of my father's had lent us his name. My father had a dry goods store originally and all transactions went through under his friend's name. We used it for years.

When we reached Bucharest, the family chipped in and helped my father open a small jewelry business right in the centre of the city where most of the Nazi officers were stationed. My mother's second language was French, but she had studied German at school and spoke it pretty well. She became the saleslady. My father wouldn't open his mouth at all and tended to his watchmaking and repairs. They made a pretty good living right under the noses of the Germans, and most of their clients were high-ranking officers.

We stayed with my grandparents for three years, always living in fear that we would be discovered and taken away. Somehow we managed to survive, and then the Russians came. We still had the store, but we had more problems because the Russians weren't too sympathetic to merchants. It was against the law for anyone to sell or buy gold, and one day a soldier came in and tried to sell my father some gold coins. He must have stolen them, and my father was afraid to buy them. Eventually the soldier was caught trying to dispose of them elsewhere. He must have been interrogated, probably tortured and named all the places he had been trying to sell the coins. Among them he probably mentioned my father's store because the police picked my father up, arrested him and put him into prison for a few months.

It must have been a very bad experience for him because when he was released, he decided that he had to leave the country. He couldn't live that way. Between 1950 and 1951, the Communist regime wasn't too good to Jews who lived in Roumania and did its best to dispose of them by encouraging emigration. At first Jews were allowed to take their furniture, but after a few months, even this was stopped. All an emigre was permitted was forty pounds — nothing else. Because we were limited this way, my father melted down some of his platinum and made nails which he banged into the corners of a small, wooden box he filled with personal papers. That was what helped us survive after we left.

I will never forget the scene at the train station when we said our good-byes to my only sister. She had married a Gentile, and he wouldn't leave because he had his family in Roumania. Life was much easier if you weren't Jewish. It was a very painful separation. We didn't think we would ever see her again.

We had decided to emigrate to Israel and from the train went to a port on the Black Sea. From the beginning it was one set of traumas after another for me. I was the youngest child of a large peripheral family — many, many relatives — and as a result had been very sheltered. Perhaps it was too late to make the arrangements or maybe my parents couldn't afford it — I don't know what it was — but we didn't have a cabin and had to sleep on mats on the deck under the stars when we boarded the ship. For me it was a shock. In addition, we didn't have access to the cafeteria. I don't recall how we ate or what we ate, but I remember my mother had taken a large salami with us and some cutlery. She cut a slice, and the meat was full of worms. It was so hot it had spoiled quickly. We had never had a garden, and I had never seen worms. I screamed. She threw the meat overboard and after that I couldn't bring myself to eat. I must have gone into some kind of shock at that point, because when I met other children on the boat with whom I had been in elementary school years before (I was now in high school), and they asked me what grade I was in and what subjects I had taken, my mind was a complete blank. I couldn't remember a thing although I had just finished the school year a month before. Part of my problem was living such a sheltered life. Later when you have to face reality, it can have a very damaging effect on you. I had gone through the bombardment during the war when both German and Allied planes were attacking, and to this day, I can't stand loud noises — even a door slamming triggers this fear. Also, I was never aware when my family lacked things, when there was no money or not enough food. My parents kept everything from us. They meant well, I suppose, but later the reality hit me harder and was destructive emotionally.

When we arrived in Israel, we had to live in a tent for four months. We were kept in quarantine for the first three or four weeks along with thousands of other people who were displaced — people who had survived the death-camps, the war, and had been forced out of countries that were hostile to Jews. They came from all over Europe, the Middle East, anywhere and everywhere. The new state of Israel wasn't what it is today where you get a job and a house when you arrive.

For the first time in my life, I was exposed to sights I had never dreamed existed. Suddenly I was seeing Jews from the isolated areas of Yemen who were squatting to eat their meals, were eating with their hands, didn't know what it meant to take a shower or bath, and were using the shower to urinate and defecate. We had always had a maid at home, and I suppose I was finicky. This was a shocking experience for me.

During the quarantine, we were given all kinds of shots and examined for medical problems. At first we were in a tent under the blistering, middle eastern sun, with sixteen people — entire families — adults and children packed together, one cot beside the other. After the quarantine was over, we were given a small tent to ourselves. And then the Chamseen began, those hot, desert winds that blow around the end of July or beginning of August. Everything was flying by. Particles of needle-like dust, hot as a poker, got into our clothes, food, eyes, noses and mouths. No matter how hard you tried to protect yourself, it was impossible to get away from it. It made life, as bad as it was, even more unbearable.

For the first time in my life, I had to help with the cooking and cleaning. My parents would go into Haifa and Tel Aviv during the day, looking for a small place where my father could start all over again as a watchmaker and jeweller. I was alone all day, washing, cooking and cleaning, trying to help them.

My parents tried everthing and even that wasn't enough. In the cities they met Jews who had been there during the 1948 War — some had been there for forty years — and they asked my father why he hadn't come forty years before. Newcomers would have to wait their turn. They were resentful and just wouldn't give him a chance. With the help of relatives who lived in the United States and sent us money, we moved into a hotel room in Tel Aviv to get out of that tent. We slept three in a bed for eight months.

Things were bad economically. My father couldn't get into a trade or business. You either had to work in a kibbutz* or you were out of luck. He was fifty-four years old and couldn't do farm work at his age. To become a merchant was almost impossible. We had to leave. There was no other choice.

A Canadian woman my aunt had met in the United States said she could get the papers for us from immigration. At that time no sponsor was needed. This woman was coming to Israel on a visit and she brought the papers with her and charged us $300. She could have mailed them, but we were so desperate at this point that my father paid her. We didn't have much money left.

We were finally on our way. In Holland we stopped for three days and had to be examined. My mother had a spot on her lungs. She had had tuberculosis when she was young and there was some scar tissue which she still has to this day, but it had healed. There was nothing wrong with her, but the doctors wanted to keep her there and told us to go on without her. There was no way we would agree to that. I think the doctor took pity on us in our misery and finally let us go.

We arrived in Canada in August, 1951. There was a family who said they could help us. They owned a house on Ste. Catherine Street near St. Matthew. They rented us one room on the second floor that came with a small kitchen, a cupboard, bathroom and two double beds in the room for $80 a month. It was a high price for 1951, but we wanted to live there and make a store out of it. However, we discovered that no one would come to a watchmaker on the second floor unless he was established and had a steady clientele. So my father had to make other arrangements.

It must have been about three or four months after we arrived that our bell rang for the first time. The only people we knew were those who collected the rent once a month. We were so alone, we had no one here and we went into a panic. We had been the first ones of the family to come to Canada, and there was always the fear that remains with you when you come from a police state or Communist country. We thought it was the police coming for us and were afraid to open the door. It took us a while to get rid of the fright whenever the bell rang.

*Farm commune.

There were a lot of things to which we had to adjust. Some of them were embarrassing. I remember one situation when my mother called up the Irish janitor when the bathtub was blocked and we couldn't use it. He came upstairs, and although my mother had gone to night school a few times, she couldn't speak English too well. Her French was much better. She didn't know the word for "wash" in English and used the French translation. "My daughter wants to make 'lave'" (laver), as she tried to explain that what I wanted was to use the bath to wash myself. It sounded as if she was offering me to him, and the man looked at my mother and me as if both of us were crazy. I can laugh about it now, but it was very embarrassing then.

We stayed there for two years, and it was like a hotel for visiting family. My mother and father each had sisters and there was a cousin as well who came and stayed with us until they could find an apartment of their own. In those two years we were never without roomers.

My cousin, who came from New York, told my parents that no matter what, I should go back to school and finish my education because I would have no chance at any kind of future without one. In Roumania I had finished ninth grade. I had been going to a kind of technical school for construction in preparation for architectural training. This was part of the Russian system where you had a choice between high school and technical school. However, I was not aware that choosing this would disqualify me from entering university. I would simply become a technician and even though I had taken advanced mathematics, calculus and physics, I would not be considered good enough to go to university.

Suddenly the opportunity was there for me to start again, even if I was older than the other students. I didn't realize how the entire cultural scene, the difference in being an immigrant, would affect me. I enrolled at Montreal High School on University Street and was the only one in class living downtown. Because of the location I had no friends near me to visit. Another barrier was the language. In Roumania, the second language had been French, and once the Communists took over it became Russian. Although the students at school tried to be nice to me and talk to me, all I knew were about twenty or thirty words in English. We didn't know that there were organizations like Jewish Immigrant Aid Services that could have helped us to integrate. I had two friends, both immigrants, one from Poland and the other from Roumania. The latter worked as a mother's helper and would translate for me. So if anyone asked me a question, it would go through her. We were both in the same class, and to this day we are still friends.

But the differences between the Canadian children and the few immigrants were very noticeable and at times for us, very painful. When there were class parties, we weren't invited. We didn't belong. I think back and I know why. It wasn't only the language. I know I looked odd. I wore socks, not stockings, because in Roumania and Israel, too, you only wear stockings after you get married. As for lipstick, forget it. European kids weren't allowed to wear it until they married. There was no question about it — I did look different. I couldn't make myself look like everyone else. I was used to the old country code of dress and even if I wanted to change, I didn't have the money to keep up with the other girls. It takes time to adapt.

Another problem was that I had to study in a room where there were usually five or six people sleeping. I needed a light to see what I was doing and I had be very quiet so as not to disturb them. With my meagre vocabulary I was required to study Shakespeare and learn entire sections by heart. I couldn't understand ordinary, modern English and here I had to learn Elizabethan English from memory. There were no special classes for teen-aged immigrants like me who were dropped into the school system. But there were night classes at Montreal High School for adults, and at night I would go to those with my mother. But they weren't much use to me. The students were learning "How do you do?" and "How are you?" and I was trying to understand Shakespeare. I listened to the radio and that helped. I read with a dictionary in one hand and when I did my homework, I had to look up every single word. It took ages and I had no help.

Then someone referred me to a woman who was teaching at home as a volunteer. She had children and couldn't get out. It took me two hours to get to her house and she gave me one hour a week. Again that wasn't much good. I had to work very hard, but I think my teachers appreciated the work I was putting in. I won a scholarship the first year. We had to pay something like five or six dollars a month for school, and with the scholarship it didn't cost anything. However, when I finished high school, I was the recipient of another scholarship for $200 to go to university. This was in 1953, and I decided to go at night so I could work during the day. What was so unbelievable for me was that I had passed the English tests so well. I don't think I was given anything I didn't deserve, but what amazed me was that there were Canadian children who failed. I took the same tests they did, and I hadn't been getting any after-school help. I didn't think I had any special ability and my memory wasn't that marvellous, but what I did have was a lot of will power. Because of the experiences I had been through, I appreciated learning more than people born here. An education is something you can take with you; no one can take it away from you. To this day I have not been able to get enough of learning.

Meanwhile, my father got his start through the help of two other immigrants, one Italian and the other Jewish, a barber and a tailor. They set up a little corner for him in the back of their shops. They knew what it was like to come to a new country and to suffer while trying to adapt, and they felt it was their duty to help us. I will never forget them for their kindness.

During the day I worked for Bell Telephone, and at night I went to school at Sir George Williams University. I studied architecture. When I switched jobs, I went to work for an architect.

About this time in 1954, my parents arranged a meeting with the parents of the man who would later become my husband. They had gone to Israel about the same time as we did, but his parents came on ahead to Canada. He had to stay behind to serve his compulsory army service. When he finally arrived here, his parents told him he had to take me out and to be nice to me. He had a big problem. He couldn't speak English and didn't have a profession because he had spent three and a half years in the army. However, he had a knack for chemistry and had worked for the air force doing tests on fuel. But he couldn't get a job. He went to all the refineries and every questionnaire asked: "Religion?" He always wrote Jewish and wasn't hired. After it happened a number of times, he put down "Orthodox" thinking it could mean Russian or Greek. The first time he did that, he got the job.

We couldn't afford expensive amusements and we went on long walks together. We knew he had to learn English and speak, so we decided that every time he used a Roumanian word in the conversation, he would have to pay one cent. It was expensive for him to learn, believe me. Now we are so used to English that when our parents are here, we have to translate the language with difficulty. Our children don't speak Roumanian and they are cut off from their grandparents as a result. For them the generation gap is one in every sense of the word. But I really don't care. I hate Roumanian, I hate the country, and anything that has to do with Roumania. I have only bad memories of my birthplace. There was very little of anything good to remember. I still feel ill at ease with people who have an allegiance to Roumania. Their way of thinking is different from mine. They believe that everything that comes from Roumania is better, the air is fresher and the food tastes better. They say that this country is backward culturally, but they seem to forget that Canada is younger. I don't agree with anything they say. I believe this country is great and it makes me angry to hear anyone knock Canada. I won't stand for anyone saying anything against it.

I have been told that if I can't identify with my roots, there is something wrong with me. I don't care if there is. That's how I feel. I have no feeling for my birthplace and no links to it. Whenever I go back to visit my sister, I hate every minute of my stay there. From the minute you get off the plane, you see soldiers pointing guns at you. That's just one thing; there are many more. I find the Roumanian language restrictive. Its vocabulary is much smaller than English, and whenever I pick up a Roumanian book, I have to put it down after reading a few lines. I just can't stand it.

When I run into people complaining about things here, I get very upset. They do this because they probably were never hungry. I remember during the war we had bread in which we found nails and even pieces of wood. In Israel my mother would cook a chicken five times over because we couldn't get any meat and even the chicken could be bought only twice a month. So of course, I would feel different from people who don't know what it is to suffer and do without. Maybe it is my attitude that makes me feel I am not like others. It must be something within myself.

I used to get asked, "Where do you come from? Your accent is lovely." I tried to lose it. To this day my children still laugh and make fun of me because of the way I pronounce some of the words.

There are other differences between Europeans and Canadians. My son has a friend whose parents are Hungarian and German. I asked my son how he felt when he went to their house. He said there was more affinity because the family came from Europe, the same way his parents did. There are so many things that are old-world . . . for example, respect for property and even more so other people's belongings. Canadian kids don't have this respect. Perhaps it is because Europeans instill this respect in their children at an early age. My kids think that littering, throwing things around, defacing and marking up other people's property is the worst crime there is. They go to a high school that looks more and more like a garbage dump every day. The students don't give a damn, and my kids won't even use the bathrooms because they are indescribably filthy.

I have to admit that other immigrants like us fared wonderfully well. Immigrants work harder than established Canadians. They have to prove something to themselves and to the country that took them in. Of course, the first few years are hell, no matter how much you want to say you are doing well. It has to do with the adjustment, the breaking away, the cultural shock, the language — all kinds of things. But I don't know anyone who is worse off than they were before they left Europe.

My father-in-law was well off in Roumania. He had ten haberdashery stores, and when he came here, he started from scratch, sweeping the floors in Brown's Department Store on St. Lawrence Boulevard. The owner was an immigrant himself from Roumania, and he helped every newcomer who came to Canada and asked him for assistance. He didn't offer any high positions or pay big salaries, but no one who knocked on his door was ever turned away. And as coincidental as this may sound, the owner happened to work for my father-in-law in the old country when he was young, and now he was offering his former boss a job. Although he had had so much once, my father-in-law wasn't proud. He took any kind of work, even sweeping and cleaning up. Immigrants don't look at this kind of work as demeaning. With a few hundred dollars he started a haberdashery store out east, then went into a glass and frame business, took his son into it, and using the same business sense he had in Europe, he is doing marvellously well, even if he isn't using his mother tongue.

My father never had an ear for language, and even here in Canada, my mother would translate French and English for him. When she wasn't in the store, he would talk Roumanian and use his hands. His customers realized he was honest and kept coming back, language skills or not. Today my mother is 72 years old and a widow and because of her experience, she went to work at Birk's. She does appraisals in the silverware area, makes and suggests settings for jewelry and other things as well. Everyone in our family was a hard worker — that's an immigrant trait — and that's how she learned English. She came to Canada speaking Roumanian, French, and German and by taking courses and dealing with the public, she picked up another language.

For an immigrant, the chances you have in this country are extraordinay. My husband is the manager of a company with over a thousand people. He has to be tough, and even with his European accent, he is able to deal with workers, unions and management. He has never been called a derogatory name or given a hard time, and he is involved with many, many people. I do not think he would have had the chance to get so high in management in a country like France or Switzerland where there is so much chauvinism and discrimination against others from outside their borders.

I see this difference whenever I go back to Europe. I took my children with me to Roumania in 1972 to visit my sister who is still there. I wanted my kids to realize how good they had it here after they saw how people live over there. Like most Canadians they tend to take things for granted. They realized it while they were there, but when we returned, the complaints began again: "Why don't we have this or do that?"

"Do you realize what we *do* have?" I asked. And then I finally gave up. Only those who have had bad experiences in the land of their origin or elsewhere can appreciate what Canada has given them. Only an immigrant who has been through hard times can understand what freedom means and what it is to know where your next meal is coming from.

We have traveled extensively in the last ten years or so in Europe, and as much as I love the different cultures, the art and architecture, the differences in each city we visit, when I come back and step off the plane, it is with such a feeling of relief and love to be back home in this wonderful country.

I know how I feel, but the thing that still bothers me is, why can't Canadians appreciate what they have here?

Rolf Buschardt Christensen

MULTICULTURALISM
The Foundation of Canadian Society
By Rolf Buschardt Christensen

When I was born in Copenhagen in 1946, the war had been over for more than a year. But the scars of the bombing and occupation were still evident. Many of the destroyed buildings had not yet been rebuilt; there were very few cars on the streets, and it was not uncommon to see horse-drawn carriages. Food, mainly imported items, was still rationed, but nobody was starving.

Of all the countries embroiled in the war, Denmark had emerged with the least damage. No major battles had taken place on Danish territory. Unlike most other countries, the domestic post-war period was a continuation of the pre-war situation for Denmark. The occupation had been a grim parenthesis in the country's history, but the invasion, occupation and liberation were events etched indelibly on the minds of the Danes who had experienced it. Liberation was like being released from prison. Danes could not trade, travel or emigrate.

Some Danes wanted to get away from it all — go someplace where they could build a new life and secure future. To these Danes, the United States and Canada represented lands of opportunity. Both countries had been built by immigrants and were free and stable societies with vast open spaces and seemingly unlimited resources. And they were far enough away not to be threatened by invasion.

My parents were among those Danes who wanted to stake out a new life in North America. However, they soon discovered that the doors to Canada and the United States were as good as closed to Danes. The millions of displaced persons and refugees all over Europe had priority. The Danes had it too good at home — they could wait. South Africa, on the other hand, was willing to take Danes at any time. So in 1947 my father left for Johannesburg, and my mother and I soon followed. Two years later my brother was born in Krugersdorp. At the time, my father was manager of The Danish Inn, a resort near Magaliesburg, which offered fishing, boating, swimming and riding as well as overnight accommodation in small bungalows.

All in all, we lived in South Africa for about three years, returning to Denmark in 1950. My parents decided to try their luck again in their homeland, hoping things would be different this time. We arrived in Copenhagen, and I began school. My parents bought a small wholesale grocery business in a working-class district, which necessitated a change of schools. The business was in a basement and in addition to running this, my father worked as a sales representative selling invoices and business forms. Later my parents bought a couple of retail candy stores.

Because they wanted me to get a good education and make nice friends, my parents enrolled me in Johannesskolen, a private school, when I was in grade two. I had to take a streetcar or bicycle through the busy streets of Copenhagen to get there. The change was overwhelming. The sons and daughters of professionals, rich people and movie stars attended Johanneskolen, but after school I would play in the street with kids who had a much more common background.

My parents involved me in extracurricular activities — dancing school, Sunday school, cub meetings on Saturday, hikes on Sunday afternoons in forests north of Copenhagen or exploring the city. If I didn't go to cub camp in the summer, I would spend the summer holidays with my grandparents in Sakskøbing on the island of Lolland where my mother had come from. My grandfather knew a lot of people. He was one of the local lawyers, active in various organizations as well as on the city council. As a child it was wonderful being out in the country, going for long bicycle rides through the forest or along the fields or watching farmers unload their horse-drawn wagons at the general store next door.

As I got older I noticed outside events began to intrude on our peaceful existence. I remember the winter of 1956 and 1957 for that was when gas was rationed due to something called the Suez crisis, I was told. Also, everyone was talking about Hungary. At school we were all told to bring a pair of shoes which were tied together and thrown in a big pile in the gymnasium. They were subsequently sent to Vienna to be given to Hungarian refugees.

It was just after this that my life changed dramatically. My parents called a family meeting and told my brother and me we were going to Canada. I didn't know anything about Canada so I looked it up in my geography book. Canada covered half a page. I concluded it must be Davy Crockett territory, thinking of the Walt Disney film I had seen a short while before. I figured the first thing we would have to do would be to build a cabin up in the mountains. It would definitely be a rough life.

Wednesday, March 20, 1957 was a milestone in my life. It was the day we left Denmark for Canada. But it was also my last day at school, and when a classmate told the teacher I was leaving for America, she cancelled math and read a story to the class instead. Our ship sailed at midnight. The *M/S Bolivia,* a small freighter, had room for only twelve passengers. Our destination was New York. We sailed north of Scotland, and once out in the Atlantic had to sail south to avoid icebergs floating down from Davis Strait. We all took turns being seasick. The waves appeared as high as houses to me.

It took about two and a half weeks to reach New York with a brief call in Boston. After a five-day stay in New York to take in the sights, we boarded a Greyhound bus to Niagara Falls and entered Canada — our new home. However, this was only a short visit as we were crossing southern Ontario to get to Detroit where we spent one night. Another day and night were spent in Chicago and from there we continued to Salt Lake City and Reno. We visited my mother's family in San Francisco and then took the bus again up the Pacific coast to Canada. We crossed the border in a pouring rainstorm at one o'clock in the morning. Customs and immigration did not take long, and we were granted landed immigrant status at Pacific High on April 23, 1957.

For me Vancouver was, and still is, a spectacular city. There is nothing that surpasses the natural beauty. Canadian humourist Stephen Leacock said about Vancouver: "If I had known what it was like . . . I would have been born there."

My father's first priority was finding a job. He wanted to sell invoices and business forms as he had done in Copenghagen, and he was lucky. Within a week he bought a car and two weeks later was selling business forms in Chinatown. For the first couple of months we lived in a rooming house downtown as did many other immigrants. Then we moved to a house in Kitsilano. I was sent to a New Canadian class at downtown Dawson School to learn English. Although there were many different nationalities in the class, there seemed to be quite a few more Danes and Hungarians. In fact, a record number of Danes came to Canada in 1957 as did Hungarians fleeing the 1956 revolution. Some of the Canadian students referred to us as DPs (displaced persons). I spent a year learning English and then transferred to an elementary school in Marpole where my parents had bought a house. The following year I entered high school where I spent the next six years.

We were not really poor, but we didn't have much money. I had to take an after-school job to have spending money. At Christmas a Danish friend and I went from door to door selling Christmas tree branches and made good money. The rest of the year we would collect beer and soft drink bottles which netted two cents each. I also made a sum selling wall plaques door to door. But my first regular job was selling the *Star Weekly.* At one point I apparently had the biggest paper route in British Columbia, selling close to 100 copies a week.

Then I delivered *The Province*, a morning paper, for over four years and through canvassing for new subscribers, won a trip to the Seattle World's Fair in 1962. Some of us winners even had our picture in the paper.

I was getting too old to be a paperboy and it was hard getting up at five in the morning, so I found a job as a delivery boy for a butcher shop. Soon I graduated to a clerk behind the counter. From there I went to clean-up boy in a Danish bakery and then clerked again in a large Vancouver meat market. From the time I was fourteen I earned enough to pay for my own clothes and even paid toward my trip to Denmark in 1960 when I was confirmed in a Sakskøbing church.

Meanwhile my parents tried to keep their Danish traditions in Canada. It wasn't always easy away from the Danish environment and family. Living in Canada we were influenced by Canadian ways, but we did speak Danish at home. In addition I kept reading Danish books. My mother and father were probably stricter than most other Danes in Canada when it came to observing Danish traditions. But at home they tried to get the best of both worlds. Most Danes came to Canada to get ahead in life and the fastest way to integrate was to learn the English language. But ties with other Danes were important and my parents became involved with the Danish community in Vancouver. My father became a correspondent for the Toronto-based *Modersmaalet* paper and for *Danmarksposten* in Copenhagen. He joined various Danish organizations in Vancouver and served on the executive of several. He became chairman of the Danish Central Committee and later one of the founders and first president of the Danish Community Centre of Vancouver. He also served on the British Columbia Centennial Commitee and became a member of the National Association of Parliamentarians, chairing many meetings and sitting on many bylaw committees, within and outside the Danish community. He set an example with his involvement in public service for my brother and me. This was my legacy, my intangible baggage when I left home in 1965 at the age of nineteen.

The summer before graduation I had spent two wonderful months in Europe, taking a bus tour through Germany, Switzerland, Austria and Italy. I had traveled around Denmark, visited family and friends and fallen in love with Copenhagen all over again. I decided to try my luck there. Because I was looking for something international, I wrote a letter of application to several big Danish shipping companies just before I graduated. The companies that answered wanted personal interviews, and right after graduation I left Vancouver by train across Canada to Montreal where I took a plane to Copenhagen.

I was interviewed and wrote some exams for the Maersk Line, one of the largest shipping companies in the world. They called me the next day and I started as a trainee in August. I remained there for three years, but soon discovered it was imperative that I know something about the society I lived in. I felt like an immigrant. Even though I spoke the language, I had trouble understanding Danish humour and mentality, in general. I had to catch up quickly. I began reading the latest books and going to the theatre. Keeping informed about cultural events was necessary. In Canada there is not the same pressing need to read, for instance, Margaret Atwood's latest book. In addition, I had had no German in school, another deficiency. So I enrolled in night school to study the language. At the same time I had to acquaint myself with Danish politics, the economy and what was happening in Denmark in other areas.

To keep in touch with my Canadian world, I would participate in Canada Day activities every year, either at the Copenhagen City Hall, at the Canadian Embassy or in the Tivoli Gardens. There were also trips to Sweden, Germany and Switzerland. On my own I traveled to Norway, France and Spain.

In spring, 1968, I decided to quit my job and go to France for half a year to learn French. I had just enrolled at the Institut International d'Etudes Francaises in Rambouillet and had paid my tuition fees when France came to a complete halt. The May 1968 crisis, which brought about the downfall of President de Gaulle within a year, had broken out. I feared my dream of studying in France would collapse.

By the beginning of August, France was slowly returning to normal, and I was able to begin my studies on time. It was an exciting period. We learned about French civilization and culture and tried to understand the present crisis. On Sundays we went on excursions around the country. But by the middle of December the course was over, and I was back in Paris with no money and no place to stay. I wanted desperately to get back to my family in Denmark for Christmas. I went to La Maison Danoise on the Champs Elysees to get help and talked to a Danish pastor who knew many of the Danes in Paris. In this way I scrounged a meal here or there and found accommodation. My last francs were spent on Metro tickets as I hauled my heavy suitcase from place to place. Finally I got lucky. I found a lift back to Denmark in a rent-a-car which had to be dropped off in Copenhagen. I was home in time for Christmas.

After New Year I started school at a Danish Folk high school or boarding college in Jutland for four months, but unfortunately I had to leave a week before the course terminated because I was called up for national duty. I wore a soldier's uniform for 26 months. My call-up notice came from the Royal Guards which meant common infantry. It also meant I would have to stand guard near the end of my tour of duty at the Royal Amalienborg Palace in Copenhagen, wearing a big bearskin on my head. I don't think I have ever been photographed so much in my life. The tourists loved us. Along with other soldiers I was on hand for receptions and audiences as well as guard duty at the royal family's other residences. While at Fredensborg Palace, King Frederik IX gave us a personal tour of the palace. Among other things, the King showed us the window where Sir Winston Churchill had signed his name with a diamond.

Instead of being demobilized when my fourteen-month tour of duty was over, I was sent to Cyprus where I served with the United Nations Peace Keeping Forces. I was attached to the Danish contingent's headquarters in Xeros and had to deliver dispatches to UN headquarters in Nicosia. A marvellous year on Cyprus included some unforgettable leaves to Israel, Lebanon and Egypt. In addition to getting the best suntan I ever had, I was also able to save some money on Cyprus. This was meant to finance my continuing education. I had decided to go to university in Vancouver. And so after six years' absence, I returned to Canada. Again it took time to adjust, but not too long.

I had missed Expo '67, Trudeaumania, the FLQ and the War Measures Act reactivated in 1970. I realized that many things had happened while I had been away. Canada had become a more mature country. Canadians no longer used the excuse, "It's still a young country," to explain shortcomings. But they had not been able to rid themselves of their inferiority complex. Britain and the United States remained their ideal models and countries of reference. Canada still had a branch plant economy protected by nationalistic import restrictions and Canada continued to be an exporter of raw materials and regretfully excelled in only a few fields of endeavour.

However, it was good to be back on Canada's evergreen west coast. Vancouver had changed considerably. There were new high-rises everywhere. While Vancouver had leveled much of its history in the process, one glimmer of hope was historic Gastown, which gradually, despite everything, turned into a commercial tourist attraction. Most of the high-rises, nevertheless, were attractive and looked impressive against the majestic north shore mountains.

I found a basement suite near Vancouver City College's Langara Campus and took various courses. Then I applied to the University of British Columbia's Honours Programme in history and was accepted. In 1975 I graduated with a B.A., Honours in History with International Relations.

Again I left Vancouver, this time for Ottawa, where I did an M.A. in International Affairs at Carleton University. My sojourn in Ottawa made me realize there is more to Canada than the west. The climate, for one, is different. I was introduced to the cold, continental Canadian winters as well as the hot, humid summers. I had to adjust to a new cultural environment because the capital is bilingual. Indeed, living in Ottawa heightened my interest in Canadian society, history, culture and politics. I became more aware of Canada's "two solitudes". Moreover, to learn more about the country I started visiting other parts of Canada during my vacations. Now Newfoundland is the only province I have not seen.

While I was working on my thesis on *Denmark and the European Community,* The European community opened a delegation in Ottawa which proved useful in my research. One day I asked if there were any job openings at the delegation and shortly after I was hired. I still work there and find it extremely interesting keeping abreast of developments in Canada and Europe. My research on Denmark and the European community has led to my publishing various articles based on my findings. In recent years I have focused on ethnic history and activities in my writing. There is much material there that has not been documented or reported. I have also been a correspondent for Dansk Samvirke's magazine *Danmarksposten* and have freelanced with other articles. Most stories come from my involvement with the Danish community.

In the absence of family in Ottawa, I have felt a need to be active within my own ethnic group. In Vancouver I had been secretary of the Royal Danish Guards' Association, and when I came to Ottawa, I joined the Danish Club of Ottawa, an ethnic and social club. One of the club's objectives is to preserve and transmit Danish culture and traditions through a wide variety of activities. The aim is to bring people together either through a community project or a party. I have been honoured by serving as secretary and later as president of the club.

Our contacts with other Danish-Canadian organizations proved to be valuable and consequently we considered establishing a national umbrella organization or federation. Thus in June, 1981 the Federation of Danish Associations in Canada was founded in Puslinch, Ontario with delegates from across Canada. I was elected as first president of the federation.

Not only was the federation formed to benefit our own community, but we also hope to share our culture and heritage with other ethnic groups and in the process, make a contribution to the development of

Canadian society and culture. We want to be a part of the multicultural mosaic of Canada today.

We feel it is essential that all Canadians come to recognize the role all cultural groups have played and continue to play in the development of Canadian society. Therefore, we support the policy of multiculturalism so we can maintain and share with pride our cultural heritage with other Canadians. What is more humanistic, democratic and just than multiculturalism? Together we can ensure that multiculturalism truly becomes one of the foundations of Canadian society and not just another cliche.

Alexander Pushkin

I ONLY WANTED TO BE FREE

From an interview with Sergo Dobrovlianski

The docking terminal on the Montreal pier was deserted at 6:30 p.m. on August 31, 1974. Early that morning all passengers had disembarked from the Russian cruise ship, *Alexander Pushkin.* Moored in majestic loneliness, the ship appeared devoid of life as her crew relaxed after a busy trans-Atlantic crossing from Leningrad. There had been stopovers in various ports along the way.

A lone seaman standing guard at the foot of the ridged, wooden gangplank turned as two Russian officers clad in denim suits clattered down to the pier. One was Alexander (Sasha) Bondarenko, 32, a handsome six-foot three-inch giant with sandy hair — the type to whom women are irresistably drawn. The other, Sergo Dobrovlianski, 37, was short, stocky and quick moving. Normally he had dancing eyes and an infectious grin. That day his eyes were serious . . . and wary.

"You are not permitted into the city," said the seaman, who was replacing the officer regularly on guard.

"We are not going into the city," answered Bondarenko. "We are just getting some air and walking along the pier."

The sailor nodded.

The two officers strolled leisurely into the huge terminal. A Canadian security guard nodded in greeting and asked how they were. The Russians smiled and nodded.

Once outside the building, Dobrovlianski and Bondarenko simultaneously broke into a furious dash toward the downtown area, occasionally glancing behind for signs of pursuit. There were none. Strangely, no one was aware of the pair's defection until the following day. By then both men were in protective custody of the RCMP.

Nine years later, Sergo Dobrovlianski traced the events leading to his defection.

My father, a journalist, was a dedicated member of the Communist party from 1930 on, and my mother was involved with a Communist youth organization. He had been sent on an assignment to work on an in-house factory publication in Volkhostroi, a town about 100 kilometres from Leningrad. My mother accompanied him and I was born in that town on February 19, 1937.

I was only four years old when Germany invaded Russia on June 22, 1941, but I do remember the air raids. Almost every block had a hand-rotated siren to warn the people enemy planes were on the way. These sirens were usually placed inside the open area of the square, compound-like buildings which surrounded a central courtyard. I was very proud to be permitted to rotate this machine and help the war effort.

My father, who had flat feet and thus was exempt from military service, volunteered anyway and went off to war. His unit was surrounded by Germans in a forest and the only food he and the men had was the berries picked up and eaten along the way. The entire unit developed dysentry. Somehow some of the men broke through the German lines to rejoin the Russians, and my father was taken to hospital. I remember being rushed from the country with my family on a horse-drawn cart to say good-bye to my father. We were being evacuated from Leningrad to an area in the Ural Mountains while the Russian leaders ordered the destruction of everything that might be of use to the enemy. And that was the last time I saw my father. He died in the hospital not long after we left. We were lucky to leave Leningrad because more than one million people starved to death as a result of the German seige.

We spent the next three years with an aunt in Chelyabinsk in the Urals, and by the time we returned to Leningrad in 1944, the seige was over although the war was still in progress.

I began school when I was seven and because I was so young, the hardships I faced in those early years and the cruelty of the Stalin regime passed right by me, unnoticed. I was about twelve or thirteen when I began to realize something was wrong. My brother, who was three and a half years older and knew more than I, began stirring anti-Soviet feelings in me. Suddenly, I was thinking of justice, freedom, and equality. I could see the propaganda we were fed by adults and teachers about the beauty of the Soviet state — the goodness of the people and how dear and necessary the Communist Party — was all a pack of lies. Next, I began thinking how I should deal with it, but I realized rather late that any changes in Russia would take 50 to 100 years to accomplish. The best way to rid myself of the entire system was to leave. But how?

I had been working for eight years as a seaman on Russian ships, mainly passenger lines. Suddenly, I realized a way was open, but the price would be very high. I knew I would have to abandon my wife and son in Russia. If I stayed, the time would come when I would be a burden and a danger to them because of the things I had seen in my travels and the feelings that I had developed as a result. I knew there was something better outside Russia. In those eight years working as a singer, drummer, arranger, master of ceremonies and show stager, I had been exposed to all kinds of people. Because I had a musical ear, I had picked up languages very easily. In addition to Russian, I spoke Mandarin Chinese, English, French, Spanish and German in varying degrees of fluency. Suddenly, I was hearing stories from so many different viewpoints. Because we stopped in many European ports — in Finland, Sweden, Denmark, France, England, Spain, Poland, Germany, Spanish Morocco, Majorca and the Canary Islands — I managed to get a lot of information about the west.

The *Alexander Pushkin* was a real Russian loveboat. You expect that aboard this type of ship, but that was only on the surface. By 1973 I was already having problems with the captain and the Russian authorities. After all, I had been at sea for over seven years. I didn't see much of my family and wanted more time at home. My request was refused. Because the cruise line was short of multi-talented people, I was used everywhere possible. My employers insisted on keeping me on the ship. I spent two to three months with my family each year, but sometimes there would be only one day between cruises and off I would go again.

However, despite my anger, I had decided to stick it out, stay on the ship and go back to my family in Russia, until something happened in March or April, 1974. A musician jumped ship in London. It was a big event, and all of the staff and crew were called together by the captain and given a harranguing and brainwashing. I was surprised the musician had defected because he had only been on the *Alexander Pushkin* for about three months. I figured he had been planning this escape for a long time and took the job as a means to that end. I had never considered myself a coward, but I began to think twice about defecting.

I had been planning to jump for all those years, anywhere in the west, and now I hesitated. I had been reading Solzhenitsyn and other dissident writers and discovered things I had not known before. As I accumulated more knowledge, I became more aware of the injustices in the system.

And then I remembered the big trial in 1971 or 1972.

Some sailors had brought in western products. It was a little more than customs permitted, but everyone smuggled . . . an extra pack of cigarettes, underwear, stockings . . . things like that. Most of the time, the customs officials looked the other way, but then people began to get greedy. And so, the Communist government decided to make an example of someone to show who was boss. I happened to be in the courtroom when a few seamen were brought to trial and I saw to what an extent these poor men were degraded. The trial was blown up out of all proportion, and the men were considered to be real criminals.

When I saw the sailors sitting in that courtroom, it was terrible just to look at them. The trial was a mockery. The defending lawyer gave a magnificent speech. When he finished, everyone thought the seamen deserved medals, but no, they got exactly what the prosecutor asked for — ten to twelve years in prison. For something as small as a few packs of cigarettes smuggled into a western country, a fine would be imposed, but not in Russia. That trial intimidated me, but after an argument with the ship's captain about my exploitation, my anger returned.

But still I was going back. However, the last straw that made me leave that last day in August was an order imposed on all of us by the captain. We were told to attend a soccer match at a Montreal stadium, where two of the ship's teams were playing a game. No stores, no shopping, he said . . . straight to the stadium and back. Four of us, two musicians, Sasha and I, ignored the order and went shopping. We met some immigrants from Russia, began a conversation and forgot the time. We arrived half an hour late back at the ship.

The captain's rage was terrible. Not only were we reprimanded, but berated and threatened. The KGB officer, who is placed on every ship and usually holds the position of assistant purser, administrator or librarian, was especially insulting and asked how we dared disobey orders. We were told we would not be permitted off the ship in any port until we reached Leningrad and then we would be reported to the higher authorities. Our careers as seamen were at stake.

That did it, Sasha and I were fuming. We went to our cabin in a state of extreme anger and I said: "Sasha, come on, let's . . ." and he finished with "go". I didn't realize it but he had been thinking of the same thing as I for a year. Of course, anyone who had plans of this nature kept them to himself. It would have been dangerous to talk about it.

So we were committed. There was no backing out. Sasha had been on the *Alexander Pushkin* for five years and he had friends in Montreal. He knew where to go. At first he thought we should stay on board for another week and make a few more dollars. Although the money we were paid was really very little, as entertainment officers we got extra money for raffles, running the bingo games, tips, etc. It is a common thing on ships. I guess you could call it private enterprise. But I felt it was now or never.

Once we were running toward the city centre, there was no stopping us. We took nothing but the clothes on our backs and our money. In a way we were lucky. Usually on the night of disembarkation, there is a big party organized for the staff and crew. No one questioned our absence because everyone knew we had been punished and thought we had been confined to our cabin. If someone had come looking for us, we would have been in big trouble.

We went straight to see a friend of Sasha's who had lived in Montreal for many years. He was of Russian origin and had a small jewelry store where he also repaired watches. From there, we visited a Canadian lady who had taken several cruises on the *Pushkin* and adored Sasha. Then we went to see a musician friend, a guitarist and bandleader who was hired sometimes to perform on the *Pushkin* when the ship was in port. The guitarist was very happy to see us and walked through some Spanish restaurants where he worked. He introduced us to everyone and bragged about what we had done. He bought us drinks, and then at his own expense put us up at the Queen Elizabeth Hotel.

The three of us were in our hotel room about two hours when a knock came at the door. I opened it to find two RCMP officers standing there. They knew Sasha because they worked the harbour area and had come aboard cruising ships many times. The *Pushkin* was well known to them. Sasha was such a friendly, outgoing person that he talked to everyone. The officers asked Sasha how he was and what he was doing there. Sasha explained and then introduced me.

Congratulations, one of them said. They made some phone calls and some arrangements. One RCMP officer took the room next to ours, and the other sat outside our door. Even if we wanted to, we couldn't leave undetected, but neither could anyone else get to us. We asked the men to find us a hiding place and shortly after they took us to a hotel at Dorval Airport where we spent a week living at close quarters with these officers. Then we were taken to a chalet on a lake in the Morin Heights area.

We had asked for political asylum, and the day after the RCMP had called on us, we were driven to a Canadian Immigration office, where papers were made up. We were happy to learn we had permission to stay in Canada.

For two months we remained in that chalet up north with the RCMP officers while they questioned us. Sasha, it seems, came from a very influential family. His father, who had died two years before Sasha defected, had been a colonel in the KGB. His mother was working for the KGB and Sasha's brother was a KGB major. Because of Sasha's background, his defection was a plum for the RCMP. I wasn't very important because my background was nothing compared to Sasha's. In fact, the Communist government must have been so worried about Sasha that it allowed his mother to come to Canada three months later to try to persuade her son to return. Sasha refused. He knew he wouldn't stand a chance once he got back to Russia. His commitment to living in the west was strong, but it was different from mine. He wanted to be a millionaire — something he could never hope to be in Russia. I only wanted to be free.

The Canadian government found jobs for us once the questioning period was over. I think Sasha did better, obviously because he had more information to give. He got a white collar job — manager of a large bowling lane concern. The RCMP found me a dishwashing job at the restaurant of a Holiday Inn. It wasn't much of a job, but it was better than nothing.

Six months later, we were given landed immigrant status and four years after jumping ship, I got my citizenship papers. Sasha never made it to citizenship. He was killed in an accident that appeared very suspicious and too coincidental. Although there were five people in the car, he was the only one injured. To this day I am not entirely convinced it was an accident.

Sasha was quite a character. He had lots of friends, especially women . . . you know the saying, "one in every port". There was one woman he was seeing in Montreal, a French-Canadian girl, but there was a story she was romantically involved with someone in the Mafia. I always suspected Sasha was mixed up with the wrong people. He seemed to know such unusual types. Once he introduced me to some men in a bar and he whispered that these guys were in the Mafia. He was actually proud they were his friends. I don't think he realized what he was doing. If he was courting one of the organization's girls, he was looking for trouble.

In addition, two days before the accident he spoke to a Soviet representative at the consulate. Sasha's girl friend's apartment was in the same building as this Soviet's. Apparently all this was known to the RCMP because we were in contact with them through this early period. If the KGB was after him for his defection, that made three that wanted to shut him up. Sasha was a talker; sometimes he talked too much.

Sasha's rib cage was smashed when another car slammed into the rear of the car where he was sitting. No one else was hurt. Sasha was rushed to a hospital and doctors operated immediately. He even joked about it, but a few hours later, he went into a coma and stayed that way for nine days. I called his wife in Leningrad the day of the accident. She tried to come to Canada, but the Russian government wouldn't let her out. When he died, I called again. She desperately wanted to come to the funeral, but again she was refused permission. Poor Sasha! He was such a friendly, good-looking man. He had so much ahead of him and he died so young.

As for me, I wouldn't say I have had any great success in life since I settled here. When I jumped ship, Canada was a merry, laughing country. It is not any more. Now you can see how much depends on affluence. Because we have such big economic problems, the people of this land are not smiling very much. But I reached the point where I knew it was useless to complain. If you want to blame something or someone for failure, blame yourself. As an immigrant I never pretended or expected to have the same rights as established Canadians. I never expected a bed of roses and I knew I would have a more difficult way of life. Being an immigrant meant I had to do so much more than a native-born Canadian. But I was willing to work hard.

I went into the fur business after the dishwashing episode and worked with a man of Russian origin who had come here around 1924. Then I went into business with another Russian immigrant who made fur hats. I was the "outside man" because I could speak so many languages. But business was slow, and there wasn't enough for both of us. I left, because he had a family to feed and I was single. He needed more money than I.

I worked as a shipper but was laid off and now I have been out of work for ten months. If it wasn't for my girl friend and my savings, I would be in trouble. She has a job, and we are planning to get married this summer. She is one of the best things that ever happened to me.

My feelings about Canada were almost reverent after an incident I had in Bucharest, Roumania, when I had flown over on business with my partner's step-uncle. The old man had many connections in the fur business and knew a lot of people in the Roumanian consulate here as well as quite a few big shots in Roumania. Who would expect trouble?

We were sitting in a restaurant, and a couple of gypsy girls were flirting with us. We had a few drinks and were on our way out with them to get a cab back to the hotel. When we climbed into the car, suddenly a couple of plainclothesmen appeared almost out of nowhere and asked for our papers. I was terrified because I had been born in Russia and was a defector. I was ready to kill the old man for convincing me to make the trip with him. But when I presented my Canadian passport, the change in the men's expressions was incredible. They showed so much respect that I felt like standing at attention and singing the Canadian national anthem.

"Okay, you can go," they said.

Needless to say, our romantic mood evaporated, and we left the girls there.

On the other hand, something happened in 1979 or 1980 that both terrified and infuriated me. By chance, I caught a news item on television, and the commentator was talking about Sasha and me. Our names weren't mentioned, but we were the subjects. The broadcaster spoke of two officers who had jumped a Russian ship in 1974 in Montreal and gave information about the KGB and activities on the ships. I was absolutely furious that something like this could happen without anyone consulting me or asking permission. All this could have been traced back to me. Sasha was dead so there was no way anyone could get him, but I was afraid something might happen to me.

I phoned to complain and had a conversation with some official who said it was out of his control. He blamed the media for digging up the information and broadcasting it, but I felt that kind of cooperation or leak, if that is what it was, between government and media was dangerous. Double agents are common in every country, and where there are no moral principles involved in security systems, a man's survival could be at stake. Someone must have been looking for a good story and couldn't care less what might have happened to me or my family because of the exposure.

But despite these things, I have never regretted leaving Russia and jumping ship. There is no question about the western way of life being better than the Russian one. I find the attitude of the people here in Canada very special. Canada gave me the freedom to reflect on many aspects of social existence. I was surprised to find so many similarities between Canada and Russia such as welfare, social reforms, caring for groups, but it is on a very small scale in Russia. Canada, perhaps because of her affluence, does ten times more even with such a small population.

From all the places I have visited and all the traveling I have done since I jumped ship, I still feel that Montreal, Canada, is the best place to live.

Frank Cerulli

THE CULTURAL TRANSITION

From an interview with Frank Cerulli

I was born in Provvidenti, a small town in Campo Basso province, in 1949. My family were farmers. They grew wheat, vegetables and also had vineyards and fruit trees. They barely lived on whatever they could raise, and there was no money for anything but the necessities. My father was the oldest of four children, and if all of them were going to live on my grandfather's land, it meant dividing it up again. With the parcels getting smaller and smaller there wasn't enough to support any of us, so my father had to get out.

It must have taken a lot of courage. He was about 23 or 24 when he left for Canada in 1949. I was only sixty days old. He chose Montreal because there were relatives here who would sponsor him, but he must have been through some real traumas, coming over here without knowing the language.

I didn't know my father until I was four years old, when he sent for my mother and me. It was a hell of a shock when we moved from Italy, came to a strange country with a new language, and I met my father for the first time. I was a real mama's boy, and the first comment I made when my father met us on arrival was: "Why don't we go home and leave him here?" It must have been difficult for my parents to redevelop a relationship after four years, let alone adjust to a son.

My earliest traumatic experience, I remember, was my first day at school when I was five years old. I was sent home and I couldn't figure out why. Of course, I cried because I couldn't understand the language and I don't think I got any moral support from my parents. They just didn't realize what it would be like. No one could communicate with me, and my father got a friend of his to go to school to talk with the principal about finding someone who spoke Italian and could understand me.

I think it was from that incident that the feeling of being Canadian rather than Italian grew. There was the sense of difference in my mind about the two cultures. Clothes had something to do with it as well.

Some of the things I wore were hand-me-downs or rejects from friends of the family. From somewhere or someone, my parents got a coat with a fur collar. They thought it was terrific — elegant and warm, too — and the best part was it didn't cost much if it had cost anything at all. No one at school had a coat with a fur collar. It was so European, and I refused to wear it. I wanted to be like the other kids, the Canadian kids.

At that time our family had boarders, my father's brother, my mother's, my grandfather . . . there must have been three or four uncles who stayed with us, coming and going in this small flat on Earnscliffe Avenue. Italian was always spoken at home.

By the time I was seven or eight, I was trying to analyse the difference between home life and outside, school and friends. This feeling of being split developed even further in high school, and I remember hating my parents because they were Italian and I wasn't. I felt Canadian.

I would say, "Here you are in Canada. Why are you speaking Italian? Speak Canadian. Why can't you do all the things my friends' parents do?"

I really didn't like being Italian at all. In fact, I hated it. I was embarrassed.

When my parents would talk about the weather being better over there, or the fruit tasting better in Italy, and that the tomatoes grew bigger and better in the old country, I would say,

"So why don't you go back and live over there if everything is so much better?"

They wouldn't answer because they knew they had it better over here, but they had to have something to bitch about.

But even if I had language problems, I had to do well in school. If I came tenth or third, my father would say: "There are still more on top of you."

I was always afraid that if I got seventy-five per cent, it wasn't good enough. Immigrants always expect more from their children than Canadians do. They didn't want me to play sports — hockey and football. That won't get you anywhere in life, they said. They didn't realize that it was good for you. Their life was farming and working all the time, and they couldn't see me spending money on sports equipment. It wasn't necessary.

But even though they didn't want me involved in sports, I still got what I wanted. I can remember forging my father's name so I could join the sports activities. I needed the authorization, and I knew he wouldn't give it to me. I loved sports, still do to this day. Of course, I realize now why my father didn't want me to play. He didn't think it was important in life. Now if you compare that attitude to the British, it's part of their heritage, you know, teamwork, perseverence, play the game and all that sort of stuff.

But in spite of this, there was one touching episode I remember, and when I look back on it now, I feel like crying. I was about ten years old, and I wanted a bicycle very badly. All the kids had bikes. Almost sadly, my parents told me they couldn't afford a bicycle. They felt so badly for me, but a bike cost about fifty dollars.

I don't know how they managed it, but I came home from school one day, and after supper, my father said, "Go look on the back balcony," and there was a bicycle.

The first thing I did was take it for a ride, show it to all my friends and have a bad spill. Directly behind our house was a Jewish family who were friendly with my parents. They had a son I played with. The father was looking out the window, and when he saw me go flyng, he leaned out and said: "Frank, you shouldn't do that. It's not good for the bike."

Here I was lying on my back, scratched by the cement, scraped bloody, the bicycle twisted and lying on top of me, and he was worried about the bike. He wasn't thinking about whether I was okay or not, but that I shouldn't do that. It wasn't good for the bike.

Somehow that bike incident stuck in my mind because of his attitude and also because of what my parents must have had to do without to buy that bike.

When I was ten or eleven, we had a trauma in our family that must have been terrible for my parents. As kids you don't understand the significance of these things until you are older and look back on them.

My parents had another son. It was their first child in the new country. It had special meaning for them because he was a real Canadian. The baby had some kind of stomach disorder. He always had diarrhea. I remember my mother tearing up sheets to make diapers for this poor baby. There were three months of this at home and then four months in the hospital doing tests. My mother went to visit him every day.

Because of this I was sent out of the house and was living at my uncle's. My little brother was only seven months old when I was told that he had died. I felt something, but I wasn't quite sure what it was. It didn't hit me until a few days later when I went to another uncle's house for dinner. I was still being shoved around from place to place. My aunt said, "You miss your brother, don't you?" And suddenly I realized that he was no longer breathing, living, and I burst into tears.

My parents had another little boy the following year, and now my brother is twenty-one and a student at Concordia University.

I guess I was too busy with my own problems at school, getting Canadianized, to be aware of their suffering and some of the situations they must have had where there was conflict because of ethnic origin.

One thing though, my parents always had the common sense to know that if anybody was going to attack them on the basis of their ethnic background, then the person was not worth talking to. Why waste your time trying to be friends with someone who calls you a dirty Italian or wop?

But when I was at the age where I hated being Italian, I may have sided with those who thought or said nasty things about Italian immigrants. When you side with them, there isn't much of an argument. Perhaps it was beneficial. It was my defence mechanism. Most of my struggle was internal, trying to decide what I was — Italian or Canadian.

I was torn in two. I thought I didn't have to choose to be Canadian or Italian. I *was* Canadian, but my parents kept saying: "But you were born in Italy." I can't deny the fact, but I was so young, I had no choice. I was brought here. It's one thing when people make the decision and choose to emigrate, but it is another with those who are too young to decide and are caught up in their parents' plans.

It wasn't until I got to college that I began to appreciate the fact that I had two cultures. It finally began to sink in that I was privileged to have these two, and that you can take the best of both.

The hardest part of all this was that I had absolutely no counselling from my parents. They were unable to guide me in any shape or form. They couldn't advise me to take law, accounting, engineering, whatever. They were trying desperately to scratch out a living for themselves. My father was working at the 7-Up plant and surviving on that, don't ask me how, and supplementing that by having boarders in the house. It wasn't until I grew up that I could appreciate what they went through.

Maybe they made it too easy for me, but when I was in high school, I didn't have to struggle for anything. I worked during the summers from the time I was thirteen or fourteen and gave all my money to my parents. They would dole out my spending money.

When I was ten or eleven I had had a *Gazette* route and a bank account with $900 I had earned. I remember my father discussing with me that he would take my money, because he needed it and promised to give it back.

Officially you could say that I didn't get it back. When I was going to university, I was taking summer courses so I could finish in three years instead of four. They wanted me to go back to Italy with them for a visit, and I said I couldn't go because of classes. I also wanted to earn some money so I could pay my tuition, but my parents said, "You're coming back with us because your grandmother and grandfather want to see you. They're getting old."

They offered to pay for my tuition the next year, and that $1,000 for the cost of the trip was the $900 my father had borrowed from me. Did I resent it? I had learned to follow the path of least resistance like most immigrants. I couldn't say no.

Another thing that was expected of me when I was growing up and at college, was to play the role of counsellor to my young brother. There's a lot of love between my father and brother, but my father doesn't know how to advise. The boy respects my advice, my guidance and experience more than my father's. So I am a son and a father all at the same time. It's a funny role and first-born children are often faced with this.

You see this at certain times, for instance, when my brother wants the car. I handle it differently from my father. It is an unusual situation being the mediator and telling my father and brother what to do and what not to do.

I guess the reason for it is that I am the Canadian in the family, and my brother even more so because he was born here. My parents are still very much old-world Italian. I'm the one who made the transition. I went to college. I broke away from the land, the farming tradition. There is also this thing about respect.

It is a European tradition that the first-born always respects his parents' wishes and does what they say. It is a difficult situation at times, and even to this day, I can't say no to my parents. I am just beginning to do it more often now. I think I have outgrown them now, but it's hard to argue with them when they use this line: "You are my son", and there is no retort to that. It closes the argument. I really don't think they know what they are doing, but they are very good at it. Even though I feel I have become Canadianized, there still is this Italian trait. Children of other ethnic groups probably have the same problem.

Because of their insecurities in adapting to another country, they can't let go of their children. There's an inability to say, "It's your life, do what you want with it. I can't tell you any more." Oh, no, they can't say this, and now that I'm divorced, I hear it even more. It is a European thing.

Last week I was over there, and my mother said, "I don't want anything from you. You're thirty-three years old, you're a man and you should lead your own life. I can't tell you what to do. Do what you want, except I want you should get married again. I can't tell you what to do, but you should come over and eat here more often and . . ."

The funny part of all this it's so typically Italian, Jewish, Greek, Israeli, etc. . . . . It's so ethnic, it makes me laugh.

However, the biggest hurdle immigrants have to clamber over is language. It's bad enough trying to scrape a bare living. But not to know what's going on around you is worse.

I remember some years ago, my parents decided to take English courses. I was thrilled for them. I was willing to help them register, find where they were given and even go with them. They lasted one night and said it wasn't for them. It takes courage to at least try, but it takes a lot more to finish. I guess they just didn't have it. They were afraid and didn't want to be embarrassed in the class. They had fought so many battles just existing that they figured they didn't need this one, too. It's unfortunate, but then again if they had taken the complete course and learned the language and grammar, I wonder how much of their Italian culture would have been submerged.

My brother was sent to an Italian school when my parents were trying to preserve the culture. It didn't work. He didn't want to go. It was on Saturday and Sunday, and he wanted to be outside playing baseball and hockey. Even now his Italian is very poor . . . as mine was until I got to college. I took Italian language courses and improved. It was hard, but at least now, I can appreciate the language more.

I don't know if I would preserve or submerge the Italian background if I remarried. I don't think I could preserve it. I'm not enough of an Italian to do that. But I've been close to it long enough not to want to submerge it totally. I would probably want my kids to speak English because that's the language I am most comfortable with.

It also depends on whether I marry an Italian girl who speaks Italian. I have seen families, friends of mine, where the husband and wife speak three languages, English, French and Italian, and the child is brought up in the Italian tongue and can't speak any of the other two. That is a crying shame. The early years are the best time to teach languages to a child, and I know from my own experience that I have benefited from my ability to speak three languages.

This language problem has a tendency to isolate the older people in the Italian community. I've been involved in community affairs, and I see that those like my parents, who came from the old country, are very much Italian. They have kept their roots, guarded them, but there is some Canadian now. Then you have the first generation, like my brother, who are born here and are more comfortable with English. Because of their parents, they learn to appreciate the Italian culture. But you see Italian characteristics in their attitudes, mannerisms and even the logic. And at some of our traditional big gatherings, you can see the varying degrees of these cultures.

And, of course, there is an affinity for others of the same culture, especially in the "shopping" area. Take my mother, for instance, God love her . . . she wants to buy furniture, so who does she go to but an Italian. After much haggling and bickering back and forth, she begins yelling, "He's screwing me. He's charging too much, the crook!"

But she still buys from him. I tell her if she doesn't like his prices, to go somewhere else.

"Oh, no," she says, "I go to him because he knows what I want. He may be charging too much, but he knows what I want."

And they enjoy the bargaining and the yelling. It's part of their background.

But there is one thing I have to say about my parents, and that is they are friendly with everyone on the street. From the time they moved in, even if they didn't know everybody, they were good neighbours. They had a garden in the back yard. The minute they had some land, no matter how small, the garden went in . . . you know, that old farming instinct . . . to make things grow. No matter where they lived, if there was a patch of land, they had to have a garden, and they always shared what they grew. They gave vegetables — anything they harvested — to the neighbours, and whenever my mother baked, she always made extra so she could share it with people on the street.

I really found this to be different from the lifestyle of Anglo-Saxon Protestants. I guess they aren't brought up to share. They're not used to it, but Europeans are different. They have been raised this way. I've thought about it a great deal and I like my way better. I like to give. I get pleasure from giving. There is an importance set on this — being friendly with everyone and making sure you have a good name on the street. The family is very important, and the family name should not be sullied in any way. You have to be a nice, upstanding family, and a lot of importance is placed on this belief.

But I did notice in my family that because of this, they used to take the path of least resistance in any confrontation. They would rather suffer and they wouldn't get what they wanted because they had to be nice. And now they have a hard time trying to reverse that.

It's a common thing with immigrants — the attempt to be so accommodating that they efface themselves. My parents were never too sure of their rights, even more so because they didn't speak the language. They were always afraid that they would be sent back. I can see this fear, this withdrawal in my brother even today. You have to learn to be tough and not turn the other cheek. I can see that my brother has many of the traits I used to have, but he is maturing at a faster rate than I did. Maybe it is because he has me, and my parents are older and softer, not as fearful as they were in the earlier years.

And that's one of the things that is different between established Canadians and immigrants — attitudes in upbringing that rub off on the children of immigrants. I have had certain difficulties in adapting to the Canadian way of life, particularly the ability to say no, the ability not to take the path of least resistance, to be more assertive, to stand up for my rights and say, "I have a right, too."

The immigrant work ethic is common to all ethnic groups. My parents were no different. They worked very hard and from a cold-water flat, they ended up owning a house they built themselves. My father has some other property and he's happy. He is even happy to pay taxes, believe it or not, to make up for all the years he was too poor to pay. He felt it was a blow to his pride.

Just recently he said to me, "You know, Frank, when I came over here, I had to borrow the money to pay for my trip, so when I arrived I was in debt. I owed $700. The first thing I did was to earn enough money to barely live on and pay back the debt immediately. Now things are much better. I only owe $700,000 — in mortgages."

To him this is the land of opportunity. He has a bigger debt, but he says, "Look at what I have. I don't worry about debts now as much as I used to."

His attitude has changed and maybe so has mine. All this time, I was helping him when I was going to school and after I graduated. For a number of years I was his interpreter, and now I am his consultant. He has his own business now and he's doing well in landscaping.

Now, my parents, compared to other Italians in the community, have become Canadianized to a greater degree. They go out more, they socialize more than they used to, but I think the reason for that is they are better off financially now than they were in the early years when they first came here.

Their attitudes have changed as well. In the old days, it was "Save a penny" or "You have to make ends meet". With the money came expressions like: "Screw business! I want to go on holiday for a couple of weeks. I don't give a damn!" But I know they are saying this tongue-in-cheek, because they do give a damn, and if something happened, they wouldn't take holidays.

If there was anything I could complain about, I guess it would be that my parents didn't make me appreciate the need to want something very badly. They gave me what I wanted too quickly.

Another thing was that they weren't demonstrative enough. The total lack of emotion bothered me. Italians are supposed to be such emotional, noisy, demonstrative people. Now I know that a good yelling match would have been worthwhile.

Once when my uncle was living with us, I did something I shouldn't have, and my mother chased me around the kitchen table with a broom ready to swat me on the bum. But I was faster than she. I think I was enjoying it.

My uncle who saw this got very angry, very emotional, threw a chair over and yelled at my mother to stop. Because I had never been used to emotional displays, it disturbed me very much, and I ran off and hid somewhere. I never forgot that.

The very few times I saw some emotion, it was either loving affection or hate . . . no in-between, and the only time I sensed there was some feeling between my father and mother was when he had an accident at work. He fell off the back of a truck, landed on his head and was taken to the hospital. He was a bloody mess with his head cracked open. We went running to the emergency when we got the news.

I remember the first night as my mother was leaving to go home, she bent over and kissed him. That was the first time I ever saw her kiss him, and I didn't realize until I was older that I never saw her display any emotion toward him. They were very private about their emotions, more my mother than my father. He used to wrestle with my brother and me, kid around, which is a form of affection, and yet when my brother tries to wrestle or give my mother a bear hug, she gets very uptight about it. She says she is busy, but I think she doesn't know how to handle these displays of emotions and affection. To this day I wonder if this is an immigrant thing, if most people's concern is whether they should be doing what they want to do, what they think they should do, or what they think people want them to do.

Another thing that immigrant parents sometimes have trouble with is giving their children self-confidence. Maybe they don't have any themselves as a result of their uprooting. They probably don't know any better, I'm sure, but if I had children, I would try first to instill in them a sense of responsibility — not to decide for them — but to guide them and hope they stick with it. That's a responsibility in itself, their learning to use their own common sense, and be confident about what they are doing. I want them to know what they want out of life, because to this day, I still don't know what I want. I've gotten this far — great — but where do I go from here? And it goes back to the parents, the immigrant ethic, the fears and insecurities passed on to the children. The first generation has the hardest time of all, not just with identity, but with a whole range of inherited emotional problems. These are the ones who most often are maladjusted.

You take a look at my parents who came from Italy. They are doing very well now and love Canada. I have often asked them if they would go back to live in Italy. No, no way, they say. For them there is no other country like Canada. I have the same opinion. I've been back and seen the way they live over there.

To this day, my parents' families don't have hot running water in the house. Twice I went over and each time we wanted to install hot water. They refused. We bought them a fridge, a TV, and I even suggested we give them money to put plumbing inside, but they won't have any of it. I couldn't live that way and neither could my parents. I'm too much of a Canadian, even though I inherited my background from my parents.

As I get older, I appreciate them more. I appreciate what they've been through and I appreciate their passing their culture on to me. I know that they have contributed something to this country. It may not be on a national scale, outside of income tax, but they did a lot on a community scale.

It goes back to the early days when the first garden was planted. It was their helping, their sharing whatever they grew, mixing wine in the basement and giving it to the neighbours...all this was a community belonging, all the way up to the present day.

They live in Cote St. Luc, in a primarily Jewish community and they give Italian parties — wine tasting, women baking cakes. They get a guy down from the Regie des Alcools to participate and the neighbours come in, join the festivities and it's written up in the *Suburban*, the local paper.

They have brought to this country a dogged determination to work and work hard, which unfortunately is lacking in some of the established Canadians. And, of couse, their biggest contribution is two sons. They may not have known it before, but they are beginning to.

For me, Canada has always had a special meaning, but I think they finally realized that things are better here and not in the old country. This is their country now.

Minko Sotiron

A MATTER OF CONSCIENCE

by Minko Sotiron

The little six-year-old German-speaking boy couldn't wait. After ten days at sea, the Hapag-Lloyd liner out of Hamburg, Germany, was moments away from sight of land.

It was 1952, and soon Minko would get his first glimpse of his new country — of New York, North America, the New World.

Skyscrapers! That was what he was especially keen about seeing. Sky ... scrapers! That meant they touched the sky. He couldn't wait to put his plan into action. Strange, that no one had ever thought of it before. Why, it was simplicity itself! If skyscrapers touched the sky, then he could simply walk into one of the tallest ones and whisk upward until the elevator got to heaven. And then he would get out and talk to God and live happily ever after.

Suddenly people were shouting, and his mother came over and told him that the ship was nearing land. The little boy stared at the horizon, and soon a low-lying shape became visible. "But where are the skyscrapers?" he asked his mother excitedly, pulling her sleeve.

"Over there," she pointed to something sticking up into the sky.

"But mother," he objected, "it's so low compared to all that sky above."

His mother simply smiled at him. Quite disgruntled at the reality of skyscrapers, he paid no attention to the Statue of Liberty when it was pointed out to him. Somehow, the new land, the promised land, had lost some of its glitter and promise.

June 12, 1967 was a special day in my life. On that day, I turned twenty-two, received my B.A. from the University of California at Berkeley and a not-unexpected message from the Selective Service Commission.

I didn't have to open the letter; I knew what was in it. But I steamed it open anyway and read that I was scheduled to report for a physical examination in two weeks. I resealed the envelope, crossed out the name and wrote "Address Unknown". I sent it back.

No, I didn't want to come home in a box, and I also believed the most courageous, principled thing I could do was to leave the U.S. and never participate in anything to do with the Vietnam war. My father gave me $1,000, signed over my little Volkswagen, and both my parents wished me luck and said good-bye.

On to Canada!

Instead of taking the most direct route from San Francisco along the coast up to Vancouver, I chose a more roundabout way through Nevada, Utah (Yellowstone National Park), Montana and back through northern Idaho and Washington. I deliberately took this route because I had the feeling it would be a long time before I would get the chance to get below the 49th parallel again.

In Seattle, while filling up with gas, the attendant asked me where I was going, after noticing my California licence.

"Vancouver," I replied.

"Now why do you want to go up there for?" he asked. "There's nothing there but a bunch of trees and rocks."

I kept my secret and didn't answer. As I got closer to the border, I became more and more excited and nervous. The big adventure, the great unknown was about to claim me.

As I approached the Blaine customs office, I checked my little green car out. I hoped that all my luggage and possessions wouldn't tip off the customs that I was planning a long vacation, perhaps a permanent one, in Canada.

The customs guard, a woman, sprightly and neat in her dark blue uniform and little, round hat with a badge in front, looked at me with a level eye.

"What's your reason for coming to Canada?" she asked.

"A vacation," I lied.

"How long are you staying?"

"Only a few days," I fibbed, praying my nose wouldn't grow longer. But I didn't have to worry. I was white, spoke English rather well and I didn't look like a hippie or a potential welfare bum. Moreover, I was fairly well-heeled. Why shouldn't she let me in? And she did.

At the time — I didn't know it then — I was entering Canada on a rather significant day in Canadian history. When I turned on the radio, I learned that it was July 1, 1967, and Canada was celebrating her 100th birthday.

"And here's a toast to all of you immigrants out there," said the disc-jockey, himself from Britain. "You've come to make a contribution to a great, humane country."

Well, I thought, what a nice introduction to Canada!

I really didn't know anyone in Vancouver except for an address I had of friends of friends in Berkeley. To my relief the ex-Berkelians, an Iowa farmboy now teaching Russian at Simon Fraser University, agreed to see me and put me up. His wife, a Chinese woman from San Francisco, and he described their experiences in Vancouver up to then.

"It's too white and too British," his wife said. "Too square. I'm damn tired of having people stare at John and me as if we were freaks. It's as if an interracial marriage was against the law!"

"That's right," agreed her husband, "you know what Vancouver is? It's the world's largest logging camp."

After a couple of days in the city, I could see their point about people staring at them, although I didn't agree with their logging-camp description.

Initially, the most surprising thing I found about Vancouver was the racial homogeneity, although there were few black faces to be seen. I marveled at the Anglo-Saxon character of the city apart from Chinatown, the few token Italians in east Vancouver, the Germans of Robsonstrasse and the denizens of the lower Hastings Street area.

But I was mystified at first as to why so many oriental-looking people were drunk in what I learned was Vancouver's skid row. My experience in San Francisco had led me to believe that on the whole Asians weren't big drinkers, and they certainly didn't drink in public. Then the light dawned. They weren't Chinese. They were Indians — native people. I had never seen so many Indians in my life.

That night I had my first experience in that most Canadian of institutions — the beer parlour, and what I saw saddened me. It was in the Rainier Hotel. I was propositioned several times by teen-aged Indian prostitutes already looking as if they were forty years old and so drunk they couldn't see straight. Everyone was yahooing and carrying on, but the revelry had a desperate quality to it as if they wanted to shout away the misery and shabbiness of their lives. The thing that bothered me the most was the calculated behaviour of some of the white people. They were obviously cruising to further exploit an already down-trodden people.

One scene I will never forget. In front of an Indian, who had passed out, his head in a pool of spilled beer on the round table, stood an array of draft beers and a pile of small bills and change. As regular as clockwork, the waiter would make his round and deposit two more beers and collect his payment and, of course, a healthy tip for himself.

After a few days with my friends, I found a room for myself in an old wooden house, east of Granville Street overlooking False Creek. It wasn't a terribly fashionable street; indeed, it was no better than skid row. My room was no bigger than my VW car, but at least it was my own.

I still remember some of the people at the rooming house: Anna, the fiery-tongued German woman, who collected the rent and had to fill the sawdust furnace every three hours during the winter; Peter, the big-bellied beer drinker, who stank up the toilet so badly you couldn't use it for an hour afterward; the two Chinese students who shared the cooking on a hotplate in the hallway outside their rooms, filling the house with the scent of their cuisine. And finally, Jillian, in the attic where I later moved after she was gone. She was a nymphomaniac from Prince Albert . . . a nice but pathetic woman. I can still hear the creak of the stairs as multitudes of men visited her and the squeak of her noisy, busy bed.

After a couple of days in my room, I decided the moment had come for me to apply for landed immigrant status. I drove back to the border, since you could apply there in those days.

I was interviewed by a severe-looking official with close-cropped hair. At first he asked innocuous questions.

"Why do you wish to emigrate to Canada?"

"I've been here for a while and I like it. It's the country for me."

He asked me about my education. I replied I had a B.A. How much money? I said $1,000. To my surprise he asked me to produce it. I did, and he carefuly counted it.

Then came the $64,000 question. Oh, he wasn't stupid.

Was I a draft-dodger?

No, I said, because in the strictest sense, I wasn't. My physical examination was still in the future, and at the moment I hadn't broken any laws. Although it really wasn't any of his business what my draft status was, I didn't want to antagonize him by pointing that out. I was also getting a bit apprehensive, a feeling that increased markedly, when he asked what was my status.

1A (the most eligible), I answered truthfully. I also explained that I had not been formally drafted. The official didn't say anything, and my heart began to sink.

He made me wait while he finished his report, and then to my surprise, smiled, extended his hand and said: "Good luck. You won't have any trouble getting your landed immigration card since I've scored you very highly, including giving you the maximum bonus points."

Several days after a required physical examination in federal immigration offices at the docks, I received my landed papers. I was a bona fide immigrant to my new country, Canada.

A couple of days later, I learned that I really was a landed immigrant in every sense of the word rather than an exile. I was reading the local "underground" paper, *The Georgia Straight,* and noticed an announcement asking all draft-dodgers in the Vancouver area to come to a meeting to be held in a Presbyterian Church on West Granville

Street. Curious, I went and was surprised by the turnout. Over two hundred young men filled the basement!

Most were draft-dodgers, but some were deserters. We took turns introducing ourselves and recounting the reasons why we were in Canada. Some were bewildered, mild-mannered people who had just wanted to be left alone. Others were moralistic about the war, while some wanted to use Canada as a base to conduct anti-war activities. Most of them, I discovered, were only in Canada in the physical sense; their minds remained in the U.S.

"Man, it's like being in a time-warp here," one of them told me, "it's as if everything is ten years in the past."

"Yeah," another piped up, "I come from Akron, and even there we're more hip."

The air hung heavy with homesickness. Many confessed to missing Phoenix or Los Angeles or wherever they came from. Others regretted coming to Canada as "chickening out" in the anti-war struggle at home. It was as if they were living in a bubble, so thoroughly did they ignore the country around them. When they began discussing the need for creating an anti-war organization, I had had enough. For me the U.S. was the past. I wasn't an exile, struggling to change things in my home country so I could return eventually. I was an immigrant, learning to be a Canadian. Let's explore Canada, I thought, as I left the meeting.

During my first couple of months in Vancouver, I was a busy boy. I managed to fall head-over-heels in love with a third-generation Vancouver girl (no mean feat considering that in 1900 Vancouver was little more than an outpost surrounded by wilderness), and I made friends with a gang of British Columbian English students. The immediate difference I noticed between them and my American student friends was that the Canadians didn't experience the fear and pressure of the draft. Several of them had done extensive traveling — then virtually unknown among male American students — and were much more relaxed than my friends. Another trait I appreciated was their seeming irreverence, both politically and socially. I found the lack of hyper-patriotism and my-country-right-or-wrong attitude, so evident in the U.S., quite refreshing.

From my girlfriend, I discovered that Canada had a history and it was not synonymous with that of the U.S. I also learned that traditions and celebrations in the States were ignored here, and that Canada had a distinct culture apart from that of the U.S. — a culture it was struggling to maintain. I also discovered the existence of Canadian nationalism.

When I learned about the Canadian identity, I was doubly ashamed of some views I had had about Canada and which I had expressed several years before. On a trip to Europe in 1964, I had met a young Canadian woman in Vienna. She was a student at Queen's University and, like me, had been born in Germany. Her family had emigrated to Canada about the same time mine had gone to the States. When I recall the conversation and how arrogantly I had dismissed her assertation of a separate identity and destiny for Canada, my cheeks burn with shame. It's ironic that years later I would echo her arguments that Canada was not interested in becoming part of the U.S.A.

Ah, the confidence and occasional blissful ignorance of youth!

With my determination to explore Canada uppermost in my mind, I spent the first year doing an inordinate amount of traveling — touring the country by rail, boat, car and thumb. I only missed two provinces, Newfoundland and Nova Scotia. During that period, I learned that Canada was a vast, unpopulated and relatively balkanized country with distinct regions. I also discovered that Canada was not all snow and pine trees, not everyone spoke English, the prairies weren't all flat as a pancake, and Canadians could be just as racist in their own way as the Americans they constantly criticize about that obnoxious characteristic.

I had intended to complete my first trip to Prince Rupert on the northern coast of British Columbia in a weekend — such was my ignorance of the distances involved. Luckily, I picked up three hitchhiking hippies outside Vancouver who quickly set me straight.

When I told them my destination, one of them asked: "Man, do you know how far that is?"

"Sure, I answered, "about three hundred miles."

"It's more like a thousand," he corrected.

They invited me to accompany them to Banff. On the way, they pointed out Canada's only desert, so they said, in Cache Creek. Sure enough, it was hot, sandy and there was sagebrush floating around. We stayed in a cabin outside Banff where I drank beer, smoked dope and generally acted like a twenty-two-year-old. The only unusual thing I did was climb several thousand feet and visit a young British firewatcher perched in a cabin overlooking the valley. It was a strenuous climb and took several hours. But the view of the towering rockies and emerald Lake Louise was awesome. So was the shattering silence.

The young man admitted he was slowly going crazy up there in the single-room cabin with glass panels on all sides.

"I only look at the trees once every fifteen minutes. If you do it more, you start to imagine fires," he said.

Just before we left, we had a visit from the big-horned mountain sheep who came to lick the salt that the firewatcher provided. They were incredible creatures with their curved horns and blank, opaque eyes.

On my way back to Vancouver, some of my "Great White North" misconceptions of Canada were wiped away when I visited such places as Peachland in the Okanagan and saw that Canada grew fruits and grapes just like sunny California.

Several months later, I finally made the trip to Prince Rupert with an American friend. About fifty miles north of 100 Mile House — that name struck me as reminiscent of the frontier — my friend suddenly remarked: "See that mountain over there," and he pointed to a distant tree-covered peak. "If that were in the U.S., there would be dozens of people climbing it. But here there's no one on it."

My impressions of that trip were of mile after mile of bush, no signs, no roadside-diners or fast-food places, no houses, just wilderness. Occasionally we'd drive through a town which seemed like a leaf floating on a vast ocean.

In the north, as we cut west from Prince George (it was all so British — those Princes), then Vanderhoof, the country changed from the dry interior to lush green vegetation and constantly overcast, darkly foreboding skies. Water was everywhere, an impression that increased as we neared Prince Rupert. People wore slickers and Wellingtons as if they were everyday clothes.

What made me sad was passing through a pathetic Indian village with leaning, peeling totem poles and the infinitely sorrowful look of the people sitting dispiritedly on their front porches.

Prince Rupert was a disappointment. Instead of the fabled gateway to the Pacific, it turned out to be a rather mean little town, sodden from too much rain, the road ending at a cod-liver-oil factory whose stench immediately persuaded us to turn around and leave.

On the way back, we had our American chauvinism and cultural ignorance highlighted by the spectacle of Barkerville. We had been told by Canadian friends to see it and were surprised by the fact that it was one of the largest ghost towns, if not the largest in North America. On the trip up to Canada, I had visited Virginia City, easily the largest and most famous ghost town in the U.S.A. But it was tiny compared to Barkerville, which I discovered was at one time the largest town after San Francisco west of the Mississippi. The gold rush had come and gone like a flash flood sweeping everything before it.

In 1968, after working at the Sedgewick Undergraduate Library at the University of British Columbia, I got tired of the job I had shelving books. I quit and decided to seek my fortune out east. The University, incidently, had been quite a haven for draft-dodgers; many worked there, and when I left, a draft-dodger from Oregon by the name of Dale Liberty replaced me.

I bought a student's fare on the Transcontinental and for four days and three nights, I traveled east, sleeping like a twisted pretzel on the day seats. If I was lucky, I could turn the seats in front backwards and get a bit more room. Different people would get on — miners in Edmonton, drinking and yahooing, grizzled, craggy-faced farmers, back-packers and so on.

The mountains gave way to rolling prairies which in turn changed to rock and pine of the Canadian Shield. It just never seemed to end. I got out in Sioux Lookout, Ontario, where it was still winter in March with a fine, powdery snow and a deep blue sky.

Then, when I reached Quebec, I got my first shock. Although I knew that French was spoken, deep down, I really hadn't accepted it until I heard two elegant women conversing in French in the dining cars.

Montreal . . . I spent a month there, but felt intimidated by my lack of French and decided to go east. Back on the train I climbed and on I traveled through New Brunswick and then by ice-breaker to Prince Edward Island. Once I got the lay of the land, I surmised that when Dick, Jane and Spot of the primary school books visited Grandfather's farm with the red barn and silo, it was on P.E.I.

Upon returning to Montreal, I decided there was nothing for me there. It was March, and I picked a cold, blustery day to hitchhike. But luck was with me, and a traveling salesman knocked five hundred miles off for me, apologizing for the shortness of the trip. He left me in the little town of Thessalon, forty-five miles east of Sault Ste. Marie. Its one-horse character could be best be typified by the sophisticated fire escape in the tiny, ancient hotel where I slept. It consisted of a giant rope tied around the foot of my iron bed, complete with instructions to throw it out of the window in case of fire.

Rides were difficult the next day. Anyone who has stood for hours in the same spot at the side of the road, eventually realizes what life is all about.

One ride, though, was remarkable, but to this day I still haven't figured out what happened. I had only managed to cover twelve miles in five hours, and as I sat under a clump of trees and gazed at Lake Superior before me, the snow was gently falling. I had just opened a tin of sardines when a pickup truck with a canopy on the back drove by and stopped at my lazily proffered thumb.

Two men sitting inside, wearing red plaid jackets like Ontario lumbermen, asked if I would mind a slight detour before the Soo.

"Of course not," I said, sitting in the back and finishing my sardines.

They drove down a winding road in the middle of a forest and stopped in an Indian community. They entered a house, and moments later, they came running out of the door, shouting. They leapt into the truck, and with a roar, we lurched at top speed from the village. As I looked out, someone was chasing us, firing a rifle at us. Bullets whizzed by, but to this day it's still a mystery to me.

They dropped me off in the "Soo", after loudly denouncing "those fucking, lazy Indians". It began to snow heavily , and I got worried because I was starting to resemble a giant snowman hitchhiking along the Trans-Canada. Finally, a diesel mechanic picked me up and drove me to White River. When we arrived, I saw two things which dropped my heart into my boots. There were twelve groups of hitchhikers stretched along the strip of service stations and fast-food restaurants; the other was a giant thermometer trumpeting the fact that several years ago White River had the distinction of being the coldest place in the world at this latitude! It was snowing, and I prayed: "Oh, don't let history repeat itself!"

To this day, remembering the giant thermometer, I chuckle at how Canada goes in for that sort of thing. So far, I've seen a giant gorilla on the Trans-Canada in the Rockies; a giant oxcart in Melville, Saskatchewan; the giant Canada geese in Wawa, Ontario; the giant nickle, not to forget Superstack in Sudbury, Ontario; and finally the Kenora, Ontario moose with its balls painted fluorescent pink, the better to see them in the dark!

Glumly, I stood at the last service station at the end of the strip, looking at the snowflakes multiplying and wondering when and if I was ever going to get out. Would I survive the night in my down sleeping bag underneath the trailer parked next to the road?

Gradually, it got darker and the cars more infrequent. When a red Volkswagen pulled into the service station with only one man in it, I looked at him and thought, why not? I walked over and before I could say anything, he rolled down the window and asked me were I was going.

"Vancouver," I answered.

"Winnipeg," he said. "Hop in."

Elated, I did.

He was a pilot and on his way to pick up his girlfriend in Winnipeg,. It was already dark, and he wanted to reach Fort William (Thunder

Bay). There was no moon and there was nothing but pitch-black roads for miles. Jokingly, he said: "What a place to break down, eh?" And seconds later, we did.

The car went dead. We tried to fix it, but nothing helped. It was eerily still, not a sound, and unfortunately, no cars. A half an hour later, miraculously, a car came by and before we could flag it down it stopped. We told the man driving what had happened, and our saviour said: "You know, long ago, someting weird like that happened to me. Maybe it's the same thing."

He screwed something off in the air filter, blew into it, and told us to try the engine. It started like a charm. Friendly people, Canadians, I thought as I got back into the car. I wasn't sure that other people in the same circumstances would have done the same thing.

The next day showed me another side to the Canadian character, thankfully not shared by most. The pilot and I had reached Kenora, where we decided to have a beer. It was a typical tavern of its time — urinal modern, with furniture and decor designed to be as uncomfortable and revolting as possible.

I was talking to some Indians at the next table. I was curious about what tribe they were from and a few other things. They told me they were from the Grassy Narrows Cree. My pilot was making some disparaging remarks about how they had to work and lift themselves by their bootstraps.

The Indian tried to explain, but the pilot suddenly stood up and impatiently said it was time to leave. I looked back, and the Indian said to me angrily and a bit sadly: "That's the trouble with you white people; you never listen!"

As we were driving away, I told the pilot we should have stayed and listened to him and I felt badly about it.

"Bah," he snorted, "look, they're lazy, dirty and stupid."

"You sound just like the bigots in the U.S.," I retorted. "They use the same language except they're talking about "niggers" or "Meskins". Why is it that when people don't like someone they always put them down the same way?"

But he wouldn't admit he was wrong. "Keep 'em on the reservations," he said.

I left him in Winnipeg, took a train back to Vancouver and started Graduate School at Simon Fraser University.

In 1972, I passed my citizenship test with flying colours. (Note the "u" in colour.) I had Canadianized myself sufficiently to put that letter in the necessary word endings and also to pronounce the letter z as "zed" and not "zee". But I could never bring myself to pronounce lieutenant as "leftenant", khaki as "kharki" and call a candy bar, a chocolate bar. I still haven't learned to call a rubber band an elastic band. I only missed one question when I said that the Northwest Territories had one member in the Senate.

By the time my citizenship was official, I had also received my Master of Arts degree from Simon Fraser University. It was at this time that my hankering to go to the Bay area became increasingly pronounced. I had no wish to return permanently to the U.S., but over the years I missed the opportunity to visit occasionally.

When something is forbidden, it becomes even more desirable. Outside of a one-day drunken excursion to Seattle with three friends, I had not been to the States for five years. Berkeley, San Francisco and California loomed in my imagination like some fabled golden place just beyond my horizon. After five years, I wanted to visit what had once been my home.

After my citizenship ceremony and graduation, I decided to go. After an enormous party with all of my friends, another friend drove me quietly over the border, and I flew to San Francisco from Seattle.

It's sad how dreams are quickly and ruthlessly altered by reality. After the initial excitement of seeing and smelling San Francisco, I felt like a stranger in what had once been part of me. Familiar things, to be sure, but I felt out of place in them. I just didn't feel I belonged anymore. The few remaining friends I had there weren't overly excited to see me. My left-wing Canadian perspective on just about everything clashed with their more imperio-centristic American viewpoint. Their accents jarred my sensibilities, as I'm sure my ending all my sentences with "eh" bothered them. All in all, after three days, I was bored and quite ready to go back home to Vancouver. American concerns — their preoccupation with crime (I was shocked to see an armed guard patrol downtown McDonald's), and the horrendous bombing of North Vietnam — weren't mine.

Then disaster struck. One morning as my parents and I were planning to go to a shopping mall, the telephone rang.

"Is this Michael Sotiron from Vancouver?" a female voice asked.

"Yes," I answered stupidly.

"This is the operator. We had a long-distance call which we were unable to transmit because our trunk lines were jammed. The party will call back."

It appeared suspicious, but then, it could be nonsense. I didn't have a chance to reflect about it because as I hung up, the front gate bell rang. You can't see the gate from the front door, so my father asked who it was.

"FBI," came the reply. "Mr. Sotiron, I'd like to speak to you about something."

Quietly, I tiptoed to the basement stairs, then bolted down them, hoping to make a break through the back door and out into the garden. There was a crashing sound, and two men burst through the garage door just as I was unbolting the door to the rear.

"Against the wall, hands in front!" one of them yelled, pulling a revolver, crouching in a two-handed firing position.

"Going anywhere, Mike?" the other asked, while frisking me.

By this time, a third one, an older man, sporting a small American flag on his lapel, and obviously in command, arrived at the same time as my parents. He read me the Miranda Act, while my mother shouted "Gestapo" at them. My father was arguing that they couldn't touch me because I was a Canadian citizen.

They ignored all this and ordered me to take off my belt.

They handcuffed me and looped the belt through the cuffs. After putting my long leather overcoat on me, they led me away, two on one side, one discreetly holding the belt like a dog on a leash. Cleverly, they had parked their car a block away so I couldn't get suspicious. I felt numb, almost in shock, like a trapped and trussed deer. As I looked up at my neighbour's window, there she was, looking out at me, and I knew how the FBI discovered I was back.

"You know, Mike, I've been looking for you for a long, long time," the older man with the flag pin said. "You're my oldest case. I never thought I'd get you. So how was it up there in Canada?"

I didn't answer; I was pretty uncomfortable sitting in the back of the car, my hands still handcuffed in back of me, and the two agents sitting on each side. We arrived at the mammoth, fortress-like federal building downtown and went in by a special entrance. We used a different elevator complete with bars diagonally across it. After we arrived at the 17th floor, we walked down a corridor, passing a long series of large photographs of wanted terrorists, Weathermen and the like.

"Know any of 'em, Mike?" one of my captors asked me.

"You've got to be kidding," I answered.

Then, all of the things I had seen on TV or had read about happened to me. First, I was fingerprinted, then they put a numberplate around my neck and took frontal and profile photographs of my face. When that was finished, they led me downstairs to a courtroom where I saw my parents waiting anxiously. A judge was there, and another man, a prosecutor, started the case as soon as I entered.

He spelled out the case against me: I was accused of failing to notify my draft board of my whereabouts. This was punishable by a maximum of five years in prison and a $10,000 fine.

The judge asked how much bail should be set.

"Would $1,000 be sufficient?" he asked the prosecutor.

Oh, let it be that, I thought. A thousand isn't much; I could easily skip the country and return to Canada where they couldn't touch me.

"No, your honour. He's our oldest case. It should be more so as to prove a deterrent in case he is thinking of leaving."

"Two thousand dollars," said the judge. It sounded like an auction, I thought, with my freedom going to the highest bidder.

"Your honour," objected the prosecutor, "we've traced Sotiron all over Canada, to England, Hamburg, Germany, even Bulgaria. That isn't enough."

"Five thousand," decided the judge, and bang went the gavel.

My father agreed to pay the bail, and I agreed to the restrictions. I couldn't leave the Bay area without special permission. I was free, but only temporarily. Stunned, my parents and I arose. But before we could leave, the judge summoned me to his chambers. He was surprisingly sympathetic to my situation.

"Do you earn much money?" he asked.

"No!"

"Good, because I am declaring you indigent and eligible for federal assistance in legal fees. And here's the name of an excellent draft lawyer. Good luck!"

The lawyer turned out to be good, indeed, and very sympathetic. Initially, with my father's agreement, I was thinking of jumping bail, and he'd forfeit the five thousand dollars. But the lawyer persuaded me to go the whole legal route, and if all else failed, I would know what to do. (He told me he couldn't advise me to break the law, but by saying that, he as much as advised me to.) In a special hearing he obtained permission for me to go back to Vancouver, claiming that I would be fired if I didn't. I found this ironic since I didn't have a job at the time.

What a relief it was to be back in Canada! It's truly my home, I thought. My Vancouver friends were extremely supportive and advised me to stay. The Americans couldn't touch me in Canada and I had broken no Canadian law, so extradition was out. But I went back. I simply didn't want to give the American government five thousand dollars. When I arrived, I phoned my lawyer, and he told me that he had planned a giant defense strategy, pulling out all the media stops.

Later that night, he phoned me back. "You're not going to believe this," he said, "but the government has dropped all the charges. Don't ask me why, but they did. You're a very lucky man."

Lucky! What an understatement! It was as if a huge weight had been removed from my chest. Up to now, my life had been filled with sleepless nights, nightmares and the crushing anxiety of knowing that I had literally screwed myself. It's always worse when you have no one to blame but yourself.

There's a sequel to this story.

When I returned to Vancouver, life somehow seemed flat and pointless, almost anti-climactic. I picked up and moved east to Toronto. Several months later, my mother sent me a letter. It was from the Selective Service Commission, assigning me a new draft classification — 1Y.

"It never ends," she wrote.

That was ten years ago. Now I'm happily married and have two children and live in Montreal.

One ironic twist to my saga as an immigrant involved my daughter. My wife, who is Quebecoise, comes from a family rooted for at least three hundred years in Canadian soil.

However, when my daughter, Veronique, was born in France in 1976, I was the one who gave her Canadian citizenship.

My wife didn't have her birth certificate with her, only her passport, which is considered to be a travel document and not proof of citizenship. It's rather stupid when you know it is impossible to get a passport without producing a birth certificate.

I, who had only been a Canadian citizen for four years and had my citizenship card with me, bestowed that proud birthright on my daughter. My wife, whose ancestors came to Canada from Normandy in the 17th century, was denied this privilege.

She was understandably upset, but I felt proud and pleased in spite of the irony of it all. I value my Canadian citizenship even more highly as a result.

Tom Nacos

I'LL FIGHT:
From an interview with Tom Nacos

It's almost dawn and Montreal is slowly awakening. A lone jogger in bright orange shorts and tank top is running up Cote des Neiges Road toward Beaver Lake.

On the opposite side of the almost deserted street, a blue Chrysler with two men in it stops at a red light. The driver leans out the windows and shouts at the jogger as he goes by.

"Run, you asshole!"

Tom Nacos slows in mid-stride, turns slightly and yells back.

"Go screw yourself!"

He keeps running.

Something tells him to look back, and he notices the big car has made a U-turn and is coming back on his side of the street.

As Nacos approaches Remembrance Road on his way to the lake, the car pulls over and stops a little way ahead of him. Instinct tells him they are waiting for him.

There's going to be trouble, Tommy boy. Be prepared, he thinks.

The man on the passenger's side opens the door and steps out, and before he can do anything, Nacos lets fly with his fist and belts him on the chin. He slides to the pavement in slow motion. His friend in the car freezes behind the wheel.

Barely breaking his stride, the jogger hops over the prone man and continues his pace up Remembrance Road. He glances back once and sees the driver emerge from the car and help his friend into the front seat.

The car pulls away from the curb and gathering speed, heads toward Queen Mary Road.

Tom Nacos is unflustered. "They figured they were two to one and could beat me up, but the element of surprise cuts down the odds. I never run away from a fight. I won't start one, but if someone's out to get me, I'll fight!"

Born in Siastasta near Kozanis in northern Greece, Tom Nacos comes from hardy Macedonian stock. The entire village of 8,000 people is involved in the main industry — furs that are imported from all over the world. People from surrounding towns converge on Siastasta during the day to work on the pelts. At least 3,000 are from outside the village.

Although Nacos' father was in farming, wholesale meat and real estate, the young man chose the fur industry. A family tiff sparked the decision.

"I came to Canada in February, 1957 when I was eighteen years old. I wanted to go into my father's business as a partner. He wanted me to start from the bottom, sweeping floors. I wasn't going to accept that, so I left.

"I had an uncle, an American, who was married to a Montreal girl, and he sponsored me."

Nacos rented a room from a Greek family in Outremont and stayed with them for five years. When the family returned to Greece, he kept the apartment.

He went to work in the fur industry as an errand boy and swept floors in the back, precisely what he had tried to avoid in Greece, he chuckles.

He muses about the early days and his "sink or swim" introduction to Canada.

"I arrived on a Friday night. Saturday morning I was taken to the factory on St. Alexandre Street to be shown where I would be working on Monday morning. All I had was my clothes and $66 in American money.

"My father thought I wouldn't be able to make it and would go back. Not having much money made things difficult for me. I had to make it. I wasn't giving in."

To augment his $20-weekly salary, Nacos gathered all the empty pop bottles during lunch hour at the factory and collected two cents on each at a nearby store. This money would pay for a Vienna roll, a piece of ham and a soft drink.

"That was my lunch for years. I used to take orders from the other workers to get their lunch, and I would get angry if someone ordered coffee instead of a soft drink. That meant I couldn't make two cents on the bottle.

"On the weekends, I would wait for the Rialto Theatre on Park Avenue to empty so I could earn a few dollars on Friday and Saturday night cleaning up — sweeping the floors."

He smiles wryly.

He went to work early in the morning and came home late at night.

"I would stay after work on my own time so I could learn English and French and as soon as I had a command of the language, I enrolled at McGill to learn business administration."

At the end of nine years, he was manager of the fur company and a year later, he opened his own business with his brother and a friend, another Greek immigrant.

"It's not easy being an immigrant," he admits. "When I first came here, I didn't speak the language. You have a tendency to be quite timid and try to stay out of trouble. But people push you around.

"I remember one incident when I was asked for a cigarette by someone on the street. There were four guys in the group and they tried to grab the whole pack. I would have given them one, but not the whole thing. I didn't make much money then and I couldn't afford to give the pack away.

"One of the guys pushed me, and I hit him. I walked into a restaurant where I was meeting a friend, and two hours later, when I left with him, the gang was outside waiting for me. I knew what was going to happen, and I saw there was no way to run. By now there were six guys in the gang, not four. Three were ahead of us and three behind, closing the gap."

Nacos figured either way he had no choice. He told his friend to keep walking, and as the three in front approached, he jumped them.

"I didn't give them a chance to hit first. I attacked fast and ran like hell. But you can't run forever."

He had to fight because he wouldn't tolerate being pushed around, he says.

"It has always been my principle in life to take the initiative and not wait for something to happen. That's my personality — 100 per cent. I have to face things head on. For a long time, I always tried to be diplomatic, but somehow it never worked out that way. I had to go back to my own beliefs and follow through.

"But you have to understand I'm not a tough guy. I am easy to get along with, but sometimes people don't understand or know when to draw the line. I don't enjoy getting tough."

From the time he came to Canada, every minute of his time was organized. For the first five or six months, he associated only with Greeks. As soon as his language skills in English and French increased and he had more confidence in his ability to communicate, he began mixing with all kinds of people, especially the Irish and Jews.

"You should hear me speak Jewish," he grins.

"I always had good relations with people, you know, the mutual respect thing. Once everyone knows what your beliefs are and what you stand for, there is respect. I got invited to different ethnic groups' homes, parties, dinners and holiday celebrations. Somewhere down the line you get recognition.,"

In addition to working and going to school at night, Nacos tried to have some social life. Sometimes he would meet "the boys" and go up north for part of the weekend.

"We all chipped in for gas and the motel room, and for two dollars we spent Saturday afternoon and evening and part of Sunday up there. There were always friends who would invite us to their homes.

"On Friday nights we would play cards all night. The next day, I would go with my friends to the Y on Park Avenue near St. Viateur Street to swim, exercise and box, and in the summer we'd play field ball on the Outremont High School grounds or on Fletcher's Field.

"I don't have bad memories of the early years here. It was a hard life, but they were the best years — making it on my own in a strange country. It was a challenge."

After a year in business, he bought out his partner and that first year on his own, became engaged and married.

"That was in 1966 and by the end of the year, I had moved into new and larger premises on de Maisonneuve Boulevard and I employed 25 to 30 people."

The business kept growing and by 1972, he was in an even larger building.

"You see, when I came to Canada, I made a bet with myself. I said I was going to be a millionaire by the time I was 35. I only missed by one year. I was 34 years old." He smiles proudly.

"I think I owe my determination to my father. He was the cause of it all. You have to understand that Greeks are fighters. They are tough! This characteristic goes back thousands of years," he says. "The men fought and the women provided everything else. Fighting was an honourable profession. A warrior spent his time training for the fight and a philosopher hung around the cafes and 'philosophized'. It still exists today.

"You get all this toughness when you are young. My father wasn't tough because he was a Greek, but because he was a man. He was a strong and determined individual. He left Greece as a child and grew up in the United States," Nacos explains.

"He served in the American army in World War I and became a captain. In France his horse was shot under him and he was thrown and broke his leg."A tone of pride creeps into Nacos' voice as he continues.

"My father got gassed trying to put his mask on his horse before wearing it himself. That's the kind of man he was. He thought of the animal first."

Nacos says he had to work from the time he was eight years old, even though the family was wealthy. His father didn't believe in wasting time or money, no matter how young his son was.

"He toughened me up . . . taught me everything I know. This is a Greek tradition handed down from father to son.

"There was no doubt in his mind that I couldn't face life in a strange country without knowing the language. He did it, too. Although he wanted me to stay, it was our stubbornness that pushed us apart.

Many times over the years I wished I could go back to Greece to my father, but my pride wouldn't allow it. I didn't speak to him for ten years."

His father's basic philosophy was the care of the body." He believed in a sound mind in a sound body," says Nacos.

"He would exercise for an hour every morning. I used to do the same in my room every day. Even now, I'm not in a good frame of mind and feel uncomfortable if I don't exercise."

Because of this need to look after his body, he played semi-professional sports back in Greece.

"I was young and fast. I had good reflexes and I was disciplined. The other team members were in their twenties. I was only thirteen."

The other players used tactics he didn't know, and he would take things into his own hands and play aggressively, even dangerously, he admits.

"My game was destructive. I played to win. My coach tried to tone me down, but I took the game very seriously. It was hard for me to accept defeat."

When he learned that defeat wasn't a disgrace, he became a much better person, he says.

"Now, I can accept it almost as well as victory, but I don't enter anything, not even a game of cards, thinking I will lose. I'm out to win, but if I lose, that's part of life and I have no excuse. It's not because the other person was better than me, but only because I didn't try hard enough to win."

From his father, Nacos inherited a streak of patriotism. His father fought for the United States in World War I, went back to Greece and got caught in the middle of World War II, unable to leave the country. Although he was an American, he was still part Greek and couldn't get involved in partisan activity.

"He had to keep his nose clean, but he believed you owed something to your country. He was very civic-minded as well. He was elected mayor of his village and he felt it was his duty to serve.

"I feel the same way. I feel close to the United States because of my father; to Greece because I was born there and lived there for eighteen years, but especially to Canada. I owe Canada a lot.

"As an immigrant," says Nacos, "the best way to succeed in life is to set goals, use determination, hard work and honesty."

"I don't believe in stepping over bodies to get there, but determination is my first priority. Equally important is getting a good education."

He insists his children do well in school. It's better to get an education when you are young, he says.

"It's too difficult to get one when you are older and involved in other things. Although I was good in math, geometry and physics, I didn't have much patience for subjects that needed application and study. But if I had to do it all over again, the only thing I would change would be to get more education."

He admits he is not a reader. Except for the newspaper he reads little else. The things he enjoys are being with friends and associating with people who know and read a great deal.

"I admire intelligence and I learn from others. I don't even have the patience to take notes. I get others to do that for me. As my business gets bigger and bigger, it is more difficult for me. I can't keep everything in my head and have to get others to do it for me."

Nacos says he is a man of principle, but he is not the kind to use the pen. "I use the sword. I'm not proud of it, but it happens that way."

He insists he doesn't like to fight, but he won't run away from it. Scraps seem to follow him around.

"You don't plan these things, they just happen. If someone is out to hurt you, you fight. However, once you establish you aren't looking for a scrap, but will fight if necessary, people will leave you alone."

Meanwhile, the government has planned to interview Tom Nacos this year for its Business Blue Book. As an immigrant who has made it up the ladder of success in a relatively short time, he is an ideal subject.

Nacos doesn't want it. He doesn't enjoy exposure and he feels modesty has nothing to do with it.

"I don't like being exposed to the public eye and I feel the less people know about me the better.

"There are people who like to be known wherever they go, but I am the opposite. I'm not impressed with people recognizing me when I walk into a place or making me feel like a celebrity. Inside I am really a shy person, even if people think I am friendly, happy-go-lucky and charming."

He grins disarmingly at the last description.

"However, I am not shy in business," he says. But achieving his goals in Canada hasn't stopped Tom Nacos from demanding more of himself. He says he never liked the fur industry — in fact he hated it. He wanted to diversify. He preferred the real estate business. Although furs provided his living, he felt it was a limited field.

"You can reach a certain level, but it's not a business you can build an empire on. I wanted to build an empire, start a dynasty. I haven't succeeded, no, but I still have the feeling in me. I might some day . . . the same way I started . . . keep working, keep expanding. I'm not trying to prove something, but I don't believe in doing things halfway. I haven't given up and I want to be in business to the last day of my life.

"And Canada is the ideal place to do it."

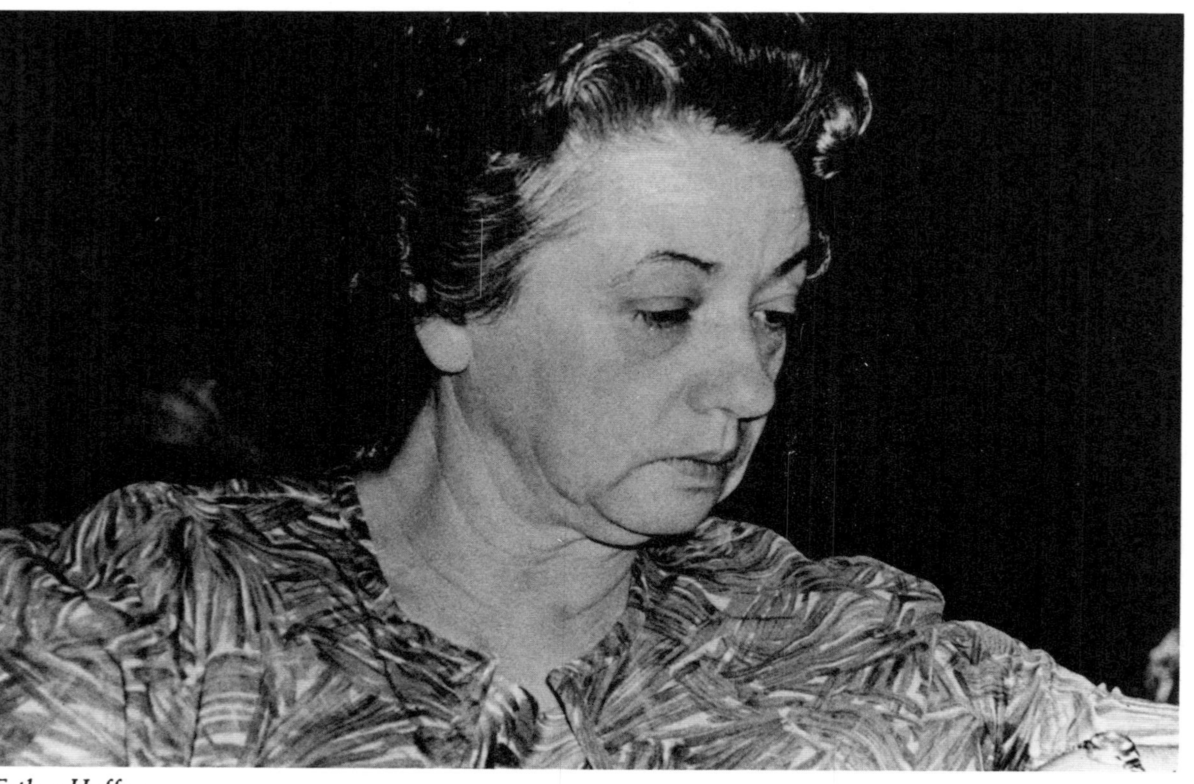

Esther Hoffer

A NEW WORLD ROMANCE

by Esther Hoffer

Clara Schwartz and Israel Hoffer met on board a ship bound for Canada in 1905. Their final destination was the territory which would become Saskatchewan that year.

At first glance, there was nothing remarkable about this young man. He was of medium height, stocky, clean shaven and had thick, wavy black hair and hazel eyes. But the eyes . . . they turned an arresting, steady gaze. One sensed strength and determination.

Clara was a slender, young girl with soft chestnut-brown hair and green-flecked grey (sometimes blue) eyes. There was nothing remarkable about her either, but she had a quick wit, logical intelligence, a love of life and optimism.

These two had something in common.

Israel's father, Moishe Hoffer, was the son of a wealthy landowner in Wiznitz, Galicia. Perhaps Moishe would not be as successful as his father, but he had a future of promise. He married, had his own small plot of land in Kossow, twenty kilometres from Wiznitz, and a growing herd of cattle.

But suddenly the promise of a future disintegrated. His young wife died, and he was bitten by a rabid dog. He was sent to an asylum where he was expected to die. But he recovered and when he returned, it was to an impoverished farm.

Moishe met a woman he fell in love with. She was the daughter of another wealthy landowner. But both young people were disowned for their choices and Moishe knew that if he regained the promise of his future, it would be without the help of their parents.

They married and their first child was a daughter, Eva. On March 10, 1885, their first son, Israel, was born. A third child, Mayer, was born three years later. Slowly the farm was rebuilt and life was good.

When Israel was six years old, his mother died. With no support from either family, the three younger children were brought up by a sister, still a child herself. Moishe, helpless, harassed and struggling to provide for them, retreated into the security of his religion. He became puritanically strict. The bonds between the children strengthened, but Israel grew up a vulnerable child, afraid to show affection for fear of rejection.

Clara Schwartz's father, Schmaya, born in a Russian-Jewish ghetto, had a less auspicious beginning than did Moishe, Israel's father. Young boys in the Russian-Jewish ghettos often simply disappeared off the streets — "inducted" into the Russian army. The sons were lost to their families and to Judaism. Many parents, rather than face the terror of losing their sons, took the train to the Austrian border and walked through the forests to offer their sons to Austrian-Jewish families. Schmaya's parents were among them.

Schmaya was raised as a son by a man who already had at least six sons of his own. In fact, his acceptance into the family went further than he might have wished. When an older brother, betrothed to be married, died, Schmaya was expected to fulfill the obligation, as tradition demanded, and marry the bereaved bride-to-be. Schmaya rebelled. So bitter was the ensuing battle that he never had contact with his family again.

Shortly afterwards, Schmaya married the cause of the rebellion, Zelda, with the soft, chestnut hair her daughter, Clara, was to inherit, and striking blue eyes. They settled in Davidenny and on December 5, 1887, Clara, who was to be one of nine children, was born.

Clara was a slender, graceful, inquisitive child. Schmaya loved her fiercely, recognizing in her something different, a feeling that she was destined for something different. At first, because there were no schools in Davidenny, Schmaya taught Clara at home. But he recognized his sources were limited. When Clara was nine, he moved his family to Storozynetz, a town twenty kilometres away where there was a *gymnasium*, a high school.

Although they were reluctant to take Jewish students, Schmaya managed to get her into the *gymnasium*. From an orthodox point of view, Schmaya probably bent the rules a little, but when the principal put obstacles in the way of his Jewish students, such as setting final exams on religious holidays or Saturdays, Schmaya assured Clara that God would not want her to lose her education because of one man's stupidity.

School, violin lessons, and friends filled the childhood years clearest in her memory. She formed a friendship with two other girls in the school, the "triumvirate". They were inseparable, in school and out, up to both good and bad. There were enticing meadows and orchards around Storozynetz which were owned and patrolled by a wealthy landowner. They were off-limits. But the girls explored them anyway, and to assuage their guilt, did their best to ignore the fruit.

One day the blue sky, the soft air, the smell of the grass and the fruit ripening in the warm sun was too much for them. One of the girls climbed into an apple tree and began throwing apples to the other two. Suddenly there were barking dogs and a guard. They froze. Penalties were always swift and sure. They waited.

The guard looked at them. He called back his dogs. Perhaps he felt as they on this mellow day; perhaps he had children of his own.

"Don't let me catch you again."

They fled — with their apples.

While Clara was going to school, Israel was battling with his father. He was thirteen years old now, a man. Moishe wanted him to begin rabbinical studies. During this period there was a growing movement of young people who began to look to the new world and to Palestine as an opportunity to regain their dignity and self-respect. Opportunities to own land in Russia and Europe were rare; opportunities for their children were minimal. They lived in constant fear.

A man now at thirteen, Israel ran away to agricultural school. The principal of the school was Dr. Landau, whose purpose was to train young men so they could go out and take their place in the world as farmers — perhaps to Palestine, perhaps to the new world where they could be part of building, a part of new values. From Dr. Landau, Israel learned a love of truth and justice and, fiercely loyal to anyone who had ever helped him, Israel never forgot him. Perhaps Dr. Landau was the father and mother he'd never had, and Israel truly and deeply loved him.

Israel ran away, and Moishe followed. But what could he do? His son was happy there, and the school was kosher. He went back home to worry about keeping his second son at home.

When Israel finished school at seventeen, he was suddenly of interest to his grandfather Schulum, Moishe's father, who saw the youth as a trained agriculturalist and useful as a manager. Israel tried working for him but his nature was no more submissive now than it had been under his father's roof. When Dr. Landau approached him with the idea and the fare to go to Canada, Israel was delighted. In return he promised Dr. Landau that he would estabish a Jewish colony in the new world.

Meanwhile in Storozynetz, tragedy struck. Zelda became ill first. When she recovered from typhoid fever the following spring, she learned she had lost five of her nine children to the disease. Anguished and angry, Schmaya decided to emigate. Certainly the obstacles to the education of his children, the lack of opportunity for all of them, had made him consider it, not to mention the endless epidemics — diphtheria, smallpox, cholera, tuberculosis — and David, his eldest son, nearing military age. He knew Pearl, Zelda's sister, and Jacov her husband had settled in a valley, the Qu'appelle Valley in Assiniboia, Canada. They could go there.

Friends and neighbors sat *shiva* for them as one does for the dead, wailing, "You are going to a land of ice and snow." Indeed, their premonition of ultimate separation was correct, for those who stayed behind were eventually lost to the many epidemics or, finally, to the Holocaust of World War II.

But Clara, although she was sorry to leave her friends and the violin lessons, looked forward to new places, new experiences . . . and a new world.

Israel left for Canada with his father's prediction, "You'll be eaten by wolves!" ringing in his ears. He left a promise that he would send for Moishe and Mayer, his brother, when he had saved enough money.

It was a crowded cattle boat, crammed to capacity with refugees, some fleeing the Russian pogroms and others the Russo-Japanese war. Israel and Clara met almost immediately. They shared their dreams of the new world: hers, the excitement of new lands to discover; his, the colony he would establish; both, a place where Jews could be free to own land — to live as others had for centuries. They recited poetry together and sang German *leider.* They were in a world of their own. They didn't see the hunger, sorrow and fear around them, only the sea, sky, sunsets — a preparation, perhaps, for the treasures this prairie would offer.

They docked in Quebec and separated — Israel to continue on to Hirsch, Clara to go on to Montreal with her family to wait for their luggage. They separated, fighting back tears, and gathered their memories in silence: Israel's of a young woman with chestnut hair, who was intelligent, serious, spirited, and laughing and Clara of a handsome young man who knew what he wanted — and who had said softly that with her beside him, he would accomplish it.

The Schwartzes remained in Montreal for six weeks, anxious to begin their new life, anxious to leave the dire predictions of their new friends.

Israel had already arrived in Hirsch in falling snow, with no one to meet him. Rabbi Berner, who just happened to be there and took him home, fed him and put him to bed on a pile of hay on the kitchen floor. Rabbi Berner liked Israel immediately and asked him to work for him for $125 a year. The Rabbi could then spend more time on the spiritual concerns of the community. His own family of five children were cared for by the oldest daughter, who was fourteen, the same as Israel's brother and sister had been cared for by Eva. The Rabbi's wife had just died that year.

While Israel was working for Rabbi Berner (work that proved to be mainly teaching the Rabbi how to farm), Clara's friends were trying to convince her to stay in Montreal. They had jobs in factories. She could get one, too.

Clara sneaked into the factory one day to try it out.

"Whatever you do," she was warned, "if the foreman comes around, keep your head down, and keep the machine going."

She was led to a bench among rows of women. Rows of women in a huge, dingy room, heads bent, afraid to stop, afraid to look up. No air, no light, no heat. Clara managed to maintain a submissive nature for the day. But she was appalled. And she had no intention of doing it twice. Hadn't Schmaya said it?

"It is not the elements I fear. It is hatred and indignity I run from."

The Schwartzes were welcomed into Pearl and Jacov's spacious two-room cottage, or shack, as Clara referred to it, after a long train trip to Lipton. It was "spacey" but not spacey enough for two families. And Schmaya and Jacov argued as much here in the new world as they had in Bukovyna.* As far as Schmaya was concerned, Jacov, with his disregard for daily Jewish ritual, was a heathen. In addition, Schmaya was getting nervous about supporting his family. His funds were dangerously low.

Jacov, the heathen, offered the use of his horse and wagon, and the wood on his land. Schmaya could cut and sell wood. When it came time for haying, Schmaya and his family could cut and stook some of it. Jacov would sell it for him. And a neighbour had a small shack that was vacant for the summer. Schmaya could rent it.

So they moved and were alone as a family for the first time in months. In spite of some rather unpleasant surprises (the necessity of straining their only source of water free of bloodsuckers and gopher-proofing the shack), this country was not yet a disappointment for Clara. There was the wonderful space for man and his soul, there were

*One of three eastern provinces of the Austro-Hungarian Empire.

red and gold sunsets and letters from Israel. Schmaya was busy supporting his family, but not too busy to have his mind on other concerns as well.

Schmaya returned from delivering a load of wood in Lipton one day with the news — a proposal — for Clara.

Clara was amused. "Did he propose to you?"

Schmaya was not amused. Schlomo was a good catch. He owned a grocery store, and his family was not poor. Furthermore, Schlomo had promised to help Schmaya settle on his homestead.

Clara's sense of humour began to fade.

"I am not a chattel!"

Uncle Jacov took up Schmaya's cause. Who would want Clara? She was poor and thin as a toothpick, he said. No prize!

Now Clara was both annoyed and amused. Hadn't he seen her stooking? Carrying water from the slough? Milking? Did he want to see her callouses? And she could sew and cook and do lace work as well.

But some people took this engagement proposal seriously. And Clara was horrified when a party to which she and her family were invited, turned out to be an engagement party. Her coming marriage was announced as Schlomo's mother fitted a black diamond ring on Clara's finger.

By now, Israel was working for another farmer and earning $40 a month — $40 a month closer to realizing his dream of establishing a farm on this land that he already loved with its open grassy plains, the rolling hills, the broad skies. Moishe, that cantankerous old man, and Mayer, Israel's younger brother, would arrive soon. They would work together to build the dream.

When they finally arrived, Mayer was excited and delighted with everything he saw, while Moishe's first fears were confirmed. The old settlers loved to pass on their knowledge to the newcomers — stories of being lost and frozen in blizzards, of sod shacks collapsing and of prairie fires. Moishe felt Israel had become a heathen in the two years he had been in this country. Did he bless the Lord in the morning for His gifts — of sight, of his two legs? Did he give thanks for a glass of milk? For the smell of a flower? But maybe there wasn't so much to bless in this country. Fifty miles for supplies! They could be dead a year. Would anybody know? In that case he should ask God for protection in this wilderness where there weren't enough men to form a minyan, the quorum required for services.

Moishe muttered and complained, but he took care of his offspring. He cooked, cleaned and he chased flies. And one day, rather than go to Hirsch for the High Holidays, he stated his intentions of staying home to watch over Basha, the cow. God would understand.

In the middle of the battles with the elements and his father, Israel had, at least, the relief of letters from Clara.

But suddenly her letters stopped.

When Zelda and Schmaya, ashamed, followed their daughter home after the engagement announcement, they found her crying on the bed.

"Is it so terrible," Schmaya fumed, "to want your daughter to marry a good provider? She talks about Israel, Israel, Israel. Israel is always visiting. He visits only in his letters."

"He'll come when he can!" Clara flared up.

A meeting was arranged between Clara and Mr. Levine, the spiritual leader of the community of the Sonnenfield Colony. Maybe he could talk sense into her.

But what could Mr. Levine say that Shmaya had not? That Schlomo was a good provider? Clara had her answer for that.

"We also need food for the mind. Schlomo and I have nothing in common. Living with him will be like living in an empty shell."

What about that beautiful ring?

"It is only a stone. There is no warmth in a stone."

This young woman knew what she wanted.

Mr. Levine took the ring from her. "I will give it back to Schlomo."

"No," Clara said, "To his mother."

Clara went home, relieved, excited, grateful, light as a feather, but expecting a storm.

Schmaya met the news with a sigh. "I only wanted you to be happy."

Soon they had to move again. The owner of the cabin was back. Jankel was dirty, unkempt, argumentative, demanding — and always hungry. They couldn't afford either the emotional or financial drain. Inquiries turned up some neighbours who offered to rent them two rooms at the back of their small cabin. It was clean and there were wooden floors. It was heaven. They received $125 for the hay they had cut for Jacov. Schmaya would sell the wood. They would make it through the winter. They had worked hard, all of them. But they were stronger and healthier than they had ever been in Europe. Here, no one spoke of epidemics. Winter was coming. There would be more time to relax.

And so, the young people decided to form a cultural club. They would take turns meeting at each other's houses — weather permitting. Weather on the prairies could be deceptive. A blizzard could blow up out of a glittering, clear day as quickly as hail can appear out of clear, hot skies in the summer.

One of their meetings was to be held on a day that began as clear and promising. Hrisha and Solomon Jampolsky, who lived on an adjoining homestead, came to collect the club members. Once installed under blankets on the hay-coverd wagon, they were off to the Jampolsky farm where Mr. Jampolsky had killed a calf and his wife was preparing a feast. As they jingled over the snow, they snuggled under the blankets, sang, gossiped, occasionally peeking out to look at the starry sky.

It was some minutes before they noted that they were no longer moving.

"Hey, Hrisha!" It was a jovial call.

No answer.

"Have we arrived?"

Stillness. They pulled their heads out of the blankets.

There was silence, an open snowy field and no horses. No Hrisha, no Solomon, either.

They waited, perplexed . . . then became concerned.

Finally Clara announced, "I'm walking."

No one else wanted to leave the sleigh, but Clara had heard stories about what happened when one remained immobile in the cold.

Clouds were covering the stars, and snow was beginning to blow. Joining hands, they all set out together. Finally, a flat, boat-like shape formed out of the darkness. The sleigh. They had walked in a circle.

By now, they were wet, tired and cold. They huddled under the blankets. But one of them noted a light in the distance. It was faint, but a light nonetheless. They set off, fearing disappointment. The light led them right into the hallway of Mr. Jampolsky's house where worried, little Mr. Jampolsky held a lamp aloft as a signal.

Hrisha and Solomon, frosted with snow, were not far behind. There were questions and explanations. The horses had broken loose, and Solomon and Hrisha had chased after them. There was no time for explanations then. The horses had to be found. A tangled bush had stopped the animals.

With everyone safe, sound and warm, they feasted, sang, danced and talked until the blizzard blew itself out in the early morning. How soon would the opportunity to laugh, to be young, come again? Mr. Jampolsky left his two sons in bed and drove contented young people home to their worried parents.

Some of the group were forming romantic alliances. Clara refused.

"Israel," Zelda said with disgust. "He visits only in his letters."

Now, there were not even the letters. He had stopped writing. She thought of a hundred reasons. Something was wrong. He had been hurt. He was sick. He was too busy. Someting must be wrong, but what?

She began to hear rumours. Rabbi Berner had a very pretty daugher — a daughter with soft brown eyes. That must be the fourteen-year-old one . . . the oldest girl. She would be seventeen by now.

While Clara waited, the rumours grew. Israel was interested in the girl — the girl with the soft brown eyes.

The rumours continued while she waited. Rabbi Berner was very fond of Israel. He was impressed by his determination, his energy, his sense of purpose. Israel would make a good son-in-law.

Finally Clara's father arrived home one day with mail . . . for her. Who could it be from but Israel? But why was he writing now after such a long silence? Was he writing to tell her about Rabbi Berner's daughter? Would he write to tell her that?

She read it.

He was coming! He would would be there for Chanukah!

Moishe stood in the doorway, fussing and fuming as his son set out for Lipton, 150 miles away.

"Is she so special?" he complained to the heavens. "He'd walk to the North Pole. He'll be eaten by wolves. He's a stubborn mule." Finally he addressed his son's retreating back. "There could be a blizzard. Who knows in this country?" His son turned to wave. "All right. Good-bye. I hope I'm still here when you get back."

It took some time to relax, but eventually the walk calmed him. It would take three, maybe four days. If he was lucky, there would be traffic occasionally to help him out. He had time to think. He had asked the neighbours to keep an eye on his father. And Clara . . . three years . . . it was a long time. What was she like? Had she changed? Why hadn't she written? Finally, he had more than a dream to offer. He was living on land that was his. His land, his farm.

A day's walking and the land began to change from the rolling hills to the dead flat plains of Weyburn. Another day and a half, and the dead flat around Regina, a railway town with a creek running through it. Israel's interest was on the other side, about 25 miles north of Regina . . . the Qu'appelle Valley . . . Lipton.

Suddenly, the flat plains opened to the valley. Israel got a ride from Lipton to the Schwartzes with a Mr. Davidner, who asked a lot of questions.

"Where are you coming from? Sonnenfield Colony? That's a long way. You didn't walk all the way, did you? Where are you from in the old country? That's around where the Schwartzes are from, isn't it? You wouldn't be coming to visit one of the Schwartz girls, would you?"

They turned into the Schwartz yard with Mr. Davidner still asking questions. Mr. Schwartz met them as they drove in. More questions, more conversation. What was the land like? Any forest? No trees? What did they do for firewood? He'd heard that they hadn't gotten their matzos in time for Passover and had had to eat potatoes for eight days.

Where was Clara?

Clara was nervous. She'd been sick. She was still pale and weak. Zelda braided her hair and washed her face while Schmaya stalled Israel outside. And she was ready . . . or as ready as she could be.

When Israel came in, Clara was startled. He'd changed. He was older, leaner and thinner. In the midst of all the hubbub — Zelda serving tea, Mr. Davidner giving news — Israel came over and took her hand.

Other visitors arrived, a family with two young girls. Mr. Davidner, a bachelor still, assumed importance. He began to impart news to the girls. "Oh, no, he didn't come to marry her. And if he doesn't like her, he's going back."

Clara looked at Israel, startled. He didn't seem to have heard. Eyes flashing, she got up, went to the bedroom and came back to deliver a package of letters to Israel. His letters.

He looked up innocently. "What am I going to do with them?"

Finally the guests had gone. Schmaya and David went to get the cows. Israel and Clara followed behind.

"Why did you want to give me the letters?" Israel asked.

Clara, still angry, explained what she had heard. Israel laughed heartily.

"Would I tell a stranger that?"

"But why didn't you write?"

"Why didn't you write?"

"I did write."

"So did I."

But neither had received the letters. Would the fact that Schlomo was involved with mail in Lipton have had anything to do with it?

He took her hand again and asked her to marry him.

It was a wonderful time. Schmaya still did not approve, of course. After all, on the boat coming over from Europe, when the other men were at prayers, where was Israel? Sitting with Clara, reading Heinriche Heine's poetry.

But Israel was used to obstreperous old men, and tried to convince Schmaya to move south to the Sonnenfield colony. There was still land available near his homestead. The growing season was longer, the land seemed more promising.

Israel stayed until Purim. They parted, with tears in Clara's eyes and a lump in Israel's throat. Schmaya was disgusted.

"Crying. Kissing. In our day, did we even see each other before we married?"

Zelda turned clear blue eyes on her husband. There was a hint of a smile. "The world is changing, Schmaya."

This time, Israel went in luxury. He went from village to village with the mailman.

Even though he missed Clara, it would be nice to be back at work on the farm, and even nice to see his irascible old father, who, hiding his delight at seeing his stubborn son, grunted, "Oh, you're back. It's about time."

The next thing in the order of business was a pre-emption of land for Moishe and Mayer. It meant a trip to Estevan. And it also meant a week of waiting and sleeping on the sidewalk in front of the land office. Getting out of line could mean losing the land.

But Israel got the land.

The Schwartz family might never have moved to the Sonnenfield Colony if nature had not taken matters into its own hands. Their home burned, destroying all but their papers and a few blankets. So five Schwartzes moved into the three-room shack with three Hoffers.

It wasn't long before the two fathers were, in prairie metaphor, "at each other's throats". Israel was able to escape the tension because his work was outside, but Clara had nowhere to go.

And Israel had other things to do. His beautiful stacks of flax, the result of a blue-blossomed field of promise, had been caught in a prairie fire. He would have to find another way to finance the wedding . . . and the winter.

One day when Israel was away in Estevan, Moishe informed Schmaya that any wife of his son's would be picked by him and furthermore, he had written to Europe about a woman there.

Schmaya countered with the information that he had certainly never been happy with his daughter's choice of a husband, either, nor with what he could offer her. And they were moving out.

Once again, after so many moves, wanting a "permanent home", as Schmaya put it, so desperately — once again, they were looking for a home. Again, they were rescued by kind neighbours. In spite of crowding (this time they moved in with a family of eight) their hosts, Mr. and Mrs. Greenstone, were most concerned about Clara.

Clara was miserable. She escaped to take long walks over the rolling hills. But now she did not see the beauty. She was alone and lost against the expansive land. Maybe she had made the wrong decision. Maybe she should have stayed in Montreal. Maybe Israel didn't really love her. Maybe he really was thinking of a woman from Europe. She had fought her parents for him. Maybe he didn't care enough — or wasn't strong enough — to fight for her.

All at once, she noticed a killdeer fluttering in front of her. It was lame. She bent down to pick it up. It fluttered just out of her reach. Clara followed, and reached again. Again, the black and white bird fluttered just out of reach . . . and suddenly took flight. She watched it, startled. And she laughed. She'd heard about the tricks these birds played to lure potential enemies from their nests. Only a greenhorn was taken in by a killdeer.

The bird had led her alongside a slough — a clear jewel blue, busy with ducks, long-legged shorebirds, even muskrats. She sat down on a knoll and realized that whether Israel loved her or not, this was where she wanted to be. She loved the prairie and its promise.

And as Clara relaxed and smiled with that decision, her attention was caught by a horse on the horizon. Israel . . . his horse. She stood up. He waved. She waited.

They were to be married on November 30, 1909.

Their wedding would be an event. It would be the first in the district, and the first official use of the Torah, which had arrived just in time. It would be held in Israel's shack.

"Here," Israel said, now that the date was finally settled. He pulled $75 out of his pocket. "It's for whatever you need for the wedding. If we hadn't lost the flax crop, we would have had more, but . . . ."

They both made a trip to Estevan. Clara bought fine white wool for her wedding dress and navy blue wool for practical wear.

So they were married.

And the irascible old men?

Well, Schmaya had said often enough to his daughter, "I only want you to be happy." And Moishe, since Rabbi Berner was officiating, was somewhat mollified. Rabbi Berner, most enthusiastic, was a decided contrast. As he confided to Clara's daughter years later, "Nothing could have prevented me from coming to officiate at your mother's and father's wedding. I can still remember him the day I picked him up at the Hirsch station. He was shivering on the platform and only eighteen years old. But he had that same pride and courage in his eyes."

It was a Jewish wedding with a difference. This was not a European Jewish ghetto. All of the neighbours took part in the celebrations.

Chairs, table and improvised benches were moved aside. A Swedish neighbour pulled out a comb and cigarette papers, and the dance began. His repertoire relied heavily on "Turkey in the Straw," but, even so, they danced late into the night, in all languages.

To the end of his days, any time his daughter wanted to see Israel tapping his foot to music, she had only to begin "Turkey in the Straw" on the piano. His foot would tap, a private smile, a special shine, would appear in his eyes.

To the end of their days, for Clara, that stocky young man remained a man who would — and did — perform miracles as he wrested a thriving farm out of bare prairie.

And to Israel, that slender, grey-eyed girl performed her own miracles. As he said, "Whenever I came into the house, discouraged after a difficult day, I felt as if I had come into a palace. I knew she would be there." He paused. "Even if we had been in a desert, your mother would have found a way to make it a home."

To the end of their days together, Clara always changed into something clean and pretty before Israel came in from work. And he never entered the kitchen without looking for her with the same first question: "Where's Mama?"

EDITOR'S NOTE: The town of Hoffer, Saskatchewan, named after Israel and Mayer Hoffer, is located a mile from the Hoffer homestead.

Dick Chen

THE LAND OF OPPORTUNITY

From an interview with Dick Chen

The fingers on Dick Chen's left hand move imperceptibly as the cleaver in his right hand chops stalks of celery at lightning speed. Seated in awed fascination, the students in his cooking class watch uneasily for a spurt of blood as the razor-sharp cleaver moves dangerously close to Chen's fingertips. There is an audible sigh of relief when he lays the implement on the chopping block.

He keeps up a steady patter of instruction on cooking techniques, interspersed with historical facts, trivia and anecdotes about China.

"Seafood is good for you. There was a famous Chinese emperor about 1,000 A.D. who had eighty-one girls in his harem. He had a painting made of each and every night would send one of his servants with a painting to identify the right one to bring her to his apartments. He ate mostly seafood — at least three hundred different dishes were prepared in his court kitchens. He had a kitchen staff of over forty workers. Seafood gave him strength."

And Chen grins.

His agility with kitchen utensils is matched by his ability with Chinese brushes and ink techniques. A graduate of the Taiwan College of Art, Chen is equally adept at teaching his two main professions. He has several others in which he was trained in his transplanted homeland, Taiwan.

Although he spent a number of years studying mechanical engineering, Chen also learned martial arts. When he was 23 years old he was a member of Chinese leader Chiang Kai-shek's palace guard. For two years Chen taught self defence at the YM-YWHA and Neighbourhood House, Montreal community organizations.

"One movement can immobilize a potential attacker," he says and demonstrates.

Born in Shanghai two years after the Japanese invasion of China in 1937, Chen remembers the early years as fairly secure ones. When the Second World War broke out, his parents took him to a small town somewhere between Shanghai and Nanking. Firmly ensconced at the family farm, Dick spent the early years in relative safety while his father and others who had business in Shanghai commuted back and forth.

"My father and his family had cooked for kings, princes and company presidents for more than a hundred years in Shanghai. We catered food to the government, to banks and to all kinds of institutions. Because my father was a strong nationalist, he felt it would be better for us away from the city."

At times there were food shortages, but because many things could be grown on the farm, the family managed to survive.

"There wasn't too much killing in our area. Sometimes Japanese soldiers passed through on patrol and helped themselves to our chickens and food, but as long as we didn't object, they didn't hurt anyone," he says.

As early as 1943, Chen's father had accompanied government officials and forces to Taiwan, where the Nationalists were trying to keep the Japanese from occupying the entire island. Japanese bases had already been established in the north prior to a planned takeover. However, other political changes were affecting the Nationalist government. The Communist movement had accelerated, and after a number of confrontations and battles, the Nationalists made plans to move to Taiwan rather than face prolonged war and eventual defeat.

Chiang Kai-shek was elected president in 1947 when the first general election in Chinese history was held. Communist troops lost no time in attacking. By 1949, Nanking, the capital, fell to the Communists and Chiang's government was established in Formosa, now Taiwan.

"My father had sent for the family and me around 1945 or 1946 before the Communist takeover, and we moved the entire household and business to Taiwan. We started a new life. I took art and at the same time helped my father in the food business. After I graduated from high school I spent two years in the compulsory military service where I participated in sports and learned the martial arts. I became so good at it I was recommended for palace security, and after six months of intensive training, the military department admitted me to Chiang Kai-shek's personal security branch."

Chen wanted to go to university, but it was difficult to pass the government tests given every year. From the time he was 13 or 14 years of age he had been working in his spare time for a relative who owned an aircraft factory. He learned all about machinery, and between 1963 and 1964, he worked for the Far Eastern Air Transport Corporation where he was taught to assemble aircraft. A year later he changed companies and became a third-class mechanic in Taiwan's biggest aircraft plant, The Air Asia Company. Along with its main American shareholder, the company had built the famous Flying Tiger planes flown by General Claire Chennault and his pilots. Originally on the mainland, the company had moved to Taiwan with the Nationalists.

Chen stayed four years, and every six months was raised to a higher labour category. The company sent him to learn English and recommended he take tests to qualify him as an aircraft engineer. He was given books to study as well as learning on the job. At the end of two years he passed exams that usually take at least ten years of work.

"Just about this time, a notice was handed around the company that Canada wanted immigrants with aircraft experience. I applied along with many others. A Canadian representative came to Taipei to interview us, and I passed the test I was given. Then came a health examination, and in three months all the arrangements were made. For me it was the beginning of a new life in more ways than one."

The other way involved a girl. Chen had met Masa when he was 22 and she was 17. She worked part-time at the library where he had been studying in the hope of getting into university.

"However, there was something called professional discrimination in my country, which kept me from developing any relationship with this girl. Because my parents were in the food business, we were considered to be very low on the professional scale. The girls I dated came from families well-placed in the government — many of them with titles and money. They looked down on me and wouldn't allow their daughters to date me. In defense I became a playboy, acting as if I didn't care. In addition to this prejudice, there was regional discrimination. Because I was from Shanghai, I wasn't acceptable. Some regions were more class-conscious than others, and many believed that people from Shanghai were the worst in China . . . shifty, sneaky and prone to changing their minds at a moment's notice. But that is the sign of a quick thinker, a person who can shift thoughts and methods of action when one avenue of endeavour is closed. Anywhere else it is a sign of intelligence and shrewdness, but not in China. People from Shanghai were sneered at for this trait."

Actually it was an exceptional business sense developed over centuries, and most of the businessmen in Hong Kong had originally come from Shanghai which had a long history of exchange with the West, as a port. In the early years when the West established colonies in China, there were foreign compounds held by France, Germany, Russia, United States and Britain as a result of three treaties signed in the middle 1800s.

"In fact, there were so many foreigners on Chinese soil they began establishing rules as if they owned the country. In one of the Crown areas where the foreigners lived, there was a sign at the entrance to a park: 'Dogs and Chinese not allowed.' We were considered to be lower than dogs in our own country. Eventually we rebelled and threw out the foreigners. There were some who remained and others came later, but this terrible practice persisted right up until the Japanese invasion in 1937."

Chen was affected as a result of this centuries-old prejudice. Masa's wealthy parents refused to let him take her out. This went on for years. He would go to her family's small department store at least once a year just to see her. They would joke and ask the same questions year in and year out.

"How are you? Are you married yet?"

"No, are you?"

"Why not?"

And both would burst into laughter. "Because nobody wants us."

Eight years later both were still single. Many men had asked to marry her, and Masa had refused them all. She wanted someone sincere, who wasn't fooling around and didn't drink, gamble or smoke.

"She may have thought I was a 'bad boy' because I ran around with many girls, but I didn't gamble, smoke or drink. One of my friends, a very talented artist, who had moved to the United States and become well known, actually pushed me toward making a decision where Masa was concerned. Here I was already thirty years old and she was twenty-five. We began dating in secret after nine o'clock at night when she closed the store. Chinese business people work very late hours. After a year of sneaking around in this way, we married secretly in November, 1968. I got two free plane tickets for a week-end honeymoon to East Taiwan from the airline where I worked."

Chen was married only two months when the opportunity to go to Canada was arranged. He had to leave his new bride and fly alone to set up a new life in a strange country. He arrived on February 6, 1969. Luckily he had written "engaged" on his papers and all he had to do was apply immediately on arrival for papers to bring his wife to Canada.

"Just before she left she broke the news to her family, and they cried. They couldn't understand why she would give up such a big business to start from nothing in a strange country."

At the time an American aircraft company had offered Chen a contract which he turned down. When he was in Canada and already working, he was approached again and asked to come to the United States and work for the company. He refused.

"I felt I could do better in Canada. Even though I had friends in the United States, I knew Canada was a new country — new in every way, including industrial potential. I was sure it would be good for a

Chinese person. Where there is a small population, there is less competition and a better chance for a good future. And that is why I didn't go to Vancouver or Toronto. I picked Montreal which didn't have many Chinese people. I knew I could succeed here."

He arrived with a job offer at Air Canada, but when he showed up at the plant's employment office, it was layoff time and there was no work available. He had several thousand dollars and decided he could survive for about three months. If he didn't find anything by then, he would return to Taiwan. About twenty days later, he found a job at Aviation Electronics Company in St. Laurent, but just as he was about to take it, a friend told him of a new restaurant, the first of its kind to specialize in Shanghai cooking in Montreal, and whose owner was looking for a chef. Because his family had been in this line for generations, he went to apply. He cooked a meal for the boss, who tasted it and hired Chen on the spot.

"The job paid more than the aircraft company had offered; it kept me inside so I couldn't run around and spend money or get into other trouble. My meals were free, and I saved quite a bit."

Three months after his arrival a letter came from Masa. She was coming to Canada. Not that he wasn't happy about it, but he knew that working eleven hours a day all week long would be impossible for her to put up with. She was a stranger to the country and would be alone all the time.

"So I decided to find a job with shorter hours and again I applied at Air Canada. I was hired to work on fire-fighting planes and eventually was transferred to jet aircraft. But I only stayed a year and a half because my wife took a look at my salary and said: 'You work for that kind of salary? I should have stayed in Taiwan because I made in one week what you make in a month. We can invest together and start our own business.' She asked me what I did best of all and I said, food."

And so the two went into the restaurant business. Advisers said it was a big investment and a risk. They would fail unless they had a partner to help with the initial $40,000 investment.

"Well, I said my wife was my partner and I didn't need anyone else. She invested her money, and we did everything ourselves. I decorated the entire place, and it cost less than one-third of what was predicted. It was the first Mandarin restaurant in Montreal and specialized in spicy Mandarin cuisine. But it only lasted three years. Just as we were beginning to do well, the place burned under suspicious circumstances, and I am convinced it was arson. There was evidence to that effect. Obviously I had enemies who resented the competition."

The Chens lost everything including his art work which he had displayed on the walls. While insurance paid for some of the loss, none of the art work could be replaced.

"I tried to rebuild from scratch, but no one would insure me if I stayed at the same location. They were afraid it would happen again and rather than operate without insurance and risk the same thing, I sold the restaurant. With the money I bought a house, where I now live on one floor and on the other I teach Chinese cooking, calligraphy and Chinese painting. It was the first school with this combination of subjects."

In addition to Chinese cooking, Chen teaches Kosher Chinese cuisine. In 1981, the Atlantic Jewish Council hired him and flew him to the Maritimes to teach Kosher Chinese cooking in different synagogues. He taught in Fredericton, Moncton, Glace Bay and Halifax. While the Jewish communities were not as large as others in Canada, Glace Bay has one of the oldest Jewish synagogues in Canada. Chen has taught in synagogues all over Montreal and in the suburbs. As a joke some of his students gave him a Jewish name — Dick Schwartz.

"I know people here in Canada are surprised that there is Kosher Chinese food, but what many don't know is that Jews came to China, escaping the Greek and Roman invasions, over 2,000 years ago and again in the sixth century there was another migration. It goes back to the Kwon-Si province settlements in the Tong dynasty. There is a province in south-west China were the food is close to ninety per cent Kosher. The Chinese Jews have changed over the centuries through intermarriage; they look Eurasian and have Chinese names, but they are still Jewish and practise their religion and traditions."

However, on the mainland, religion has all but vanished since the Communists took over, but Chen says it is an old country and changing all the time.

"We have 4,000 years of history and we keep the traditions of our ancestors which is not a religion, purely a belief and a way of honouring our forebears and respecting our ancestry. We take this belief with us wherever we go.

"No matter where Chinese people move, and they migrate all over the world, they are not afraid to learn new ways and new languages. In China every province has a different language. Why should it be different elsewhere? For a country like Canada to have two languages is very good. Why fight about that? But no matter, it isn't easy starting over somewhere else, and when immigrants come here with little or no funds, they have to depend on themselves.

"I have seen some of them, and it is very sad. But I feel that no matter what you do, even collecting garbage, you should be happy, work hard and look for something else to do. If you want a good future, you have to study. If one thing doesn't work, another will, but you have to keep trying. As an immigrant, you have to plan your life and fight to survive. You must have other interests and hobbies because one of these may become your life's work. When things look black and you are fed up, turn your life around. Walk away and try something else and don't get upset. When you come back to the problem, you will be able to solve it. That is the way to survive.

"Every time I go back to Taiwan, I feel the change in the lifestyle. When I arrive there, I want to come back here. I feel I no longer belong in Taiwan. This is my home. Even though my blood and bones are Chinese, my desire to go back is only to visit family and friends. But I find there is too much socializing in Taiwan. About forty-five per cent of people's incomes are spent on eating, drinking and parties. I can't live that way here. I have too busy a life. My wife goes back fairly often, and many times she calls me long distance and cries she wants to come back right away. She is so homesick for Montreal and our way of living. Once the lifestyle changes, there is no going back.

If I had to emigrate all over again, I would still come to Canada. For me Montreal is the most beautiful city there is. I have been to many places, but there is no cleaner nor friendlier city anywhere. There are flowers, trees and grass everywhere, and the mountain in the middle of the city is very unusual. Whenever I visit friends in other countries, they try to persuade me to move there, but I am staying right here. It's still the best place.

Canada is a beautiful country and a big land where there are so many opportunities for a good future. You are free to do anything you want. Where else can you find this?

Jean Robert Milord

MATTERS OF CHOICE

by Alice Levesque
from an interview with Jean Robert Milord

Cote-des Neiges residents in Montreal often stare in surprise when they see Jean Robert Milord drive by in a squad car with his partner. It is unusual to see a black policeman covering a beat with his white "buddy" seated beside him. Few people know there are only two black policemen on the Montreal Urban Community Police Force. What is even more surprising is that Robert Milord is Haitian, a member of an ethnic group that has been subjected to an abnormal amount of prejudice and racism in this city.

Most of the attacks have been directed at Haitian taxidrivers in Montreal, and coincidentally Robert drove a cab before he joined the police force. It was during this period that he had a number of unpleasant experiences.

"Once," he said, "I stopped in front of a disco, and two girls and a guy climbed into my cab. They looked at me and climbed out, saying, "I don't want any damn nigger!"

Or sometimes, someone would make a sign that he wanted a cab, only to wave it away when he noticed Robert was black. And many times passengers rudely ordered him about, speaking to him as if he was their servant.

"I felt very bad," he says. "I was angry and humiliated, as if I didn't exist as a human being. But you have to have good control and not let people like that change you. Because they did that to me doesn't mean that I should do the same. I try to remember that all people are not like that."

In Port-au-Prince where Robert comes from, he had heard about discrimination, but it was only when he reached Montreal that he realized it was real.

"I learned in school that there is racial discrimination in North America, but because I had never seen it in Haiti, I didn't know if any was directed at me. I wasn't looking for it, and it wasn't in my mind. After I began to know the country and the way the people talked and reacted, then I recognized it."

Robert Milord's education began early. When he was seventeen and a half, he had finished school and was prepared professionally to be a medical technologist. But he wasn't prepared for his mother's ultimatum. As Robert remembers it, she gave him a choice. "Listen, man," she said. "You are almost eighteen and you have a profession.

It's very hard to work in Haiti, so make your choice: New York, Montreal or Paris."

"Just like that — bang! Man, you've got to do something. You've got to earn your money. So I said all right; I knew I had to decide."

Robert had a happy life in Haiti, growing up with his four sisters. His family wasn't rich, but they were closely knit.

"Family ties are closer in Haiti than in Canada. My family ties are still very close. I had a very happy childhood, and we always had fun.

"When I was young, my father worked on commercial boats traveling between Haiti, the Bahamas and Florida. Sometimes he was gone for over a year. In the meantime my mother had to work and she worked hard for us. She was a private vendor. She bought yard goods and traveled around Haiti in a big truck selling the material. She paid a housekeeper to stay with us. Sometimes she was gone for two days and sometimes for fifteen."

At eighteen, Robert felt adventurous and ready to heed his mother's advice and look for better opportunities elsewhere.

"There are opportunities in medical technology in Haiti, but you've got to know someone, otherwise you wait, wait, wait. Anyhow, if you always stay in the same place, it's no good. You can't get experience. You have to learn from other people."

Robert made his choice — Montreal. "Everyone," says Robert, "wants to go to the States — to New York — when he leaves Haiti. I'd studied English in Haiti, but my English wasn't too good and I decided I'd rather go to a French country. But first I wanted to see what was happening in Quebec. I figured that if it was good, I'd stay; if it wasn't, then that would be it."

Robert landed at Dorval on November 20, 1971. "At that time there was no Canadian embassy in Haiti. You just got enough money, bought a ticket and you went! It was the first time I'd been on a plane. I flew Air Canada, and it was fantastic and exciting!

"At Dorval, the immigration officer wanted to know whether I really wanted to stay or was just coming for two years. I told him that I was a medical technician, that I wanted to get more experience and, if I had an opportunity to work, I wanted to stay. They asked strange questions. I had over a thousand dollars, and they wanted to know why I had come. They said, 'You've got money, you have some training and your family is over there, so why do you want to come to Canada?' They asked questions like that. It gave me the impression that here in Canada they don't judge people by who you are."

Happily, Robert had a friend in Montreal and he went to stay with him on St. Hubert Street. However, his friend was working in a factory and didn't have either the time or knowledge to completely orient Robert to the new environment.

"Everything seemed very strange," Robert recalls. "I had never seen snow. It was fantastic! We knew, in Haiti, that there was snow, so I was dressed for the weather, but it was very hard adjusting because I had to try and do everything myself.

"I wanted to go to school, but I arrived in November, and the schools start in September and January. Every time I went to Immigration, they gave me different answers . . . one thing the first time I went and the opposite the next time. If you don't use your head, you can really be in trouble! In the meantime, I didn't have anyone to direct me, to say 'Bob, you've got to do that, Bob, you've got to go to Quebec City, Bob, you've got to go there.' I lost about six months just trying to find out where to go and whom to see. If I couldn't go to school, I wanted to know where to go to learn Canadian laboratory techniques. I didn't even know how to get a social security card. And then, they tell you they want Canadian experience, but they don't tell you how to get it.

"A thousand dollars doesn't go far, and I had to pay my rent, my food — everything. So I called my mother and said, 'This country is like hell. I don't want to stay here. In the first place it's too cold and secondly, I can't find anyone who can tell me what I have to do to get settled, and my money is almost finished. I want to take a plane and return to Port-au-Prince!' "

Robert's mother wasn't unsympathetic, but she didn't want him to give up. "Listen," she said. "If you ever come back, I'm going to buy another ticket, put you on a plane and send you back to Canada. You've got to try and find your own way."

Robert shrugged. "Why fight it?" With his money finished, he began to look for jobs. "I tried to find work as a medical technician," he says. "I applied to various hospitals, but no one would hire me because I didn't have Canadian experience. And they said that my Haitian certificate was no good. Now I had to have both Canadian training and Canadian experience. They wouldn't take me in school because it was the wrong time of the year, and after a long time, I found I had to send all my papers to Quebec City to get an evaluation of my medical technician's courses from Port-au-Prince. At the same time I was supposed to be getting Canadian experience.

"My mother had told me that I had to try to do everything I could to stay in Canada, but she tried to help by sending me money every two weeks. Then, one day, my money was low and I felt desperate. I didn't know what to do. You know the first thing I did in Montreal? It was very, very bad, and I'll always cry in my heart when I remember. My first job was distributing advertising flyers from house to house. It was hard for me because in my country I never did anything like that. In my country I wasn't rich, but I was proud and I had a nice life and money in my pocket.

"I wondered why I had gone to school and what my schooling had done for me? What was I doing here? I kept that job one month."

That winter was the worst for Robert. He was unhappy and depressed and with only one Haitian friend in Montreal he felt alienated and lost. The enclosed feeling of the long Canadian winter reinforced his sense of imprisonment — a sense of being cut off when he asked questions and didn't receive answers. It was too great a contrast to the pleasant climate and easygoing ambiance of Haiti. Nothing was familiar — not the people, not the food, not the lifestyle. Robert was homesick for Port-au-Prince.

"In Haiti," Robert says, "all the doors are open. People visit and talk. Here, all doors are closed. It's like being in jail. I like to pass and say 'Hi, how are you' and stop and talk. Here, people say 'Hi' and pass. You can't talk."

After a month distributing advertising flyers, Robert went to school at night to learn English. He also tried to go back to school to take courses in medical technology, but he had to be a landed immigrant, and the courses cost much more than he could afford.

"I was willing to take any kind of job and I ended up working in a clothing factory, cutting elastics for waistbands. I worked five days a week — 8:00 a.m. to 6:00 p.m. — for about fifty dollars a week. It was easy but terribly boring. My mother was still supporting my four sisters in school in Haiti so I couldn't have her sending money, money, money. I had to think about the others, too. So I decided to think of nothing else and just make money. And I ran around a lot, did disco dancing and things like that.

"One day I said to myself, 'Bobby, that's enough now. You have to do something. You can't just work in the factories.' I tried to go to school again, but there was no way. It was just too expensive.

"In the meantime I had been going to the gym. In Haiti I had boxed in school. I love boxing. I don't know why I love it — I just do. I started boxing at about age thirteen. We used to have competitions between schools. One day in Montreal, I was reading the newspaper and saw the name of a gym advertising a boxing competition. That was the first gym I went to, on Park Avenue. There I met Dave Campanelli, who told me, after I said I'd boxed in Haiti, to come to the gym and work out whenever I wanted. So I cut elastics during the day and at night I worked out at the gym.

"Then I changed gyms. I went to George Drouin's gym on Mount Royal. I'm sure George is the best man in boxing in Canada. Drouin's gym was more my style; they box like Joe Frazier. Then George told me he wanted me to train for the Golden Gloves. Drouin said, "I'm sure you could win' and I said, 'Are you sure?' and he told me he was really sure. My first match was in Trois Rivieres in 1974, and in 1977 I won the Golden Gloves for Quebec.

"After the Golden Gloves championship in 1977, I had the choice of going professional. But there's a big difference between amateur and professional boxing. You do amateur boxing because you like it. My manager started putting the idea of going professional in my mind. But I know what happens in boxing. I know that when you are good there are so many people after you who are pushing to make money. They use you.

"At the same time I made an application to the Montreal police. They didn't say they didn't want to take me, but I had to have a diploma from the CEGEP (Quebec's junior college system) in Technique Policier. I could either continue boxing and forget the police application or work in the daytime and go to school at night. So, just like that, I quit the gym and boxing and went to school at night. I held a lot of jobs while I was studying."

After finishing CEGEP, Robert went on to the Institute de Police du Quebec, the police academy at Nicolet. Robert says that it is not usual for the inhabitants of Nicolet to see blacks, but he was treated well and police training was "fantastic — super fantastic!"

Two parts of Robert's life came together at Nicolet when he started giving fellow cadets boxing instructions. Even some of the teachers came to those workouts in the gym. It was so successful that the academy added Robert's training program to their physical fitness program.

In 1980 Robert finished the academy with an 86.8 per cent average. When the Montreal police department came to Nicolet to look over the candidates with the highest grades, Robert was chosen immediately, the second black officer with the Montreal police.

Robert works both in plain clothes and uniform in an area of Montreal with a growing black population, and he is often chosen to work in special programs dealing with blacks. He feels that he is being accepted in the community since he's often greeted when he drives by in the squad car. And Robert's partner says to him: "It's the first time I've passed here, and they've said 'Hi' to me. They never used to say 'Hi' before; it's because you are here."

Robert says that with all the training police receive "there's not the same mentality as before. For example, you learn how to talk to people. Before the police wanted a big man. Now, well, look at me. I'm only five feet ten inches tall. Before you had to be six feet tall or something like that. Now you have to use your brain rather than your brawn. I find police work an intellectual challenge."

His presence, Robert thinks, helps the community by changing the mentality of the police themselves. He says that when he's not there and a black is brought in, some of his fellow officers might say stuff like 'Hey, come over here, nigger,' or 'shut your mouth, nigger.' When they know I'm there, they don't fool around."

Robert says he doesn't accept this kind of behaviour from anyone, not from blacks or whites. "I respect everyone," he says. "And you should be honest with everyone."

"We're a good group," Robert says of the men he works with. We work well together, we have fun, and the department tries to help. They pay for the guys to go to school at night. I want to go back to school. I was thinking of criminology or maybe law. I'd like to learn something so that if I go back to Haiti one day, I can use my experience from here to help my people."

Robert hasn't traveled much in the rest of Canada, only in Ontario and New Brunswick. "When you're some place where they don't see many black people, they appreciate you. They are curious; they want to talk to you. But when you go to places where there are a lot of black people, they say, 'Of course, we know what they are like', and they are often scared. They don't want you to come and steal their job or steal their wife, or whatever." Robert laughs as he mentions these old myths.

But no one ever told him he should have stayed in Haiti, and if they had, Robert would have answered: "The world is for everyone."

Though he now feels at home in Montreal, Robert still misses the ambiance of Haiti, and, of couse, the sun. If he had to do it over, Robert says he would still come to Canada, but he would try to get more advance information. He thinks the Canadian Government should do a better job of informing potential immigrants what to expect.

"In Haiti we had little to explain Canada, or Quebec. We might hear on the radio or read in the papers some trivial thing about this or that, or we'd hear that there are two languages. But they don't explain procedures you must follow for whatever you want to do. They should tell the newcomer, or person intending to come to Canada, whether his schooling is any good and what else he might have to take in school and to what schools he should go. What they say is: 'This is a beautiful country. Welcome to Canada,' and that's that. It's the same for all immigrants, wherever they come from. The government, and society, often loses the experience, knowledge and useful intelligence of newcomers."

Today, Robert's parents live in Florida, and his mother has extended her business acumen, buying goods in Haiti to sell in Florida. And she is able to visit her son in Montreal more easily. She is proud of her son. And Robert has chosen well, gained experience and is a fine addition to his adopted country.

THE ETERNAL IMMIGRANT

Milly Charon

Up from the holds,
Crammed in third-class steerage they come;
Down from the skies,
Ejected like eggs from a huge bird;
They lug their belongings,
Clutching infants close to their breasts;
Their faces etched in anxiety and fear
As they face an uncertain future,
Strangers in a foreign land.

White, red, yellow, brown and black,
Scattered by the winds of time spanning centuries,
Like autumn leaves fleeing before the blast;
Driven and dispersed by hunger, fear, poverty and
persecution;
They come seeking sanctuary on our shores.

The trains and buses rumble eastward and
westward,
Containers of human cargo,
Moving day and night across an indifferent
continent;
So many unloaded here, others dropped there;
They gaze bewildered,
Their tongues mouthing words no one
comprehends.

A hand outstretched, pleading for understanding;
Who stops to help these poor and weary travelers,
Embarked on an endless journey in time,
A journey only their grandchildren can complete
As one with the new land?
The children straddle the void, incomplete,
Torn by the weights of both worlds,
Leashed like dogs to the past.

APPENDIX

For centuries after the discovery of America, pioneers and adventurers moved westward from the Old World. What began as a trickle in the days of the tall ships increased to a flow as transportation improved. The sailing vessels gave way to the steamships, and then with the aid of modern ocean liners and air travel, the journey to the new world was facilitated even further.

Up from the holds they came in the early days to stagger onto shore, clutching their meagre possessions. The next wave traveling in third-class steerage had their first views of Eastern Canada as their vessels approached Nova Scotia and Halifax harbour. Those who proceeded farther up the St. Lawrence River disembarked at Quebec City.

Before 1850, immigration had been relatively low. The 1820s saw 15,000 settle in Canada. In 1832 there was a peak year — 66,000, and 1847 was to remain the record at 90,000 because of the failure of the Irish potato crop in 1840. Starving immigrants literally flooded North American shores.

Between 1842 and 1881, 768,123 came to Canada.

The despicable practice of importing thousands of British children, aged from eight to twelve, to work on Canadian farms between 1870 and 1930, added another page to Canada's immigration history.

For most of the 15,000 Chinese workers imported to labour on the Canadian Pacific Railway in the late 1870s and 1880s, the sight of Victoria harbour nestled among dozens of islands was the beginning of years of near-slavery conditions. Laying track across uncharted wilderness was the only life they knew. Thousands died in the process.

The years between 1881 and 1914 saw the greatest Canadian ingathering ever — almost four million people. From the mid-1600s on, the eastern European scene had been one of constant slaughter and torture of hundreds of thousands of Jews. From the steppes of the Ukraine westward to Galicia, part of the Austro-Hungarian Empire, bands of Cossacks murdered and raped, disrupting and destroying a flourishing Jewish culture. Between 1881 and 1914, sixty per cent of the Jewish population emigrated from Galicia, settling in Canada and United States. Between 1870 and 1914, over two million Jews left eastern Europe.

During this thirty-three-year span, Canada admitted approximately 170,000 to 200,000 Ukrainians. About 97 per cent of these were peasant farmers fleeing oppressive social and economic conditions in the Ukraine and nearby provinces of Bukovyna and Galicia.

Most of these people had been encouraged to emigrate by the policies of Clifford Sifton, Canadian Minister of the Interior, who was determined to populate and develop the prairies with sturdy farmers. To attract this type of immigrant, Sifton mounted a massive publicity campaign in central European regions, arranging with booking agents to encourage settlers from the Austro-Hungarian Empire and the Ukraine. As incentive, the Canadian government offered free 160-acre farms on the prairies to every male immigrant.

In the history of Canadian immigration, 1912 and 1913 remain record years — 375,756 in 1912 and 400,870 in 1913. Perhaps a portent of the terrible "war to end all wars" sparked the exodus, coupled with a more liberal Canadian immigration policy.

However, from 1914 to 1940 only two million people were admitted to Canada. The stock market crash of '29 and the depression that followed brought immigration nearly to a halt. This policy was applied until 1945 and because of economic conditions, immigration was discouraged unless people had relatives in Canada or were bringing substantial amounts of money.

Regrettably, Canada closed its doors from 1941 to 1943 to refugees fleeing the European Holocaust. In these three years, a mere 25,409 were accepted. Most of those turned away were Jews fleeing Hitler's "final solution".

World crises are the major cause of mass immigration. Once again this was the case in 1956 and 1957. The 1956 Hungarian uprising against Soviet Russia helped raise the number of people who entered Canada during those years to 347,000.

Expo '67 brought many visitors, a number of whom returned to settle. The Czechoslovakian Revolution in 1968 brought more newcomers to Canada. In those two years alone, Canada's population increased by almost 407,000.

The Vietnam War protests in the United States in the 1960s sent a flood of conscientious objectors and draft dodgers northward. There are no exact figures of the number, but Canadian immigration statistics show anywhere from 40,000 to 100,000 sought refuge from the political and military policies south of the 49th parallel.

By 1971, almost one-third of Canada's population were first-or second-generation immigrants.

The years 1976 to 1979 "painted an Asian landscape of distress. As combat escalated, the conflict in war-ravaged Vietnam, Laos and Cambodia sent hundreds of thousands of starving, frightened refugees rolling like tidal waves across borders in search of food and shelter".

The plight of the boat people during this period was brought to world attention and after initial indifference, countries around the world began accepting small numbers of the remnants who survived. Between 1975 and 1981, 53,074 entered Canada as new immigrants. More are being sponsored by relatives every day.

There are many more who have fled harsh economic conditions and repressive governments. Over the last thirty years there was: Nasser's clampdown on religious minorities in Egypt; the Indian-Pakistani conflict; Uganda's persecution and expulsion of its citizens of Asian origin; the fall of Isabel Peron's government in Argentina; the civil war in Lebanon and the collapse of the Allende regime in Chile. All these have sent waves of refugees seeking sanctuary to our shores.

To this day, no one knows how many illegals have entered over the last century and a half. Although many immigrants have remained, hundreds of thousands have used Canada as a steppingstone to the United States.

BIBLIOGRAPHY

A Critical Guide by the Law Union of Ontario. *The Immigrant's Handbook,* Montreal: Black Rose Books, 1981.

Asi, Harry. Critical article, Toronto, July 24, 1962.

Bagnell, Kenneth. *The Little Immigrants,* Toronto: Macmillan of Canada, 1980.

Bedoukian, Kerop. *The Urchin,* Frome and London: Butler and Tanner Ltd., 1978. Files and Case Book of Kerop Bedoukian courtesy of Harold Bedoukian and Linda Ghan.

Dennis, Eric. Article, "Marked Man On Stalin's Books. . .", *The Halifax Mail,* December 1948.

Directorate of Multiculturalism, Department of the Secretary of State, *Canadian Family Tree, Canada's Peoples,* Don Mills: Corpus, 1979.

El Salvador: Central America in the New Cold War. New York: Grove Press, Inc., 1981.

Employment and Immigration, Canada. *Annual Report,* Ottawa, 1980-81, 1981-82.

Employment and Immigration, Canada. *Annual Report to Parliament on Immigration Levels,* 1983.

Newspaper Article, *Halifax Mail* and *Halifax Chronicle.* December 23-24, 1948.

Newspaper Article, "Red Cross to Exhibit Art Works", *The Halifax Mail-Star.* January 18, 1949.

Handlin, Oscar and Mary F., *A Century of Jewish Immigration to the United States.* New York: American Jewish Committee, 1949. Reprinted from the American Jewish Year Book.

Kennedy, Peter, editor. *Folk Songs of Britain and Ireland,* London: Cassell, 1975.

Lady Dufferin. "Lament of the Irish Immigrant". (1807-1867)

Newspaper Article, "Secret Messages Link D'Aubuisson. . .", *Los Angeles Times*. Reprinted in The *Gazette*, Montreal, May 4, 1983.

Manpower and Immigration Statistics. Canada, 1982 and 1983.

Manpower and Immigration, *Perspectives.* Canada, 1976.

"Korea", *The New Encyclopedia Britannica.* Fifteenth Edition, William and Helen Hemingway Benton: Chicago, London, Toronto, 1973-4.

Rasky, Frank. "Our Baltic New Canadians", *Liberty,* January, 1959.

Soules, J. *Recollections* Volume 1, No. 3, Special Edition 10th Anniversary, New Horizons Program.

Newspaper article, "Estonian Artist Painted Horror of Slave Camps", *The Toronto Star*, July 14, 1972.

Tables from *The Canadian Pocket Encyclopedia*, 35th Edition. British Columbia: CanExpo Publishers, Inc., 1981.

Tate, O.A. Newspaper article, "Press Club Stages Party. . .", *The Toronto Star*, February 25, 1978.

Newspaper article, "A Gallery of Torture and Terror", *The Toronto Star*, February 25, 1978.

"World War I", *Universal History of the World*. New York: Golden Press, Inc., 1966.

"World War I", Universal Standard Encyclopedia, New York: Wilfrid Funk, Inc. 1954.

"Asia", *1980 Year Book, The World Book Encyclopedia*, Childcraft International, Inc., 1980 and Field Enterrises Educational Corporation, 1961, respectively.

If you enjoyed this collection of immigrant experiences and if you have a meaningful story for Volume II, which you would like to share with Canadians across the country, please write to:

Milly Charon, editor
Between Two Worlds
7481 Ostell Crescent
Montreal, Quebec H4P 1Y7

Writers must be landed immigrants and/or Canadian citizens. The stories should have something of the country of origin as well as the Canadian experience to fit the two-world concept.

First-generation stories are especially valuable for the children are often caught between the two worlds. All ethnic groups are important.

If you have no writing skills, you may submit tapes providing they are clear and understandable. Your name, address and phone number must accompany each submission. I will also require a short blurb on your ethnic background, some family history and the date of arrival in Canada of you and your family.

The Editor

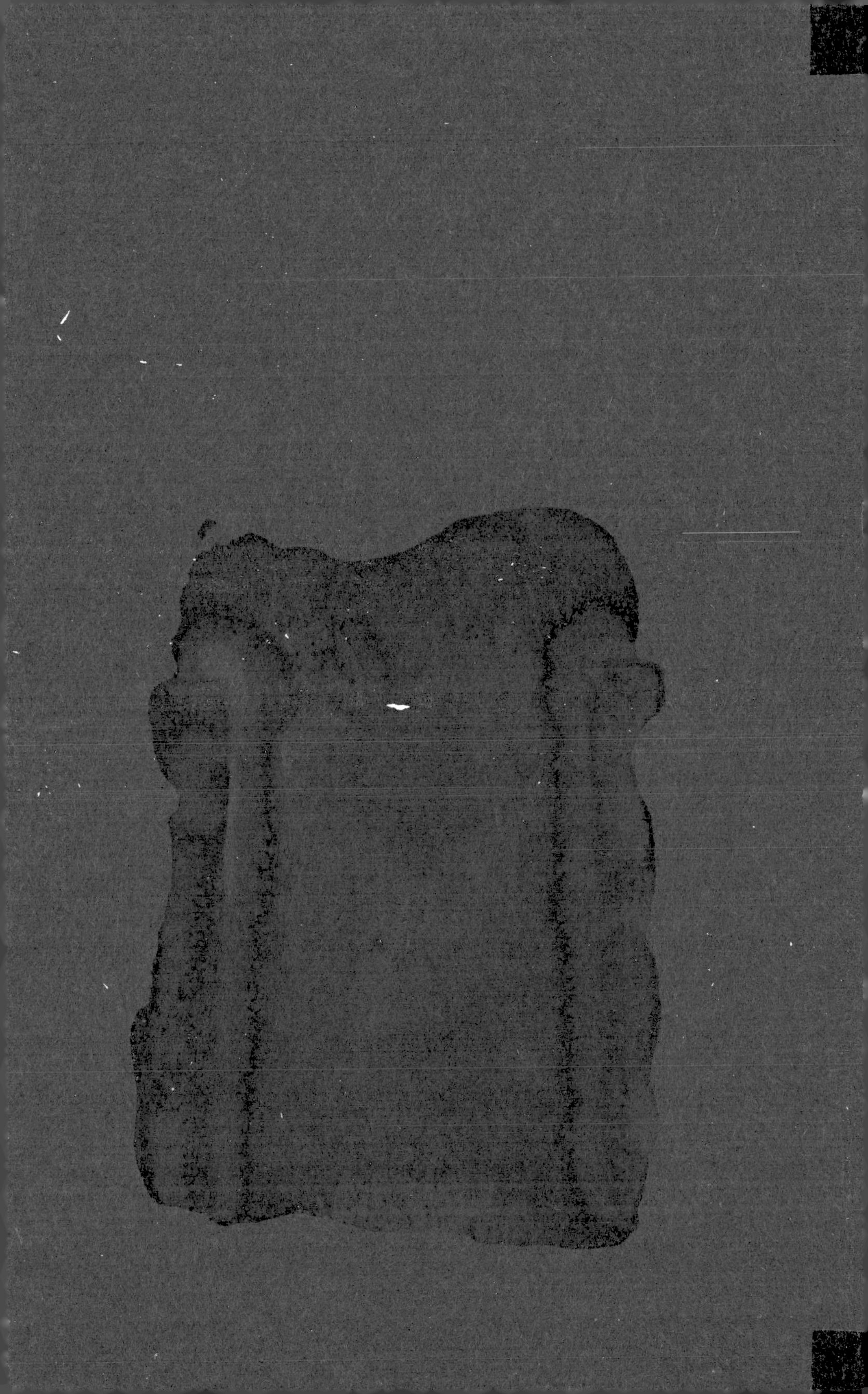